*f*P

WINNING THE GLOBAL GAME

A Strategy for Linking People and Profits

JEFFREY A. ROSENSWEIG

THE FREE PRESS

NEW YORK   LONDON   TORONTO   SYDNEY   SINGAPORE

THE FREE PRESS
A Division of Simon & Schuster, Inc.
1230 Avenue of the Americas
New York, N.Y. 10020

THE FREE PRESS and colophon are trademarks
of Simon & Schuster Inc.

Designed by Michael Mendelsohn of MM Design 2000, Inc.

Manufactured in the United States of America

10 9 8 7 6 5 4 3 2

Library of Congress Cataloging-in-Publication Data

Rosensweig, Jeffrey A.
    Winning the global game: a strategy for linking people and
profits/ Jeffrey A. Rosensweig.
        p.   cm.
    Includes bibliographical references and index.
    1. International business enterprises—Management.   2. Economic
forecasting.   3. Twenty-first century—Forecasts.   I. Title.
HD62.4.R67 1998
658' .049—dc21
                                                          98-17194
                                                            CIP

ISBN 0-684-84919-4

Pages 9–10:   "Rubber Ducks in the Net," *The Economist*, July 26, 1997,
              pp. 56–57. ©1997 The Economist Newspaper Group, Inc.
              Reprinted with permission.

Page 78:   "Shrinking," *The Economist*, November 9, 1996, p. 64.
              ©1996 The Economist Newspaper Group, Inc. Reprinted
              with permission.

Dedicated to the memory of my father,

PAUL S. ROSENSWEIG

CONTENTS

PREFACE

Anyone reading this book will conclude that I am an optimist. Donald Keough, when he was President of The Coca-Cola Company, commented that Coke is one of the most highly valued companies in the world, thanks largely to the more than 80% of its growing profit that comes from overseas. Keough jokes that if Coca-Cola's leaders had not been optimists, Coke would never have gone beyond Macon, Georgia! Clearly, optimism fueled Coke's global expansion and its resulting huge increases in stock market valuation. Forces of technical progress can globalize the economy. I hope to argue in this book that a more global, open capitalist economy can help the world's people while enabling profit growth for firms with the foresight to help lead the charge. My secondary goal is to make clear that two starkly alternative scenarios are possible for the world as it moves into the new century. Policy actions and strategic decisions are crucial as the world economy is currently poised on a knife-edge.

When the increasingly wealthy 26 nations that dominate the world's economy, yet comprise less than 20% of the world's people (what I term the industrialized trading nations or ITN of the "traditional triad" detailed in Chapter 1), are contrasted with the widespread poverty and environmental destruction in the increasingly more populous "rest of the world," it is easy to envision a pessimistic scenario. World population could explode by the middle of the next century. Increased poverty and environmental degradation could join with this population explosion in a "vicious circle" feedback loop as shown in Chapter 4. Pressures of immigration, global environmental decay and resource depletion, and spreading disease will have an increasingly negative impact if this pessimistic scenario is allowed to dominate.

The most populous areas of the world are now largely outside the focus of the world's largest and most advanced business firms. Chapter 1 will show that nations comprising more than 80% of the world's people are involved in less than 20% of the international business "action," even when I define "action" using a variety of measures. Chapter 3 will illustrate that almost all of the world's projected population growth is in this poor, often neglected, developing region. If the status quo continues, and no visionary leadership is forthcoming, the pessimistic scenario is a quite possible outcome.

Fortunately, we can also envision a more optimistic scenario for the world into the 21st century. Importantly, people can make a difference. Current business leaders and those with the potential to become constructive business leaders can help to move the world onto the path of the optimistic scenario. They can help save billions of people from a lifetime of poverty, one often linked with a lack of literacy and of natural resources or a healthy environment.

We will need a new generation of business leaders. These leaders can move the world onto the more optimistic trajectory if they respect the environment and the human potential of diverse people throughout the entire world. The ultimate point of this book is that this respect, and the attendant need for business to take positive actions to help ensure that the optimistic scenario prevails, is the "right thing to do." Fortunately, with sufficient foresight we can make a truly global growth strategy the profitable path of action. Enlightened self-interest should give visionary business leaders the incentive to "do the right thing," as detailed in the win-win strategy portrayed in our concluding chapter.

It is for this new generation of potential leaders that I write this book. Current students in many fields, young executives, disgruntled lawyers or doctors, middle-level managers or government workers who are told they are "not essential"; you are all essential and you must strive to keep up your spirit while steadily building your skills. Chapter 8 presents a road map indicating the needed skills. There are babies born in Africa and Southwest Asia today with less than a 75% probability of living until age five, and almost no probability of realizing their vast human potential. Business could try to run from them, but we cannot hide from the resulting global environmental and human degradation. We can make a difference; indeed we must develop our skills and global vision in order to win the global game. I am optimistic that a truly global strategy which looks to invest in children worldwide (and open capitalist policies in these potentially developing nations that enable these investments) will be the way to achieve profit growth. I know it is the *right* thing to do.

ACKNOWLEDGMENTS

A ny book has strengths and flaws. This book's flaws reflect weaknesses of its author. However, this author hopes the book is useful for you because I am in intellectual debt to many superb people. Without them I could not hope that the strengths here and in my teaching more than compensate for the flaws. I especially owe three groups.

First, the distinguished lecturers who have graced my International Perspectives courses at Emory and taught me along with my students: The Honorable Jimmy Carter, the Honorable Michael Manley (deceased), the Honorable P. J. Patterson, and the Honorable Andrew Young are inspiring leaders of truly global vision who put people first. Chairmen or CEOs Jan Leschly of SmithKline Beecham, the late Roberto Goizueta of The Coca-Cola Company, Ed Artzt (former CEO of Procter and Gamble), Bernie Marcus and Arthur Blank of The Home Depot, Donald Keough of Allen & Co., and Dan Amos of AFLAC are leaders who prove that a global vision can grow people, jobs, and profits. In my own state of Georgia, President Carter and Ambassador Young, along with leaders such as Jim Blanchard, Bishop Eddie L. Long and Dr. Alfred W. Brann, Jr., inspire me with their selfless efforts to improve the lives of all the people, by extending opportunities for decent housing, education, and health care.

Second, my own teachers and professors of the past twenty years: Rudiger Dornbusch, Lance Taylor, Richard Eckaus, Stanley Fischer, Olivier Blanchard, Jeffrey Sachs, Larry Summers, and Paul Krugman all taught me and inspired me while somehow getting me through my Economics Ph.D. at MIT. They are now contributing in institutions and nations throughout the world, but I was fortunate they were all in Cambridge, Massachusetts, in the early 1980s. This group of great teachers, researchers, and enlightened policy advisors includes potential Nobel laureates. However, I am sure they join me in looking up to Nobel laureate James Tobin of Yale. I would not be a professor, let alone one who cares deeply about teaching, if not for this role model. He and his brilliant wife, Betty Tobin, took the time to mentor and open their home to numerous undergraduates such as myself, even while performing pathbreaking economic research. As I strive to share my ideas and conviction with a new generation of students, I hope to give something back "intergenerationally" to such a great set of teachers. They answered the raging "teaching vs. research" debate, with their great talent and energy; they do both superbly, finding synergy as each aspect of their professional contribution informs the others.

Senior colleagues at Emory have also served as trusted advisors and friends. This group includes former Dean John Robson, professors Al Hartgraves, Benn Konsynski, Jag Sheth, Jeff Sonnenfeld, Jim Gustafson, Jim Fowler, Robert Pastor, and especially my mentor at Emory, George Benston. George has personally and intellectually supported and inspired my research and writing.

Third, the superb set of students who have helped as research assistants the past few years while inspiring me with their potential as constructive future business leaders: Brent Cobb, Gil Winters, Jason Kindland, Crystal Mario, Jean Wu, Kevin Bassler, Laura Hosbein, James Lanzone, Henry Lee, Eric Levin, Ari Straus, Mike Discenza, Lado Gurgenidze, Levan Vasadze, Chris Markou, Kathy McLane Gersch, Tara Whitehead, Noel Schmidt, Tim Peacocke, Christophe Van Riet, Ying Qiu, Lee Ward, Thomas Amster, Russ McDonough III, Jun Ma, Evelyn Greiner, and Charles Davis.

Lori A. Sullivan (Cornell, B.A. 1991; Emory, M.B.A. 1998) was an invaluable participant in the research and writing of this book. Students such as Lori and those cited above make teaching a rewarding profession.

My assistant at Emory, Randi Strumlauf, contributed high levels of skill and enthusiasm, and was instrumental in the writing of this book. Rose Flynn significantly improved the graphics.

Senior Editor Bob Wallace and his whole team at The Free Press, notably Abby Luthin, are the best in the business.

Most significantly, my wife, son, and daughter have provided tremendous support and immeasurable patience throughout the process of completing this book and in all my endeavors.

GLOBALIZATION OR "GLOBALONEY"?

A list of the most ubiquitous business buzzwords of this decade would surely include the following: empowerment, reengineering, and *globalization*. Overused though they might be, each term summarizes a trend or strategic process absolutely critical to business as we move into a new millennium. Identifying trends of globalization in the world economy and outlining strategies firms and individuals might employ to profit from these trends are the major focal points of this book. The empowerment of diverse people, particularly women in Africa and South Asia, will play a central role as well.

Before you decide to read this book, however, I must assume a burden of proof. Is "globalization" merely a buzzword, or is it indeed the future of business? Is all this talk about the economy globalizing useful for strategy, or is it just a bunch of "globaloney"?[1] My goal is to answer this by delving deeply into the actual data trends, while portraying data in useful, often visual, ways. I hope to demonstrate that globalization is indeed an emerging reality. The implication of this emerging reality is that we all must create informed business approaches and personal strategies not only to survive, but also to prosper, in the coming global economy.

In order to test if globalization is a reality, we need to get a handle on what constitutes international business. The best way to begin our analysis is to realize that, essentially, international business has two major components: international trade and foreign investment. First, consider the case of a domestic firm starting to exhaust growth possibilities in its local market. The firm may decide to sell its products overseas, by producing in the domestic market and then selling its wares to foreign nations. Hence, the firm begins to engage in the first realm of international business, *international trade,* where trade is merely the selling of a product across a national border.

Next, as the international markets grow, the firm may decide that it makes more sense to produce its wares in foreign nations themselves. This represents a more mature phase of the product life cycle. The firm may source production overseas in order to avoid transportation costs or import restrictions, or to take advantage of cheaper labor costs in foreign markets. By establishing a subsidiary abroad, or investing in a joint venture abroad, the firm has entered the second realm of international business, *foreign investment.* If the firm has a controlling or major interest in business units abroad, it is termed *foreign direct investment* (FDI). In contrast to this, if a firm or individual invests abroad, but does not gain a controlling or even a major interest in the foreign entity, it is termed *portfolio investment.*

In this introduction we will examine the recent record regarding globalization. We begin by studying trends in international trade, followed by international investment transactions.

GROWTH IN INTERNATIONAL TRADE: THE U.S. CASE

In terms of U.S. dollars or other nominal values, trade is clearly booming, which has led many casual observers to trumpet this as the "era of globalization." The numbers are indeed stunning, both on a total worldwide basis and for the United States alone. We will quickly move to a more sophisticated analysis, but pause here to highlight the striking growth in world trade in terms of nominal values. Exports of good and services by the United States should exceed one trillion (a thousand billion) dollars in 1998, and imports will approach $1.2 trillion. By contrast, in 1963, neither exports nor imports of goods and services reached even $30 billion in the United States. Indeed, as late as 1972, exports from the United States were barely $67 billion; thus, in the succeeding quarter-century, U.S. exports increased nearly fifteenfold.

Readers with a background in economics or finance will no doubt realize that I am exaggerating the case here. To be sure, it is true that imports to the United States grew (fortyfold!) from less than $26 billion in 1963, to a figure far in excess of a trillion dollars in 1997. But these are nominal dollars, not adjusted for inflation. Obviously, the United States has experienced inflation in the period since 1963. Yet inflation has increased the price level not even close to 40 times, but rather, just a few times. Consequently, even if we corrected for inflation by measuring imports in "real" terms, that is, inflation-adjusted terms, we will see that they have grown tremendously.

Examining trade figures is one way to show that there has been something of a globalization of the U.S. economy. But the first, or most basic, measure of a nation's openness to trade is the ratio of a nation's exports or imports to its total production, its gross domestic product (GDP). This ratio is often the main measure employed to establish the extent of globalization of a nation's economy. Let us examine the rationale for using this ratio in more detail.

For the most part, economies grow over time, and most of the relevant macroeconomic magnitudes grow as well. This is particularly true of successful economies, such as that of the United States. Even correcting for inflation and measuring things in "real" terms, macroeconomic magnitudes typically grow. As a result, a simple analysis of export or import levels, for example, will usually show an increase over time. So we need a more descriptive measure of globalization.

Thus, analysts usually portray economic magnitudes as *shares* of a nation's total production, in order to see if the magnitudes are growing more quickly or more slowly than a nation's total economy. Analysts normally use either GDP or a very similar concept, gross national product (GNP), as the best measure of a nation's total economic output. Total economic output is a very close proxy for a nation's income, because income is earned only by production that is valued by the market. That is, if you produce something that has no value in the market, you do not earn income from it, and it is not counted in a nation's GDP or GNP. Therefore, GDP (or GNP) is a good proxy for a nation's income, because it shows the total of a nation's production in a given time period (usually one year), as that production is valued by the market.

Figure I–1 illustrates the case of the United States, with three *global* macroeconomic magnitudes expressed as a share of GDP. Indeed, rather than just showing exports as a share of GDP, we also show imports to provide added insight. Also, we portray the U.S. trade balance as a share of GDP, where *trade balance* is defined as a nation's export revenues minus its import expenditures. Note too that Figure I–1 counts exports and imports of *both* goods and services, since goods and services are each an important aspect of the U.S. economy and of U.S. trade. A number of interesting trends can be noted from the figure, but two important ones deserve special emphasis.

First, Figure I–1 provides concrete evidence that globalization of the U.S. economy is much more than an en vogue cliché; indeed, we see that

Figure I–1   GLOBALIZATION: TRADE RISES AS A SHARE OF U.S. GDP

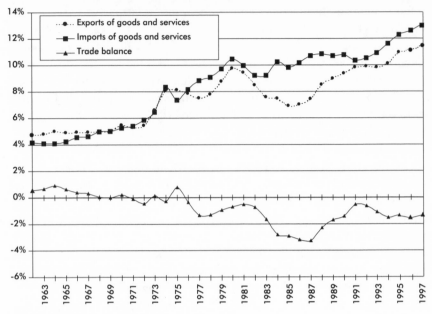

Data Source: U.S. Department of Commerce

it does have an empirical reality supporting it. Both imports and exports have risen sharply as a share of GDP since 1962; and this trend toward globalization of overall U.S. production shows no sign of deceleration. You may ask if I chose the starting point, 1962, in order to best present this case. The answer is no, because if we go back in time even further, for example to 1950, we would notice globalization to an even greater extent, if we define "globalization" as increasing shares of trade in overall GDP. By 1962, where our graph begins, exports had reached 4.75% and imports 4.2% of U.S. GDP. The corresponding figures for 1950 are only 4% each of U.S. GDP.[2] So we have not prejudiced the case by beginning our analysis in 1962. Thus, the first clear trend in Figure I–1 is that the U.S. economy is becoming increasingly more global, as proxied by import and export trade shares of total production.

The second clear trend is not such an optimistic one. The U.S. trade balance on goods and services as a share of GDP has shifted from significant surpluses throughout the 1960s to rather massive deficits in the mid- to late 1980s and 1990s. Some of the many reasons for this trend toward trade deficit will be discussed throughout this book, especially in Chapter 7. However, the simple explanation for this deficit is clear from Figure I–1: exports have risen strongly as a share of GDP, but imports have risen even more dramatically.

The overall picture for the United States is one of increasing exposure to the global economy. But the more rapid increases have been on the import side, leading to a shift in the U.S. trade imbalance from habitual trade surpluses to successive and large trade deficits. Again, the most important point here is that these trade deficits have arisen *not* because of any declines in the export position, but rather, because of the more extreme opening or globalization on the import side. The export share did decline in the early 1980s, because the rising foreign exchange value of the U.S. dollar rendered many U.S. exports unattractive to foreigners. In other words, the strong dollar made U.S. exports relatively expensive, pricing these goods and services out of world markets. However, the decline of the U.S. dollar since 1985 has restored the long-term trend of a prolonged rise in the U.S. export-to-GDP ratio.

One reason the U.S. trade share of GDP is rising so rapidly is the formation of NAFTA—the North American Free Trade Agreement. NAFTA and other integrating forces point to globalization as a current reality for other nations as well. Canada, the biggest trade partner of the United States, was highlighted for its own globalization in a front-page article in the *Wall Street Journal,* "Canada Sees Exports as Path to Prosperity." The article stated that "exports now account for 43% of

Figure I–2   GLOBALIZATION OF BUSINESS
Trade Growth Integrates the World's Economy

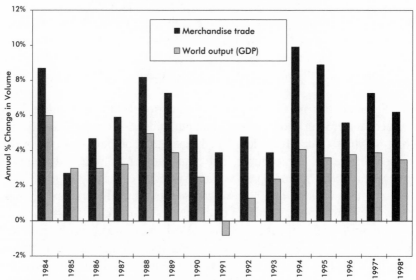

Data Sources: World Trade Organization, International Monetary Fund.
*Preliminary estimates

Canada's gross domestic product, up from just 29% in 1990. Canada's imports, in the same period, rose to 36% of GDP from 25%."[3]

GROWTH IN INTERNATIONAL TRADE: THE GLOBAL CASE

Figure I–2 provides a convenient way to illustrate the globalization, or lack thereof, of the entire world's economy. The figure does so by testing the same proposition we examined in the case of the United States above: Does the internationally traded portion of world output constitute a growing share of total world production? In order to emphasize the dynamic trend in the world economy, this figure looks at yearly percent changes over the past thirteen years. Note that both the total aggregate of world merchandise trade and the total aggregate of world output, measured by world GDP, are portrayed in volume or real terms. This means that we have subtracted or corrected for any growth in nominal values due to inflating prices, to focus on the important concept of the growth in real volumes of business.

Figure I–2 clearly shows that business is globalizing, as the growth in the part of business that is traded across national borders strongly outstrips the growth of total business, as measured by total world output. A number of interesting facts emerge from a closer analysis of Figure I–2. First, the volume of world trade increased every year in the period under study. That is, since the graph depicts growth in merchandise trade volume year to year, as long as the bars are positive, then volume has increased from the year before. Thus, world trade seems somewhat recession-proof. Of course, we do not want to push this claim too broadly, because if the world ever fell into another economic depression, then obviously trade would decline.

Secondly, we note in Figure I–2 that growth in merchandise trade exceeds the growth of overall world output. Indeed, even in 1985—the one year in which trade grew more slowly than total outputs—we see only a minor difference. By contrast, note the number of years where *trade growth far outstrips total world output growth,* especially in the 1990s. For example, looking at 1995, we can see that global merchandise trade grew about two and one-half times as much as world GDP grew.

Figure I–2 also illustrates that in 1991, there was a decline in total output due to a worldwide recession. Nevertheless, that recession did not diminish total world trade, another indication that trade is somewhat recession-proof. Indeed, the trade portion of global business continued to grow even during that recessionary period induced by the Gulf War.[4] Although the United States recovered quickly from recession, and in fact was growing by the second half of 1991, Europe and Japan remained in recession into 1992. Thus, we see only very low growth in 1992 overall world output.

Trade is pro-cyclic in the sense that trade growth does seem to move through the same business cycle as the overall world economy. That is, in years when the world economy grows quickly (e.g., 1984, 1988, 1994), world trade growth also appears to accelerate. Likewise, in years of slow global economic growth (e.g., 1985, 1986, 1990–1993), trade growth typically decelerates somewhat. However, even in the slowdown periods of the world business cycle, trade grows more rapidly than overall world output.

Thus, in many years, the world economy seems to grow about 3% or 4% percent, while world trade seems to grow at a faster rate, often between 4% and 9%. The upshot is that the world is moving forward, in the sense that total world output has grown nicely since 1983. Preliminary estimates reveal that total world output in 1998 will be at least 60% greater than the 1983 total. To avoid overstating our case, I used 1983, the year *after* the recession of 1981–82, to begin looking at growth rates. This was a year of very good economic growth and trade growth, during the height of the "Reagan boom" in the United States. The United States was sucking in a lot of imports from the rest of the world, helping other nations to grow as well. Thus, even when comparing to a good year in the world economy, such as 1983; we see that by 1998, world output volume will have increased over 60%.

The salient point for this introductory chapter is that recent decades have witnessed a much faster growth in world *trade* than in world output. Our calculations show that 1996 world trade more than doubled the 1983 trade total in volume terms.[5] If we constructed an index with the volume of world trade in 1983 set equal to 100, then preliminary estimates indicate the 1998 indexed volume of world trade will be approaching 250. In other words, global trade volume has increased by nearly 150%, reaching almost two and a half times its value in 1983. Given that total world output has "only" increased to 1.6 times its 1983 value, we can calculate that the ratio of trade to world output (2.5/1.6) rose by over 50% between 1983 and 1998. This is strong evidence that *globalization is more a reality than a mere buzzword,* because even though the world economy has grown very steadily since 1983, the truly dynamic aspect of output growth is the internationally traded portion. Furthermore, Figure I–2 shows no apparent deceleration in this rapid growth of world trade volumes; if anything, world trade growth appears to be accelerating.

What accounts for this rapid increase in global trade volumes and can we expect it to continue? Two key factors are: (1) the advance of communication and information technology that facilitates doing business internationally, and (2) institutional progress in removing barriers to international trade.

First, the spread of modern distribution, communication, and information technology has clearly facilitated international trade. The global transport of people (hence, services they perform), ideas, information, and goods, is both cheaper and easier, thanks to modern telephony, jet transport, and containerization. The accompanying "spotlight mini-case" highlights the importance of technology, particularly the ability to trade or perform "electronic commerce" over the Internet, in driving a recent further acceleration in the globalization of business (even for small firms). These trends are so powerful and clear that to further detail them risks resorting to clichés such as "the world is getting smaller."

INDUSTRY SPOTLIGHT
Electronic Commerce Helps Small Business Open Global Frontiers

Modern information and communication technologies, especially the Internet, are accelerating the forces currently globalizing markets, as I noted in the Preface. In the past, only rather large firms could approach customers worldwide, as a result of the massive fixed costs of international business, such as maintaining a sales force or hiring local agents in numerous distant nations. Now however, the exploding growth in access to the Internet and the World Wide Web is thrusting a long-hyped new mode of transacting global business to the forefront. This new mode of conducting global business is termed *electronic commerce*.

Bill Gates in his book *The Road Ahead*[6] gives us a clear and useful view of how the Internet (and new information technology more broadly) will change the way most of us communicate, learn, and conduct our daily business. Change will be dramatic and generally for the better. Gates describes how electronic documents, stored in digital form, will spawn a "content revolution." He recounts (p. 131) how the Internet helped him write his book, a process that represents one more way we can learn from Bill Gates.

This book would have been much harder to write without e-mail. Readers whose opinions I valued received drafts electronically, made electronic changes to the drafts, and sent the altered documents back to me. It was helpful to be able to look at the proposed revisions, see the rationales for the proposed changes in electronic annotations, and see the electronic record of who made the revision suggestions and when.

Clearly my own business, teaching and writing books, is being fundamentally transformed by the Internet. I use it to find the latest data to upgrade my figures and trends; search for relevant articles; and send e-mail messages at virtually no cost or time delay to former MBA students scattered around the world. As I write this, the Teamsters Union has temporarily crippled United Parcel Service (UPS) by calling its workers out on strike. In the past this would have delayed my sending chapters of this book to my editor, Bob Wallace, in New York. Now I just e-mail them, and Bob can edit my 'electronic chapter' and reply promptly over the Internet. I can respond instantly (and at virtually no cost): "You think it's a silly example, but I want to keep it in." You can judge for yourself who won this round of electronic editing.

A recent article in *The Economist,* "Asian Electronic Commerce. Rubber Ducks in the Net" (26 July 1997, pp. 56–57), aptly shows the potential impact of the Internet as a globalizing force. It highlights the capacity of the Internet to empower even small firms to seek customers globally, through the cost efficiencies and ubiquitous reach of electronic commerce. Thus, I reproduce most of the article here.

At the heart of Asia's electronic-commerce boom is the Asian Sources Media Group (ASM), a publishing company based in Hong Kong. The firm's Web site serves as a shopfront for more than 7,000 Asian suppliers, mostly small-to-medium-sized factories in Hong Kong, China, Taiwan and Korea, selling everything from cheap plastic toys to multimedia electronics. Before the ASM sales representatives came calling many of these factories did not even have a personal computer, let alone an Internet connection. But that hardly made a difference: ASM got them what they needed, trained them in how to use it, and included them in its on-line catalogue of nearly 200,000 products.

The point about ASM's site is that most of the commerce is genuinely electronic—by e-mail. About 70% of the firms on ASM's Web site have e-mail, mainly thanks to ASM's efforts. In about half of the cases, ASM provides the e-mail account, which the customers can dial into, but many have their own addresses. In either case, it has proved invaluable. E-mail is fast, considerably cheaper than international fax or telephone (especially in parts of Asia where local monopolies have kept telecom costs high), relatively insensitive to time-zone differences, and less psychologically daunting for wired buyers than a call or composing and sending a fax. . . .

At first, Hong Kong firms were the most receptive to ASM's efforts: not surprising since the city is the centre of Internet activity in the region. They have now been overtaken by Taiwan, whose electronics-parts makers supply much of Silicon Valley. Eventually, Chinese firms may prove the most numerous: a third of those on the site already list an e-mail address.

In America, the first groups to adopt the Internet were universities and consumer-services companies; in Europe, it was students, hackers, and a few brave publishers. But in commerce-minded Asia it is the keychain and rubber-duck makers that are leading the way. Too small to have better ways of reaching the outside world, but able to adopt a new communications technology without the fuss and bureaucracy of larger firms, ASM's prosaic customers are the perfect electronic-commerce pioneers.

Second, *institutional* agreements to remove barriers to trade have gained strong momentum. This progress includes both *multilateral,* or more truly global, arrangements, such as the creation of the World Trade Organization, and *regional* free trade areas or integrated economies. Regional progress in the 1990s includes the formation of NAFTA by the addition of Mexico to the Canada/U.S. Free Trade Agreement; the formation of a true single-market European Union in 1993 and its broadening to fifteen nations; the addition of three members (Vietnam, Myanmar, and Laos) to the Association of Southeast Asian Nations (ASEAN), and the progress of the Asia Pacific Economic Cooperation (APEC) forum. These developments will be analyzed further in Chapter 2.

Let us consider now whether the impressive record of increased globalization portrayed above is significant even in a longer historical perspective. After all, substantial integration of a global economy existed before World War I tore it asunder. John Maynard Keynes, writing in 1920, summarized this earlier "global economic era."[7]

What an extraordinary episode in the progress of man that age was which came to an end in August, 1914! . . . The inhabitant of London could order by telephone, sipping his morning tea in bed, the various products of the whole earth, in such quantity as he might see fit, and reasonably expect their early delivery upon his doorstep; he could at the same moment and by the same means adventure his wealth in the natural resources and new enterprises of any quarter of the world, and share, without exertion or even trouble, in their prospective fruits and advantages; or he could decide to couple the security of his fortunes with the good faith of the townspeople of any substantial municipality in any continent that fancy or information might recommend. He could secure forthwith, if he wished it, cheap and comfortable means of transit to any country or climate without passport or other formality, . . . most important of all, he regarded this state of affairs as normal, certain, and permanent, . . . the ordinary course of social and economic life, the internationalization of which was nearly complete in practice.

The above passage certainly provides evidence of much earlier globalization both in trade and in foreign investments. Today, however, we have entered a new, and thanks to technological advances, far more extensive global era for business. *The Economist*[8] summarizes the recent evidence.

How integrated is the "global" economy? One guide is the proportion of GDP accounted for by exports. Of the nine countries in our chart, seven now have a higher ratio of exports to GDP than at any time since 1870. Canada is the most integrated into the global economy. Its exports were worth 34% of GDP in 1995. Germany and Britain have only recently exceeded their export-GDP peaks of 1913. Argentina and Brazil still export a smaller share of GDP than in 1870—7.5%, down from 9.4% and 7.3%, down from 11.8%, respectively—although their export ratios are higher than in 1973. Mexico's exports were worth only 2.2% of GDP in 1973, but have since soared to 31.9%

Let us now turn to a discussion of international investment flows. Noteworthy data trends indicate that this component of international business may be growing even more rapidly than the trade component of international business.

GROWTH IN INTERNATIONAL INVESTMENT

International investment flows may be the key to affirming the unique power of this recent globalization era. The World Bank discusses this point, contrasting the recent era to the globalizing period before World War I:

Thus the start of the twentieth century was a period of considerable global economic integration supported by relatively liberal economic policies. Still, it differed from the 1990s. . . . Gross (as distinct from net) capital flows are very high today, and come from a wider variety of sources.[9]

These gross investment flows are indeed reaching massive and unprecedented proportions. Two-way flows of foreign investment fuel the world's biggest market: the global foreign exchange market, which the Bank for International Settlements (BIS) estimates averaged a *daily* turnover of $1,200 billion in 1995![10] Obviously, over a trillion dollars of foreign exchange transactions a day highlights quite clearly that trade is only a small part of the action. Indeed, capital is surging over national borders as individuals, firms, and investment funds truly are globalizing their investment strategies.

A common method to contrast the growth in international investment to growth in international trade is to compare the ratio of exports as a share of GDP to the ratio of foreign direct investment (FDI) to GDP. *The Economist* presents a novel and interesting way to further compare these two components of international business:[11]

A third ratio—FDI flows as a percentage of exports—compares the relative importance of each. According to ING Barings, an investment bank, the inflow of FDI to emerging economies has increased from 5% of exports in 1990 to 9% in 1995.

Thus, if FDI flows are rising as a ratio of exports, then we can conclude that direct investment in these emerging economies is growing even faster than trade (exports).

As we shall see, foreign investment is growing very rapidly within the wealthy, advanced nations. But it is useful to observe that this trend also applies to the emerging and developing economies. We will structure our analysis of foreign investment in a manner similar to our approach to trade above. First, we will briefly examine the case of the United States, and then we will discuss some trends for the world as a whole.

GROWTH IN INTERNATIONAL INVESTMENT: THE U.S. CASE

The United States is indeed becoming increasingly integrated into the global economy through international investment transactions in addition to increased international trade volume. Data on U.S. international investment is presented annually by the Commerce Department.[12] Recall that total foreign investment is made up of both direct investment (FDI) and portfolio investment. Thus, when we speak of ownership here, we are referring to *total foreign* investment. Measuring FDI at current cost of assets (accountants traditionally use historical costs, but that can lead to

Figure I–3   GLOBALIZATION OF OWNERSHIP
U.S. Net Foreign Worth Declines

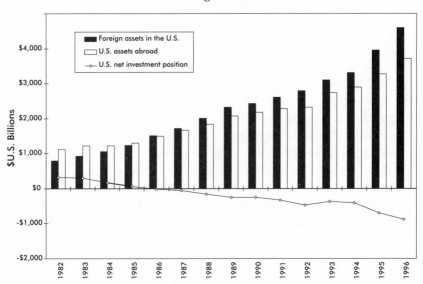

Data Source: U.S. Department of Commerce, *Survey of Current Business*, July 1997.

very misleading conclusions in an inflationary world), the Commerce Department figures are quite revealing.

Figure I–3 summarizes the trends toward *globalization of ownership* currently engulfing the U.S. economy and spurring U.S. firms. Strikingly, U.S. assets owned abroad totaled just over $1.1 trillion in 1982. This exceeded by far the $790 billion of foreign-owned assets in the United States. Thus, the United States had a net international investment position, that is, a net equity or *net worth position* vis-à-vis the rest of the world, of positive $325 billion. At this time, the United States was the world's largest creditor nation; it had the greatest net foreign worth.

We all know that the United States has evolved from the largest net foreign creditor to the world's largest net foreign debtor. However, this frequently cited fact obscures a more important point: *international investment gross totals clearly demonstrate the significant recent expansion of globalization.* The important thing to note is that U.S. assets abroad have continued to grow dramatically during the 1980s and 1990s, illustrating the globalization of ownership. The only reason we have moved to a net debtor status is that foreign ownership of assets in the United States has grown even more dramatically; indeed it has grown at breathtaking rates.

Thus, as with trade, two important trends emerge. The primary one is that *globalization is a reality,* that the gross flows in both directions are huge. Our assets abroad and foreigners' assets in the United States have grown dramatically in gross terms. The secondary trend pertains to *imbalance:* Just as import growth outstripped export growth and led the United States to huge trade deficit imbalances, the growth of foreign assets in the United States is far outdistancing the growth of U.S. assets held abroad, an imbalance resulting in the net debtor status. Of course, these two imbalances are linked. In order to fund the trade deficits resulting from our added imports, the United States must sell assets to, or borrow from, foreigners. This foreign borrowing or selling of assets leads to our current status as a net international debtor. These linkages will be discussed much more deeply in the model underlying Chapter 7.

Figure I–3 summarizes the U.S. position in international investment. U.S. assets abroad have far more than tripled since 1982, from $1.1 trillion, to over $3.7 trillion in 1996. Strikingly, even this fast growth is dwarfed by the growth in foreign ownership of assets in the United States, which has gone up nearly sixfold, from $790 billion in 1982 to $4.6 trillion in 1996. Thus, U.S. liabilities to foreigners *increased $3.8 trillion* in fourteen years.

Of course, total wealth in the United States is massive and difficult to measure precisely. So even if foreigners currently own substantial assets in the United States, we have not, as certain popular books decry, "sold America." However, one could argue that we are beginning to sell off chunks of (U.S.) America. I am not overly worried about this trend, however, as it is merely a reflection of two-way globalization of ownership. The fact is that U.S.-Americans are still buying big chunks of Europe, Canada, and parts of Latin America and Southeast Asia. The bottom line is *that globalization of ownership is a healthy trend,* because it shows a beneficial diversification of assets on the part of businesses and investors, and it makes the world a more peaceful place. Indeed, it is hard to imagine the Japanese dropping bombs anywhere near Hawaii now, given that they own so many hotels in that beach-laden state!

To see if international ownership is not just rising, but is rising even in relation to total economic output, we must compare the more than tripling of U.S. assets abroad and the sextupling of foreign assets in the United States between 1982 and 1996 to the growth of the overall U.S. economy. The key fact is that, although nominal U.S. GDP more than doubled since 1982, from $3.24 trillion to $7.64 trillion in 1996, it did not approach tripling, let alone sextupling. Therefore, international ownership did indeed rise significantly even when compared to the strongly growing GDP in the United States.

The country's deepening entanglement in a more global economy is clearly shown by the rise of servicing payments that it must send abroad. Servicing payments are income payments made by the United States on its liabilities to foreigners (e.g., interest on debt). These servicing payments flowing out of the country rose to over $250 billion in 1997; compared to only $53 billion in 1983, $14 billion in 1977, and a mere $1.56 billion in 1963. Globalization of investment income flows is clearly a reality.

GROWTH IN INTERNATIONAL INVESTMENT: THE GLOBAL CASE

An examination of globalization of ownership on a world scale reveals that worldwide international investment activities confirm and even amplify the message from international trade growth: that trends toward the globalization of business are much more than mere rhetoric. This section relies heavily on the work of the United Nations Conference on Trade and Development (UNCTAD), which publishes annually its *World Investment Report.* These reports highlight the growing importance of transnational corporations (TNCs) in the global economy, and the foreign direct investment TNCs undertake and control. A theme of this book is that more firms should follow these TNC global leaders by adopting a more international strategy over time.

Figure I–4   FOREIGN DIRECT INVESTMENT
The Level Booms with Globalization
(Stock of Inward FDI, in Billions of U.S. $)

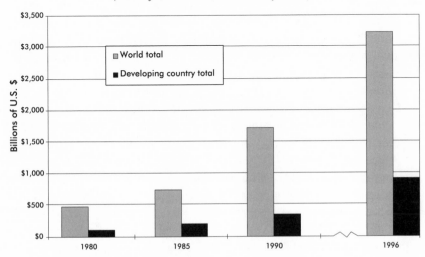

Source: UNCTAD, *World Investment Report* 1997, p. 239.

Figure I–4 summarizes the boom in the level of international investment during recent decades. The worldwide total *stock* (cumulative level)
of FDI rose from $480 billion in 1980 to $3,233 billion in 1996.[13] This
total has been rising rapidly, due to huge and increasing annual *flows* of
FDI. *The World Investment Report 1996* summarizes how the record-sized
flows indicate a globalizing force (p. xiv), and are leading globalization.

> World economic growth and the response of transnational corpo-
> rations (TNCs) to technological development, international
> competition, and liberalization propelled global foreign direct
> investment (FDI) flows to unprecedented levels in 1995.
> Investment inflows rose by 9% in 1994 (to $226 billion) and by
> another 40% (about $90 billion) in 1995, to reach a record $315
> billion. . . . In 1995, FDI growth was substantially higher than that
> of exports of goods and nonfactor services, world output, and
> gross domestic capital formation. (p. 3)

World FDI flows increased again in 1996, to $349 billion, with the
United States attracting more than any other nation. The U.S. Department
of Commerce reported that the country attracted a record FDI inflow of
$80.5 billion in 1996, up 41% from 1995 and three times greater than the
1993 inflow.[14] Indeed, the U.S. figures are instructive, as most of the
globe's foreign direct investment has been directed to the economically
advanced nations. However, there is finally an increased share of FDI
flowing to developing nations.

The total stock of FDI invested in developing nations rose more than
eightfold from 1980 to 1996, and nearly tripled between 1990 and 1996 to
$918 billion. This fast growth enabled developing countries to move from
a mere 20% share[15] of the total global FDI stock in 1990 to over 28% by
1996. The *World Investment Report 1996* (p. xvi) shows that firms' strategic plans point to a continued deepening and broadening of their globalizing investment strategies: "The future investment plans of the top 100
TNCs suggest a strong upward trend in FDI (as well as total investment),
fueled partly by economic growth in major destinations, among which the
developing countries are becoming more prominent."

Indeed, the United Nations reports[16] that FDI did continue to rise in
1996. In fact, in that year FDI to developing countries rose by $33 billion
to $129 billion. In particular, major destinations such as China and Latin
America continued to experience substantial increases in FDI inflows in
1996. The *World Investment Report 1997* neatly summarizes and highlights the major trends discussed above[17]:

Figure I-5   GLOBALIZATION: CHINA OPENS FOR BUSINESS

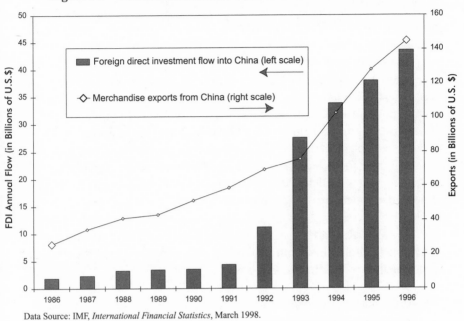

Data Source: IMF, *International Financial Statistics*, March 1998.

FDI flows set a new record in 1996. . . . Inflows increased by 10%. . . .

Developing countries invested $51 billion abroad and received $129 billion in 1996. . . .

South, East and South-East Asia and Latin America attained record FDI inflows. . . . Flows to South, East and South-East Asia increased by 25 per cent, to more than $80 billion, while those to Latin America were nearly $39 billion in 1996, about $13 billion more than in 1995.

EXAMPLE OF GLOBALIZATION: CHINA OPENS TO INVESTMENT

We have already examined globalization in the United States, the largest economy in the world. Now let us consider in depth one other major example of globalization. Given its world-leading population of over 1.2 billion people, China is a focal point for global firms, reflecting and accelerating the economic globalization initiated in 1978 with the market-opening reforms of the late Chairman Deng Xiaoping. The startling rise of China as a global business force is evident in both major components of international business: trade and foreign investment.

Figure I–5 displays the two striking trends that may help presage business in the 21st century. First, China is attracting massive and increasing annual flows of FDI, leading to a stock of investment (e.g., factories and infrastructure) that is helping China industrialize. This industrialization is driving the second trend, China's increasing exports to the rest of the world. Furthermore, Figure I–5 uses confirmed data through 1996,[18] but initial estimates indicate that China's attraction of foreign investment inflows continued in 1997 and into 1998 (despite the moderating influence of the Asian crisis).

Nicholas R. Lardy, in his excellent book, *China in the World Economy,*[19] highlights both China's market-opening reforms and its consequent growth into a global business force:

> At the outset of its economic reforms in the late 1970s, China was an insignificant participant in international markets for goods and capital. In 1977 . . . it was only the 30th largest exporting country in the world . . . prior to the late 1970s, China also was barely a participant in world capital markets. . . .
>
> By the early 1990s, China's role in the international economy had been totally transformed. . . . In 1992 it was the world's tenth largest exporter, lagging behind only the largest and most advanced industrial states. It also was a significant recipient of foreign aid and a major borrower on international capital markets. . . .
>
> Even more significantly, by the early 1990s China was attracting substantial inflows of foreign direct investment. (pp. 1–3)

The increasing linkage of China to a more global economy applies to other populous nations in East or Southeast Asia as well. For example, Indonesia has the world's fourth largest population, roughly 200 million citizens, and it is also globalizing its economy. Indonesia nearly rivals China in the growth rate of its exports and the flood of FDI it is attracting. Indeed, a graph similar to Figure I–5 for Indonesia would show somewhat *smaller magnitudes* than China, but a similar *pattern* of global growth. Even Vietnam is emerging in the global economic sense by attracting FDI, industrializing, and boosting its exports.

Globalization is increasingly real. Transnational corporations are leading this development by making direct investments around the globe, with a renewed focus on developing nations. These populous nations can only truly develop if they gain needed infrastructure, which the *World Investment Report 1996* identifies as a future source of global demand (p. 18): "One reason we can expect continued growth in FDI flows is that transnational corporations are becoming increasingly involved in infrastructure development . . . ." This report goes on (p. 20) to identify the favorite regions for firms or investors seizing such future opportunities for global infrastructure investment:

> The financial requirements for infrastructure are vast. Present growth rates in East Asia suggest that such investment requirements will be $1.4 trillion during the next decade; for China alone the figure is over $700 billion. In Latin America, requirements are around $600 to $800 billion.

Clearly, globalizing forces are extending into the developing world. Indeed, some nations, such as South Korea, Singapore, and Taiwan (Republic of China), formerly categorized as developing nations, are now wealthy enough to contain firms that are themselves globalizing—they are currently sending FDI outward as well as attracting it.

On a cautionary note, however, we must remind ourselves not to be overly euphoric. Recall that I began this introduction with the notion that "globalization" can be a hollow buzzword if it is not subjected to close analysis. Evidence in this introduction clearly shows an increased extent of globalization, thanks to both burgeoning trade and investment flows. However, we also have seen that most of the world's stock of foreign investment is hosted by nations that are already advanced or industrialized. Furthermore, the increased flows of investment to the developing world are not widely and equally distributed. Rather, these flows are mostly aimed at East Asia and Latin America, and not toward South Asia, West Asia, or Africa. The next chapter highlights this critical divergence, as it analyzes the limited geographic range of globalization at the end of the second millennium.

PART I

REGIONAL ASPECTS OF (OR ROUTES TO) A GLOBALIZING ECONOMY

CHAPTER 1

THE LIMITED WORLD OF BUSINESS AT THE END OF THE 20TH CENTURY

For billions of people on this Earth, talk of the prosperous and growing global economy is just a cruel reminder of their own abject poverty. In terms of trading or communications/information technology, many nations are still barely participating in the supposedly global network. Despite the growing power of the global business network, inequality and lack of effective access to this network still distinguish the international business environment as the 20th century draws to a close.

The decades marking the end of this century clearly represent a "mixed bag." Some nations, particularly in East Asia but also elsewhere, like Chile, enhanced their global business linkages and gained from rapid economic growth. However, other nations did not fare so well: "Economic decline or stagnation . . . affected 100 countries, reducing the incomes of 1.6 billion people— . . . more than a quarter of the world's population."[1] A recent World Bank book[2] summarizes both the overall progress and its unequal global spread:

> Developing countries as a group have participated extensively in the acceleration of global integration, although some have done much better than others . . . there are wide disparities in global economic integration across developing countries. . . . Many developing countries became less integrated with the world economy over the past decade, and a large divide separates the least from the most integrated. . . . Countries with the highest levels of integration tended to exhibit the fastest output growth, as did countries that made the greatest advances in integration.

The great challenge of the 21st century is to establish a more truly global international business network, one that can foster a much more comprehensive spread of economic progress than that which the world currently enjoys. The contrast between nations that rapidly grew their economies and trade linkages and those more numerous nations that failed to achieve this progress is discussed in the United Nations Development Program's *Human Development Report (HDR)*. The 1996 *HDR* stresses the point that inequality is still the name of the game: "The world has become more polarized, and the gulf between the poor and rich of the world has widened even further."[3] The *HDR* goes on to detail this widening inequality, stating that "the poorest 20% of the world's people saw their share of global income decline from 2.3% to 1.4% in the past thirty years. Meanwhile, the share of the richest 20% rose from 70% to 85%. That doubled the ratio of the shares of the richest and the poorest—from 30:1 to 61:1."[4]

That the richest 20% of the world's people amassed more than 80% of global income is a clear example of the "80/20 rule." This "rule" is well known to apply in many diverse situations. For example, teachers know that 20% of their students will be responsible for 80% of their headaches. Similarly, in business, it is often the case that 20% of customers render 80% of the complaints, special requests, and the like. On the other hand, wise executives and managers know that a special 20% of their customers typically generate more than 80% of their companies' profits. We will use the 80/20 rule later in our analysis of the current global economy.

THE WORLD ACCORDING TO TRADE

Let us begin our analysis by looking at the extent of international business as the 20th century draws to a close. A new perspective on the limited nature of the international trading network is provided by Figure 1–1. After many years of exhorting my students to buy an atlas and gain a focus on world geography, I now confuse them by offering this as my map of the world—one with a very different scale from that of a typical atlas. Most atlases attribute power to land mass, using geographic area as the scaling factor. My map is entitled "The World According to Trade" because it scales the world using international trade as the crucial determinant.

How do we measure international trade for this map? We cannot use trade balance as the scaling factor, because some nations, including the United States, run massive trade deficits, and therefore have negative trade balances. It would be very difficult to show a negative number as a scaling factor. Alternatively, exports (what a country sells internationally) or imports (what it buys internationally) could be used as the scaling factor.

Figure 1–1 THE WORLD ACCORDING TO TRADE, 1995

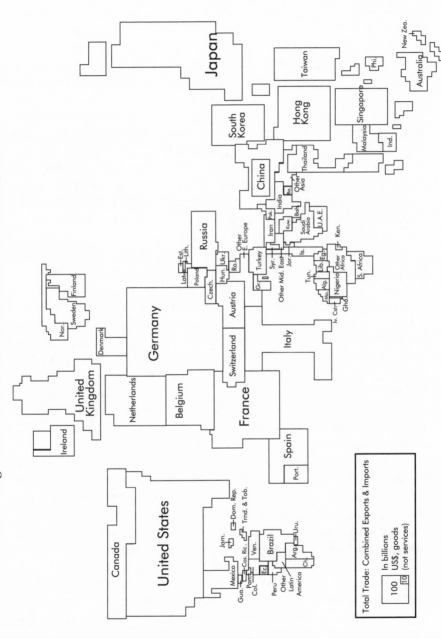

Total Trade: Combined Exports & Imports

100 | In billions US$, goods (not services)

Data Sources: IMF, CIA *World Fact Book*.

25

But exports or imports by themselves would introduce a bias. For example, if we used exports, we would be favoring nations that rely heavily on exports, such as Japan, and be doing an injustice to nations, such as the United States, that are massive importers. More importantly, using exports or imports alone would show only half the picture of international trade, as a nation is participating in international trade if it is buying or selling across national borders. Thus, the most appropriate measure is total trade, calculated as a nation's exports *plus* imports.

What does this new perspective map show us? First, *Western Europe is still the center of international business,* as it is the largest single bloc in a global trading sense. This dominance is due to intra-European trade, as well as the tremendous trade Europe does with other regions of the world, and has done since the glory days of the Dutch East Indies Company. Note that the legacy of the earlier dominance of that company continues into the modem era, as the Netherlands appears much larger on this map than it does on a geographical map.

Second, although Europe is the largest regional trade *bloc,* the United States is the largest *nation* when measured by total trade. This surprises many people, who do not often think of the United States as very savvy about international business.[5] But the United States has doubled its exports in less than a decade, and opened up to the world economy in dramatic ways, as was highlighted in this book's introduction. The fact remains, however, that the major reason we are the world's largest trading nation is the empirical reality that we import far more than any other nation. Still, one should not miss the big picture: U.S. exports are booming, and have been booming since the dollar started to decline from its peak values of early 1985, making this country the world's largest exporter as well as largest importer.

The incredible thing is not how big the United States is in this graph, but rather, how big nations such as Singapore, Hong Kong, Switzerland, Belgium, and the Netherlands appear. On an ordinary map, scaled by land mass, these nations would be mere dots. In this trading perspective, we see that these are major nations in the international business network. Singapore, of course, is an extreme case: its population is barely more than 1% of the United States, but it engages in massive trade. Obviously, Singapore's total trade is less than ours, but not all that much less, for a nation that has such a small land and population base.

The third thing to notice about Figure 1–1 is that there are three major focal points, or massive blocs, in the world trading picture. First, as noted above, Western Europe, at the center of the picture, is an immense trading bloc. Second, the United States is not only the largest trading nation, but is also part of a North American bloc that is noteworthy in this new global perspective. Finally, Japan anchors an East Asian bloc which is remarkably significant in this picture. Figure 1–1 illustrates the often-cited idea that international business essentially comprises a *triad* of three dominant focal points or regions: Western Europe, North America, and East Asia.

The fourth significant feature of this graph is a key to much of this book. Ever since the Cold War ended with Gorbachev disbanding the Soviet Union, commentators have talked about the end of the East-West divide. However, this new trade perspective makes it apparent that a major divide often talked about during the 1970s still exists. This is the divide between the "haves" in the Northern Hemisphere and the "have nots" in many parts of the Southern Hemisphere. This graph strikingly displays how much of the action in an international business sense takes place among the three blocs of the triad, and thus in the Northern Hemisphere. The contrast between this trade map and a hypothetical map of the "World According to Population" is compelling. A map that scaled the world by population would of course show China and India as the two largest nations, with several other nations in Africa, South America, the Mideast, and South Asia attaining huge dimensions. Thus, in a population sense, the major players are clearly south of the traditional triad.

We truly do have a North-South divide. Roughly 80% of the action, whether we define action in terms of total income, trade, or wealth, resides in the nations of the triad, and thus, in the Northern Hemisphere, north of the Tropic of Cancer. By contrast, most of the world's people reside in nations near or south of the Tropic of Cancer, often in the Southern Hemisphere or equatorial regions. Notably, the areas in which population is expected to explode are these same equatorial or southern nations, as we will see in Chapter 3. This picture is key to understanding the limited extent of international business as the 20th century draws to a close.

In his acclaimed book, *Borderless World,*[6] the brilliant Japanese consultant and erstwhile politician, Kenichi Ohmae, talks about business opportunities in a world where national borders have become less important. Capital, goods, and people flow with low cost and rapid speed around the world. Although Ohmae's vision of a borderless world is enticing, a critical reader will notice he only talks about nations in the traditional triad. Hardly a mention is made in the entire book of Africa or the teeming populations of South and Southwest Asia. The world of capital and labor mobility may be borderless, but it exists only among a handful of the very richest nations. Paul Kennedy, in his prescient book, *Preparing for the Twenty-first Century,* more completely develops this comment on Ohmae's vision.[7]

One of my main goals in this book is to put the 80% of the world's people located outside the wealthy traditional triad back in the vision of a borderless world. Through their own actions and policies, as well as a win-win strategy on the part of global business leaders, these people can become very much a part of the international business network as we move into the 21st century. To continue to ignore them is not only a human tragedy for these populous but poor nations, but also a tremendous lost opportunity for businesses that hope to expand. Global expansion is indeed the catchphrase of the 1990s. However, very few firms think about regions such as Africa and South Asia when they use the term global.

THE NEW FIRST, SECOND, AND THIRD WORLDS

It would be sheer madness to try in this book to provide detailed numerical analyses of every nation, or even, for that matter, of the almost 200 that participated in the 1996 Centennial Olympic Games in Atlanta. Thus, I created a "master spreadsheet" to help us analyze the international business environment in an efficient manner. I chose a subset of the world's countries, attempting to capture the great majority of global production, trade, and population. I also included those nations deemed most exciting for future business opportunity. Thus, we will examine more closely about one-fourth of the world's nations, grouped into three categories, which roughly translate to a new vision of the First World, the Second World, and the Third World.

The First World is captured by a construct very similar to the traditional triad of Western Europe, East Asia, and North America. I term our new First World the ITN. I first used this term to signify *industrialized trading nations*—those nations that are prominent in total trade, as portrayed in Figure 1–1. However, these nations are also distinguished by being linked in a global *information technology network*. Thus, the ITN is our modern-day notion of the traditional triad, comprising 26 nations that conduct the bulk of world trade and contain the vast majority of the world's information technology resources.

Seventeen of the twenty-six ITN nations are in Europe: the current fifteen members of the European Union, as well as Switzerland and Norway. These two wealthy nations opted in the mid-1990s not to join the Union, but do maintain very favorable trade relations with the Union through their membership in the European Free Trade Area (EFTA).

The North American part of our ITN construct comprises only two nations: the United States and Canada. Although Mexico is in the North American Free Trade Agreement (NAFTA), it is not included in our ITN as yet, because it is at a much lower level of economic development than its two NAFTA partners.

Finally, the East Asian/Pacific component of the ITN is made up of seven nations. Three are clearly wealthy: Japan, New Zealand, and Australia. Note that Australia and New Zealand are two exceptions to the general rule that Southern Hemisphere nations are poor. The other four nations are the "little dragons" or "little tigers" of East Asia, the aptly termed newly industrialized countries (NICS). These nations are South Korea, Taiwan (which calls itself the Republic of China, but which the mainland Chinese call the Province of Taipei), Singapore, and Hong Kong. Hong Kong was politically subsumed into the Peoples' Republic of China in 1997, but it continues as a separate economic system and maintains its own economic accounts, so we count it separately here. Although small in land area and fairly small in population, we saw earlier that they are major influences in "The World According to Trade."

Hence, in total, the ITN, the world's economic first tier, is made up of 26 nations: 17 in Europe, two in North America, and seven in East Asia or the Pacific. In the days of the Cold War, people would think of something very similar to our ITN as the First World. The Soviet Union and its allied communist nations would be considered the Second World, and the poor, developing countries as the Third World. The end of the Cold War marked the collapse of the traditional Second World, which declined as an economic bloc as the Soviet Union disbanded its empire.

Notably, the Soviet Union was falling to Third World status even before it broke apart. Indeed, Paul Kennedy, in *Preparing for the Twenty-first Century* (p. 235), summarized the situation facing the Soviet empire as follows: "Overall, the economy and society were showing ever more signs of joining the so-called Third World than of catching up with the First." The U.S.S.R. was increasingly falling behind the industrialized capitalist nations; thus, Gorbachev chose to disband the failing communist economic system in the hopes of creating a new structure for an eventual First World economy. However, this massive economic transition to a new system resulted in the economies of the former Soviet Union suffering massive dislocation. The economic upheaval pulled these nations down to economic levels that truly reflect a Third World status.

Russia's economic decline has been extreme. A special box in the *Human Development Report 1996,* entitled "Russia—into reverse"

(p. 84), supports the claim that Russia has fallen into the Third World during its transition toward capitalism:

> Since 1991 Russia's growth and human development have plummeted. Deep recession and hyperinflation sharply increased unemployment and poverty and exacerbated income inequality. Life expectancy, mortality and morbidity have worsened dramatically. Russia is now struggling to rebound from this downward spiral. . . . In 1991–94 average real wages dropped by more than a third, and agricultural wages by more than half. . . . In early 1995 the minimum pension was only about 30% of subsistence income. . . . The Russian education system is also deteriorating.

Russia and its associated republics from the former Soviet Union clearly are at a Third World economic level. However, as we look to the 21st century, it is important to note that this current low status is partly attributable to the short-term costs of a painful but necessary *transition* toward an open capitalist economy. The former Soviet Union, as it was being economically surpassed by former Third World nations such as South Korea, Taiwan, and Singapore, had to make a change; even if in the short run the massive costs of this historic transition dumped it into Third World economic status. Indeed, the presence of significant assets, particularly educated people and abundant natural resources, indicates that these republics can greatly advance their status if they continue to embrace freedom and economic reform.

Our new view of the Second World is that it is made up of nations that are *emerging* as key players in international business. This grouping is highlighted by the U. S. Commerce Department's very useful category— the "Big Emerging Markets," or BEMs. The Commerce Department originally started with ten BEMs: highly populated nations that were opening up to world trade and investment; good examples are China, India, and Mexico. Recently the Commerce Department has begun to recognize not only nations, but also regional groupings, and in particular, ASEAN, the Association of Southeast Asian Nations. So although the Commerce Department currently lists ten BEMs, these emerging markets actually comprise many more nations, at least 14 of which have such large populations and/or rapid trade growth and economic development that each deserves our own appellation of BEN—"Big Emerging Nation." Thus, our Second World consists of 14 BENs: Indonesia, the Philippines, Thailand, Malaysia, Vietnam, China, India, Brazil, Mexico, Argentina, Chile, Poland, Turkey, and South Africa.[8] Note that the first five nations listed are the largest economies included in ASEAN.[9] In counting these five

ASEAN nations separately, instead of as one big regional market, we move from the Commerce Department's ten BEMs to our 14 BENs.[10] General Motors is an example of a firm that has a strategic focus on the BENs; the five new vehicle plants it is building are in Argentina, Poland, China, Thailand, and Brazil. In response to the recent financial woes in Asia, however, the company did decide to scale back and delay the opening of its Thailand factory.[11]

Interestingly, our master spreadsheet shows that these 14 nations combined contain more than half the world's people. Although not nearly as rich as the 26 nations in the ITN, these nations have two compelling drivers on their side: the sheer scale and dynamism of their human resources as captured by demographic statistics, and the sustained economic growth that many of them are achieving. The rapid economic growth of big emerging nations is a subject we will analyze more deeply in Chapter 5. In Chapter 6, we will explore their 21st century economic potential; a massive potential that future business leaders must study and understand thoroughly.

Finally, we offer our version of the new Third World. We say "new" because some members of the traditional Third World, such as India or South Africa, have "graduated" to the Second World of BENs, while others have leapfrogged all the way to the First World of the ITN, notably South Korea and Singapore. Meanwhile, some nations, such as Ukraine and Russia, have slipped to a Third World level of despair, as the transition from command economies to a hoped-for capitalist revival bears a heavy economic cost. Again, our intent is to capture most of the world's people, as well as economic activity, in the subset of nations that we will study intensively. Therefore, in our third-tier grouping, we have selected the 13 relatively poor nations that the World Bank projects will each exceed 52 million people by the year 2030.

Tracking these 13 nations, although they are often ignored by business, is useful because huge or growing populations here should eventually command business attention. Our third tier contains Ukraine, Russia, Afghanistan, Burma (Myanmar), Egypt, Iran, Pakistan, Bangladesh, Nigeria, Ethiopia, the Democratic Republic of Congo (formerly Zaire), Tanzania, and the Sudan. Given the extreme poverty prevalent in these 13 nations, I have termed this tier the "Unlucky 13." Although blessed with many wonderful cultural and other attributes, I deem the term "unlucky" is appropriate, because people born into these nations currently face very dismal economic prospects. In many cases, even their life expectancy is tragically short. The unlucky starting point for most babies born in these populous, but poor, nations will be clear after we examine some of the dynamically linked problems that exist in this "Populous South Region" in Chapters 3 and 4.

Figure 1–2 shows quite clearly that the *Human Development Report*'s description of a huge gulf of inequality present in today's world is correct. This figure contrasts our first tier, the 26 nations in the ITN, with the 13 unlucky nations that comprise our third tier. Interestingly, these two tiers each comprise 15.9% of the world's population. Since the two groups have a population ratio of 1, we can easily compare them without further numerical manipulation. Figure 1–2 shows the *ratio* of the values of some

**Figure 1–2   THE LIMITED WORLD OF BUSINESS AS
THE 20TH CENTURY ENDS**

Total for 26 Advanced Nations (ITN) as ratio of total for 13 poor nations ("Unlucky 13")

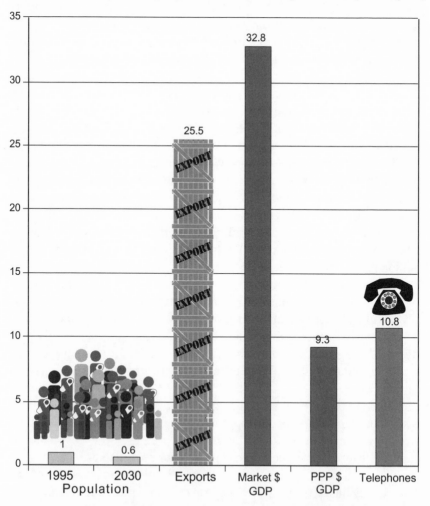

Source: Professor Jeffrey Rosensweig, Emory University, using World Bank, IMF, and ITU data.

key variables in the ITN to the values of those same key variables in the Unlucky 13 nations.

The first bar simply makes the point that the two tiers have equal current populations; therefore the ratio is exactly 1. The second bar in the graph holds a key to the future. It shows us that businesses hoping for prolonged expansion must look beyond the rich nations of the ITN because, at least in a demographic sense, future growth appears brightest everywhere *except* in the ITN! This is a major point of Paul Kennedy's book *Preparing for the Twenty-first Century:* 95% of the world's current population growth is occurring in the developing world, whereas only 5% of global population gains are in the advanced nations of the traditional triad.[12] What Figure 1–2 shows us is that by the year 2030, the Unlucky 13 nations will have a total population far exceeding the total of the twice as many nations that belong to our First World or ITN. Indeed, the ITN will total only 60% of the population that the Unlucky 13 is projected to reach in 2030. In other words, there will be *five* potential consumers or workers in the Unlucky 13 for every *three* in the ITN!

This stands in remarkable contrast to the remaining bars in Figure 1–2, which show the ratio between the two tiers for various relevant economic magnitudes. Readers can see from the third bar in Figure 1–2 why I term the 26 wealthy or triad nations in the first tier the "industrialized *trading* nations." Exports produced and sold by the 900 million people living in the ITN are more than 25 times the value of export revenues earned by the same number of people living in the Unlucky 13 nations. This 25:1 discrepancy certainly illustrates our point that at the end of the 20th century, certain nations are truly within an international trading network, whereas others are really not part of the too glibly cited "global village." This chapter is titled, "The Limited World of Business at the End of the 20th Century" because, despite the trends toward globalization described in the introduction, it is apparent that those great increases in total world trade mask a huge disparity between the first and third tiers.

DISPARITY ALONG THE GLOBAL INFORMATION HIGHWAY

Readers can also see from the final bar in Figure 1–2 why I say that the 26 rich nations in the ITN are members of an *information technology network:* they have nearly 11 times as many telephones as the equal number of people currently residing in the "Unlucky 13." It is exciting to talk about the power of commerce on the Internet, or how information technology is "making the world smaller," but it is important to realize that the Internet is not so empowering for someone in an African nation that has few or no host computers. The unequal ratio seen in the bar for telephones is an example of the gulf that we must cross if we are to have a truly global business environment.

A "teledensity" (phones per 100 people) 10.8 times higher for the rich ITN nations than for the poor nations comprising our unlucky third tier does indeed mark a large inequality. Note, however, that the ratio is actually much smaller than some of the other ratios reflected in Figure 1–2. The reason for this lesser disparity is that our third tier now contains some nations that actually *were* in the Second World, that is, in the former Soviet sphere of influence. These nations did build an extensive, albeit often inefficient and unreliable, infrastructure, and so today there are still many telephones in Russia and Ukraine.

The 900 million people in the ITN have 474 million main telephone lines available to them, or more than 50 per hundred people. This is in stark contrast to the fewer than 45 million phone lines available to the like number of people in the Unlucky 13, which is fewer than 5 phones per hundred people. An additional point I want to make here, however, is that even those 44.4 million telephones in the Unlucky 13 are dominated by the nearly 33.5 million in Russia and Ukraine. If not for the enhanced level of telephone access in these former members of the Second World, we would see a very stark disparity indeed.

This wide gulf in access to telecommunications, even basic telephones, let alone the Internet, is very apparent when we study the subset of the Unlucky 13 that are the five populous nations in the *Heart of Africa:* Nigeria, Ethiopia, Democratic Republic of Congo, Tanzania, and the Sudan. These desperately poor but highly populous nations have a mind-boggling lack of access to telephones. In fact, despite having 267 million people in 1995, these nations have fewer than 750,000 telephone lines, or one telephone per nearly 400 people. Saddest in this regard is the Democratic Republic of Congo which, with 40,000 telephone lines for over 43 million people, has less than one telephone per *thousand* people.

According to 1995 statistics, the combined population of the five nations in this subgroup is roughly the same as that of the United States— about 265 million people. The similarity ends there. In the United States, residents have access to over 164 million main telephone lines, or 62.5 lines per 100 people. The number of telephone lines available in the Heart of Africa is a mere 740,000. In other words, the same number of people in the United States have more than *225 times as many telephone lines.* Obviously, the nearly 11:1 telephone ratio bar in Figure 1–2 shows a large disparity, but not nearly as huge as when we focus on the very poor nations in the Heart of Africa.

Figure 1–3   DISTRIBUTION OF MAIN TELEPHONE LINES IN 1995:
Two-thirds in "Traditional Triad"

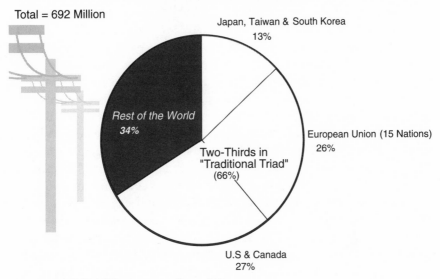

Total = 692 Million

Japan, Taiwan & South Korea
13%

Rest of the World
34%

European Union (15 Nations)
26%

Two-Thirds in
"Traditional Triad"
(66%)

U.S & Canada
27%

Data source: ITU, *World Telecommunication Report*, 1996.

Figure 1–3 is a convenient way to show that although international business is growing, with a cheap and effective communications infrastructure facilitating this growth, the extent of globalization has been strictly limited well into the 1990s. This figure isolates the nations that are truly "haves," portraying not the entire ITN, but just 20 wealthy nations at the core of the traditional triad. We see, for example, that the United States and Canada have more than one-quarter of the world's telephone lines, despite containing barely over 5% of world population. Similarly, the 15 nations in the European Union have 26% of world telephone lines, although they hold less than 7% of world population. If we isolate the most industrialized Asian nations that have fairly large populations—Japan, Taiwan, and South Korea—we see that they have fully 13% of the world's telephone lines despite having only 3.4% of world population.

The most interesting observation from a business perspective is that the entire rest of the world—all those roughly 200 nations outside the core of the traditional triad—contains only *one-third* of the world's telephone lines. This shows two very different things, depending on one's perspective. A pessimist can complain about the gross inequality existing in the world in the 1990s. The nations in the core of the traditional triad shown in Figure 1–3 have two-thirds of the world's telephones, yet they comprise less than 15% of world population. Indeed, if we add the other six nations of the ITN, such as Switzerland, Norway, and Australia, we find that less than 16% of the world's population has over 70% of its telephones.

But an optimist sees a great opportunity for business. Nations comprising over 85% of the world's population have only one-third of the world's telephones, and we will see in Chapter 5 that many of these nations are experiencing rapid economic growth. These nations will increasingly add consumers with the purchasing power to create an effective demand for more telephones. What a tremendous opportunity for companies that have anything to do with telecommunications or information technology, if only they would adopt a more global viewpoint! What we highlight here are literally billions of people without telephones, in nations which, although relatively poor *now,* demonstrate the *potential* to continue along the path of economic growth. What excites me is the notion that economic growth does not need to extend to the point where most of the citizens become wealthy, or even upper middle class. Instead, if economic growth proceeds to the point where the bulk of a nation's population just reaches lower-middle-class status, the demand for new telephony will be huge. We are already witnessing the start of this in nations such as China, which added 14 million new telephone lines during 1995, and is projected to add roughly 20 million new lines every year, well into the 21st century. Chapter 5 will look more deeply at the recent record of economic growth around the world and the implications for the emergence of a new lower middle class, which I believe can constitute "tomorrow's customers" for firms with the foresight to move toward a global strategy.

The Economist[13] recently analyzed the discrepancy in telephone access around the world, pointing out that some developing countries, notably those in Asia, are experiencing rapid increases in the number of telephone lines. However, *The Economist* also notes that Africa is desperately underserved by telephones and on some measures is falling ever further behind:

> Two out of three people have no access to a telephone. That is changing rapidly, but it is easier for countries to increase the availability of main lines if population growth is slow. China has been installing telephones at a tremendous pace, but it also has slow population growth by developing countries' standards. In Africa, by contrast, underfinanced telecoms operators struggle to keep pace with burgeoning members. In some they are losing ground. Many donors would like sub-Saharan Africa to have at least one line per one hundred people by the end of the century. At present the region, excluding South Africa, has only 0.48 lines for every one hundred people.

We can certainly sympathize with Africans or South Asians who are not very impressed by the argument that nearly costless communication is rapidly shrinking the globe and making global business a current reality. Many pundits forecast that business will increasingly shift to forms of electronic commerce as we move into the 21st century, with more and more business conducted directly over the Internet. But this exciting prospect, spotlighted in the Introduction, is not so exciting for those who live in African nations with a lack of Internet host computers and a paucity of network connections. For many Third World nations, the growth of electronic commerce raises the scary prospect that the economic information highway that will be built to the 21st century, will have virtually no on-ramps for their access. Thus, poor nations face the prospect of being excluded from the most dynamic area of growth in international commerce. As a result, these nations risk falling even further behind the nations that have more fully developed information technology networks.

Originally, I planned to include a graph showing the wide disparity between worldwide regional population shares and the corresponding regional shares of Internet connections or host computers. However, the Internet and the World Wide Web are growing so rapidly that any chart would be outdated by the time you read this book. Thus, I merely include suggestive figures to give you an idea that, in terms of linkages to the so-called global information highway, there truly are "haves" and "have nots."

The *Wall Street Journal* summarized the huge disparity in Internet access in a major article entitled "Web's Heavy U.S. Accent Grates on Overseas Ears."[14] The article showed that nearly three-quarters of the world's users of the World Wide Web are residents of the United States. A further 10.8% are in Europe, while Canada and Mexico have 8.4% of total World Wide Web users. Interestingly, the English-speaking people in Australia and New Zealand constitute a full 3.6% of Web users. Here's the upshot: the countries just listed, with about one-sixth of the world's total population, represent over 96% of the globe's World Wide Web users. The same article cited estimates by the consulting firm Network Wizards that the United States accounts for 64% of the host computers on the Internet. Moreover, the first-tier economic powers in our ITN group contain nearly 98% of the world's Internet host computers. This total domination of the Internet by the 26 wealthy industrialized nations of the triad validates my alternative concept of the ITN as an information-technology-networked grouping. The Internet can become an information highway for global commerce, but its limited on-ramps currently exacerbate the global disparities highlighted in this chapter.

CONTRASTING MEASURES OF GROSS DOMESTIC PRODUCTION

Returning to Figure 1–2, an interesting distinction can be seen in the two bars that constitute the ratios of gross domestic production (GDP). GDP is the favorite measure of national income used by economists and analysts, as well as business people and investors, worldwide. There are two distinct ways to measure GDP when making international comparisons. Both start by measuring a nation's GDP in its own currency, and then convert it to a common standard, such as the U.S. dollar. The difference lies in the conversion step.

The first method translates a nation's currency to the U.S. dollar using current *market* exchange rates. For example, if the international banks and foreign exchange dealers that constitute the world's foreign exchange market are currently trading at a market exchange rate of eight units of a nation's currency for one U.S. dollar; then we would divide that nation's GDP, as measured in its own currency, by eight to calculate its value in market-determined U.S. dollar terms.

The second method pays less respect to the market-determined exchange rate, concentrating instead on the *relative purchasing power* of various nations' currencies. This method attempts to figure out what exchange rate would give "purchasing power parity" (PPP). That is, it determines what *hypothetical* exchange rate would make the purchasing power of the U.S. dollar the same if you bought a typical market basket of goods in the United States and then went to another country and bought the same goods in that nation's currency.

A practical example should help illustrate the difference. Assume a Big Mac costs $2.00 in the United States and 8 kroner in Denmark, and that Big Macs are generally representative of relative prices in these two nations. We could then use the relative price of a Big Mac in each nation's respective currency to calculate the "PPP exchange rate," that is, the exchange rate that would make our purchasing power the same whether we spent our money in the United States or in Denmark. In this case, an exchange rate of 4 Danish kroner for 1 U.S. dollar would mean that for $2.00, I could eat a Big Mac in the United States, or I could get the 8 kroner needed to buy a Big Mac in Denmark. Thus, 4 kroner per dollar would be the PPP exchange rate.

Now, assume the market exchange rate is only 2 Danish kroner for a U.S. dollar. This implies that it would take 4 U.S. dollars to obtain the 8 kroner needed to eat a Big Mac in Denmark. Eating in Denmark would seem twice as expensive as eating in the United States. Economists would say that the Danish krone is "overvalued," since it is relatively expensive to exchange dollars into kroner and purchase products in Denmark. Conversely, the U.S. dollar is "undervalued" by the market. This type of PPP exchange rate calculation is the basis of the very clever and quite useful "Big Mac index" maintained by *The Economist* magazine for many years.

The "Big Mac indexes" show that there are often large deviations of a nation's market exchange rate from the hypothetical PPP exchange rate. Not surprisingly to international travelers, many Western European nations and Japan are typically found to have exchange rates that are over-valued by the market; thereby making purchases in these nations relatively expensive. By contrast, nations in Southeast Asia or parts of the developing world have undervalued currencies; that is, to an American, purchases in these nations seem quite cheap, as their currencies seem very undervalued by the market.

The distinction between GDP measured using market exchange rates and GDP that is converted to U.S. dollars using the hypothetical PPP exchange rates is crucial in this book, particularly in Chapter 6. We see its significance directly in Figure 1–2. Many ITN nations have highly valued currencies, as investors favor or demand them because of the wealth and stability of such nations. Germany, Switzerland, and Japan are examples of nations whose currencies are very highly valued by the market, resulting in relatively high prices there. The ITN has more than 32.8 times the value of GDP of the 13 nations in our third tier. Of course, since the groups' total populations are the same, this means that per capita market income is 32.8 times as high in the First World as the Third World.

Interestingly and importantly, there is still a wide gap, but not nearly as large, if one measures GDP using the hypothetical exchange rates that yield purchasing power equality in any country in the world. When we convert nations' local currency GDP into U.S. dollars using the World Bank's purchasing power parity (PPP) exchange rate estimates, we see that the inequality is not nearly so great. The upshot is that a dollar goes very far in most places in Africa or rural India, and if we consider what people are eating, for example, rather than asking "What is their income in terms of dollars at market exchange rates," we see that the living standard in the Third World, although very poor, is not as nearly as unequal as when we use market exchange rates.

For example, if we converted India's currency at market exchange rates, the per capita income or GDP in 1995 was roughly $340. We may wonder how people could live for an entire year on $340 per person; but in fact, India's currency goes much further than $340 would go in the United States. Indeed, the World Bank, in its *1997 Atlas,* estimates that India's per person income is more than four times higher if one looks at the actual relative purchasing power within India instead of the $340 based on market exchange rates. Thus, at a U.S. supermarket we pay a dollar for a few bananas, whereas in India we would be able to purchase those same bananas for about 25 cents. Because the purchasing power of a dollar goes so much further in India, converting Indians' incomes at market exchange rates and trying to make some comparisons about standard of living can be misleading. The rupees an Indian earns translates into few dollars at current market exchange rates, yet those rupees enable the person in India to buy bananas (and other necessities!) at prices that are relatively cheaper than prices in the United States.

We see similar ratios of three or four times higher incomes for the relatively poor nations in Africa and South Asia using the hypothetical PPP exchange rate, rather than market exchange rates. Hence, Figure 1–2 shows that the ratio of income when we look at relative domestic purchasing power (PPP) is more like 9:1 rather than 33:1. Nine-to-one still shows tremendous inequality, but at least now we understand how poor people in the "Unlucky 13" somehow manage to eat despite average per capita incomes below $300 a year when converted using market exchange rates.

Which measure of GDP is correct for making international comparisons—one based on actual market exchange rates, or one based on the hypothetical exchange rates that would equate purchasing power (PPP) around the world? The simple answer is that neither one is perfect. Both have their advantages and the best solution probably depends on what you are trying to compare. If you want to analyze the power of a certain nation or its ability to command control over world products and world assets, then you should probably use GDP converted at market exchange rates, because it shows the actual ability of a nation to purchase products and assets on an international basis. Therefore, when we talk about world power at the end of the 20th century, it is important to realize that in terms of the actual ability to get U.S. dollars or other hard currencies, people in poor nations have very little global purchasing power.

The ratio of 33:1 gives us some idea of the gross inequality when it comes, for instance, to the ability to purchase a vacation home at a desirable spot in Europe or to send children to an Ivy League college. On the other hand, if we are concerned about the actual comparative living standards *within* the various nations, then the calculations using the PPP exchange rates that give equivalent purchasing powers can be quite useful. The gap is not nearly as wide as it seems when using market exchange rates, but a 9:1 ratio still shows that living standards in the ITN far surpass those in the nations we have branded the "Unlucky 13." In Chapter 6, we will further pursue this notion of measuring national economies based on equalized relative purchasing power, in order to get an idea of the standard of living of various countries and, more importantly, the future potential of such economies.

INTERNATIONAL TRADE: THE GLOBAL GAP

Returning once again to global trade, we will now see if the "80/20 rule" applies to the huge gulf in export revenue between the first and third tiers. Figure 1–4 illustrates the great challenge of more widespread economic development looming ahead for the world as we move into the 21st century. The massive inequality reflected by an 80/20 rule is quite apparent in world trade statistics, as nations with over 80% of the world population sell only 20% of total world exports. Conversely, nations with less than 20% of the world's people earn 80% of its export revenues. The left-hand pie chart in Figure 1–4 portrays this 80/20 split by distinguishing major regions of global export trade and their relative shares of world exports. Not surprisingly, the dominant trading tier (the ITN) is mainly composed of the triad of industrialized Europe, North America (excluding Mexico in this case), and industrialized Asia. Notice, as in "The World According to Trade," the prominence of Europe in world trade, as well as the growing importance of industrialized Asia.

The population pie chart is divided in a different way than the trade chart, and shows the key areas where over 80% of the world's people live.

Figure 1–4   THE CHALLENGE OF DEVELOPMENT
The Population vs. Trade Divide
(Nations with over 80% of the world population sell less than 20% of its exports)

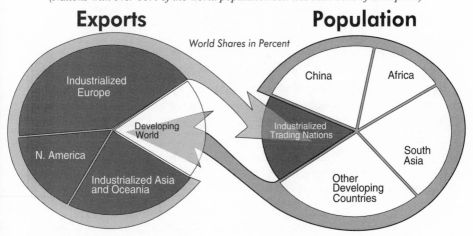

Industrialized Trading Nations: 17 in Europe, U.S., Canada, Japan, Oceania, 6 East Asian Tigers

Source: IMF and World Bank data for 1995.

Because of a lack of economic development, these areas now have only a limited share of world business (in this case world trade). Obviously, no discussion of world population shares can ignore China and South Asia, but we also see that Africa has a large slice of the world population pie and that other developing countries, such as those in Southwest Asia and South America, have a very large slice as well.

It is important to note that in this chart I have expanded the definition of industrialized trading nations slightly to include not just the usual four East Asian Little Tigers but also two more potential East Asian Tigers: Malaysia and Thailand. Why have I done so here? Recall that our goal is to see if an 80/20 rule holds for world trade. The ITN, as discussed earlier, includes just under 16% of world population and earns 78% of world export revenue. By adding Malaysia and Thailand to the ITN, we create a group that accounts for over 80% of world exports, yet still comprises well less than 20% of world population.

Finally, when we think of power in the 21st century, we would do well to consider the massive influence of the world's largest firms. *Fortune* annually ranks the world's 500 biggest firms by total global revenues. An analysis of a recent "*Fortune* Global 500" ranking15 reveals that more than 97% of the world's biggest firms were headquartered in the 26 wealthy nations of the ITN. A mere thirteen, or 2.6%, of them were based in all other nations—those comprising 84% of world population. Furthermore, only four, or 2%, of the global top 200, the truly powerful firms, are based outside the ITN.[16]

FOREIGN DIRECT INVESTMENT TRENDS: UNEQUAL ACCESS

Despite the rather limited range of most international business character-izing the era up to the 1990s, recent signs indicate some significant causes for optimism. The arena for international business is suddenly expanding aggressively, and business leaders would be wise to continue shifting some of their focus toward developing countries and away from the tradi-tional triad.

A recent edition of *Trends in Private Investment in Developing Countries,* a discussion paper by the International Finance Corporation of the World Bank, summarizes the crucial reasons for my optimism:

> In the 1990s, private investment in developing countries has undergone a marked revival. . . . Closer global integration of both the international trading and financial systems has meant that

economically and politically stable developing countries have experienced unprecedented access to international goods markets and sources of international capital with the result that economic growth rates have accelerated.[17]

Good news for some developing countries is not, however, relevant across the globe. The International Finance Corporation (IFC) paper also details marked disparities in investment, reporting that East Asia has the highest investment rates and sub-Saharan Africa has the lowest, and steadily decreasing, rates; while Latin America has seen rising rates of investment.

Thus, the two key trends are that more foreign investment is flowing into developing countries, but that the flows are concentrated in a few developing nations. The IFC report (p. 7) illustrates both trends, stating that while foreign direct investment flows (FDI) have risen during the 1990s, only five East Asian nations—China, Indonesia, Malaysia, the Philippines, and Thailand—received a total of *half* of the FDI flows to all developing nations since 1990. These trends are further confirmed in a recent World Bank book, *1996 Global Economic Prospects and the Developing Countries*.[18] Clearly then, firms are investing directly in the developing world, but are mainly targeting the five big "recently industrializing countries" (RICs) of East Asia, and to a lesser extent, the few major economies in Latin America, while essentially ignoring Africa and Southwest Asia. Using our construct, the second tier BENs are integrating into the global economy as they attract massive direct investments from globalizing firms, while the nations of the third tier are being largely left behind.

Foreign direct investment is a key to the continuing evolution of global business, as Edward Graham makes clear in his useful book, *Global Corporations and National Governments*.[19] Graham begins by validating the existence of the global forces that we discussed in the Introduction, maintaining that "a massive surge in foreign direct investment (FDI) has led to the deepest integration of the world economy in history." Graham makes it clear that FDI is a powerful globalizing force for business and the world economy:

. . . FDI does not contribute only capital to the world economy. Foreign operations of large multinational firms also help to transform the economies in which they operate through technology transfer, and by introducing new and better management techniques, providing market access to other countries, and increasing competition.[20]

Graham also points out that while developing nations once accused global corporations of exploiting the local economy, most nations now recognize "the positive contributions of FDI and global corporations to economic development in . . . raising growth levels, efficiency, and living standards."[21]

Let us now look at the recent evidence on evolving trends regarding foreign direct investment flows. The United Nations Conference on Trade and Development (UNCTAD) summarizes the unequal flow of FDI in its *World Investment Report 1996 (WIR 1996)*. This report shows that the inequality discussed above continues:

> Investment flows are concentrated in a few countries. The ten largest host countries received two thirds of total inflows in 1995 and the smallest 100 recipient countries received only 1%. . . . In the case of outflows, the largest five home countries (the U.S., Germany, the U.K., Japan, and France) accounted for about two thirds of all outflows in 1995.[22]
>
> Almost 90% of the 1995 increases in FDI inflows (and outflows) were registered by developed countries. Because of this the share of developed countries in world inflows increased from 59% in 1994 to 65% in 1995 while outflows rose from 83% to 85%.[23]

Recent data confirm the continued dominance of the triad (ITN) in world FDI flows. The United States remained by far the largest recipient of FDI inflows in 1996, as its total inflow of $80.5 billion nearly doubled China's inflow. The U.S. FDI inflow was up 41% from 1995, reaching three times its 1993 value! Furthermore, a full 90% of the FDI flowing to the United States came from just a few countries, representing a core subset of the ITN: Canada, European nations, Japan, and Australia.[24]

In absolute terms, FDI flows into emerging nations did rise sharply each of the past few years. However, even these increased FDI flows to developing countries are not at all uniformly distributed.

> South, East and South-East Asia continued to be the largest host developing region, with an estimated 65 billion of inflows in 1995, accounting for two thirds of all developing country FDI inflows.
>
> The size and dynamism of developing Asia have made it increasingly important for TNCs from all countries to service rapidly expanding markets, or to tap the tangible and intangible resources of that region for global production networks. . . . China

has been the largest developing-country recipient since 1992. . . . China has been the principal drive behind Asia's current investment boom.[25]

WIR 1996 contrasts this Asian boom with Africa, noting that Africa has remained marginalized (see p. xviii). Not only has Africa received a small and declining share of total FDI, but the trends show that southern Africa has had its share diminished substantially, in contrast to the increasing share in North Africa. The surge of private capital into emerging markets in the 1990s has almost entirely missed sub-Saharan Africa. Between 1990 and 1995, the net yearly inflow of foreign direct investment (FDI) in developing countries nearly quadrupled, to over $90 billion; but Africa's share of this fell to only 2.4%. In 1995, the whole of sub-Saharan Africa, excluding South Africa, received less than $2.2 billion in net FDI. That amount is less than the sum invested in Chile alone.

My own research shows that the United States is a prime example of a nation that contains many so-called global corporations, yet does little to integrate Africa into the global economy through foreign direct investment. Recent data[26] show that Africa's share of the total stock of FDI invested by U.S. firms has fallen below 1%, a startling drop from an already low 3% share of the total stock in the early 1980s. In addition, African firms or investors hold only 0.2% of the stock of FDI invested in the United States. Thus, so-called global firms are doing little at this time to integrate Africa with the United States.[27]

I conclude by offering *three key trends*. First, the vast majority of FDI still originates in the wealthy triad of developed nations and remains mainly invested in other nations in this wealthy network. Second, developing countries are generally attracting a rapidly increasing flow of FDI; but third, these increased FDI flows to the developing world show a great deal of concentration or inequality.

SUMMARY AND IMPLICATIONS

Obviously, trends such as the massive flows of private foreign direct investment to China and ASEAN nations indicate there are reasons for optimism in major portions of the developing world. Wide disparities continue, however, not only between the advanced and the developing world, but increasingly within the broad grouping called the developing world. Business is most interested in the big emerging markets, particularly those in East Asia and Latin America. These markets seem set to join the global trading club, an exciting development for business, as we will see in the next chapter.

The important point, from the perspective of businesses that hope to grow, is the vast potential stemming from a more global approach to business. First, we have seen that going beyond one's own nation to do business throughout the nations of the traditional triad can open up a huge level of economic and international business activity. Traditionally, business has been able to expand internationally and gain access to a large proportion of world purchasing power through a focus on only two dozen nations. That is the strategy, for instance, implied by most of Kenichi Ohmae's writings. However, the intent of this book is to show that a strategy aiming to ensure growth well into the 21st century needs to embrace a more truly global perspective. Although up until recent years a vast majority of the action in international business was confined to the traditional triad, we have seen in this chapter that big emerging nations are becoming increasingly interesting to business.

Furthermore, most of the world's population, and almost all of its population growth, are in nations outside the traditional nexus of international business. Thus, in the next few chapters we will study the likely evolution of the global economy, focusing on the most probable growth pattern for the international business network. We will examine those countries most likely to graduate into the more advanced economic status captured by our concept of the ITN. Recall that for the ITN depicted in Figure 1–4 to achieve fully 80% of world exports and closer to 20% of world population, we needed to add Malaysia and Thailand to it. This foreshadows what I hope to do in Chapter 2, where we develop our strategic theory that the traditional triad is becoming an outdated concept, and introduce the new concept of an "Extended Triad." Then, in Chapter 3 we will examine the many nations that are still not a part of the network of international business, be it trade or investment, to any significant extent.

CHAPTER 2

———————— ⊕ ————————

BUSINESS STRATEGY INTO THE 21ST CENTURY:

Extending the Triad

The arena for international business in the years leading into the new century has changed spectacularly since 1990. At that time, most international business was confined to the "traditional triad," as portrayed in the preceding chapter. Economic integration in the Americas was largely limited to the Free Trade Agreement (FTA) between the United States and Canada. Japan, with perhaps a minor assist from South Korea or the other East Asian newly industrialized countries (NICs), represented the Asian part of the triad, while the twelve nations then in the European Union made up the European segment. There was no World Trade Organization (WTO) and very little movement toward a global economy.

Based on the events and actions of the 1990s, we see great cause for optimism that businesses can prosper from a much more global strategy now and in the new millennium. A main reason for optimism is that trade integration has already begun to occur on a macro-regional scale, primarily through the expansion of the three triad areas. Our model predicts continued expansion of this main arena for international business, in part supported by the substantial momentum already achieved within each of the three areas. Although this expansion still adheres to the structure of a triad, we predict a much more *extended triad model* than that which dominated global business through the early 1990s. We will explore the expansion of the triad in more detail below.

A second main reason for optimism is the success of the last and largest round of global (termed "multilateral") negotiations toward liberalizing

Lori Sullivan significantly contributed to the research and writing of this chapter.

47

trade. In April 1994, after eight years of negotiation, the Uruguay Round of the GATT (General Agreement on Tariffs and Trade) finally reached its belated but successful conclusion, which led to the formation of the World Trade Organization. The WTO, based in Geneva, is the primary international body dealing with the rules of trade between nations. Operating under a number of international laws governing commerce and trade policy, its primary goal is to facilitate the free flow of trade, but it also works to further liberalize trade and to resolve trade disputes. This agreement was critical because, even as trade expands through the formation of trading blocs at the *regional* level, the WTO represents a parallel process aimed at achieving open trade and investment *worldwide.*

Readers desiring a more detailed description of the evolving multilateral trading system, particularly a deeper assessment of the implications of the Uruguay Round and the formation of the WTO, should read the recent book by John Whalley and Colleen Hamilton, *The Trading System after the Uruguay Round.*[1] Readers should also be advised that some analysts are less optimistic than I am about the world continuing toward a more global, free-trading economy.[2]

THE REGIONAL PATH TO A MORE GLOBAL ECONOMY

The path to a truly global economy leads well into the 21st century. Thus, business leaders are wise to focus now on the emerging and evolving regional entities that may hold the key to business structure, strategy, and success. Kenichi Ohmae has shown business leaders and scholars alike the strategic importance of thinking about regions, and not just nations, as natural economic units. Ohmae, a prolific author and former senior partner of McKinsey & Co., is an erstwhile Japanese political leader and reformer. In a series of influential articles[3] and in his book *The End of the Nation State: The Rise of Regional Economies,*[4] Ohmae has taught many of us the importance of thinking in *regional* rather than only national or only global terms.

Ohmae favors what he terms the "region state" as the natural business unit in today's global economy.[5] Region states, such as Hong Kong/southern China or San Diego/Tijuana, often ignore national or territorial dividing lines. Ohmae states his case as follows:

In a borderless world, these are the natural economic zones. Though limited in geographical size, they are often huge in their economic influence. . . . These region states may or may not fall within the borders of a particular nation. Whether they do is purely an accident of history. In practical terms, it really does not matter. Like Singapore, many are, in effect, city states. . . . [6]

It is important to realize that other leading scholars, while concurring that global or regional economies often transcend national borders, do not predict the demise of the nation-state. For example, management guru Peter F. Drucker, in a recent article in *Foreign Affairs*[7] also concludes that the nation-state will survive:

Since talk of the globalization of the world's economy began some 35 years ago, the demise of the nation-state has been widely predicted. . . . Despite all its shortcomings, the nation-state has shown amazing resilience. . . . So far, at least, there is no other institution capable of political integration and effective membership in the world's political community. In all probability, therefore, the nation-state will survive the globalization of the economy and the information revolution that accompanies it.

Still, most observers agree that business will generally transcend national boundaries and that Ohmae's concept of region states is useful. In my teaching, I refer to Ohmae's original concept of region states as "micro-regions." His region states are powerful, but small.

Region states tend to have between five million and 20 million people. The range is broad, but the extremes are clear: not half a million, not 50 or 100 million. A region state must be small enough for its citizens to share certain economic and consumer interests but of adequate size to justify the infrastructure—communication and transportation links and quality professional services—necessary to participate economically on a global scale.[8]

Ohmae's region states may indeed be natural economic or business units, but I believe that they prosper more when they attain the economies of scale available to members of larger free trade areas. I term these evolving large regional free trade areas "macro-regions" and will detail their emergence and evolution later in this chapter. These macro-regions encompass Ohmae's region states or micro-regions. But by removing national barriers to free trade among constituent parts of region states that may lie in different nations, macro-regions enable them to further prosper.

The three key macro-regions discussed below will each contain greater than 500 million people by early in the 21st century, according to my forecasts. As such, they are an entirely different order of magnitude than Ohmae's region states. However, the two ideas are *complementary:* both show the importance of thinking in regional terms, not merely national terms, as the path for business strategy. Clearly, firms need to consider both micro- and macro-regions as they set strategy along the road to a more truly global economy in the 21st century.

Let us trace a possible scenario for the gradual but significant extension of the triad, hoping this portrayal will help guide a time-phased strategy for international business expansion.

EXTENDING THE TRIAD

I. AN EMERGING INTEGRATED AMERICAS ECONOMY

In December 1994, government leaders resolved to achieve significant economic integration of the Americas when they met at the Hemispheric Summit of the Americas in Miami. Thirty-four countries in North, Central, and South America, as well as the Caribbean, reached preliminary accord by accepting the U.S. Hemispheric Proposal to build a Free Trade Area of the Americas (FTAA) by 2005. Such an integration would be very exciting, for it would allow businesses to adopt an "Americas strategy for growth" in the next decade.

Since the early 1990s, integration in the Americas has proceeded along two very important but distinct tracks. First, the free trade agreement between the United States and Canada was extended to a true North American Free Trade Agreement (NAFTA) with the addition of Mexico on January 1, 1994. Second, integration is proceeding in Latin America itself, notably through the unexpected success and probable future expansion of Mercosur, an emerging free trade area in South America.

One possible scenario for integration of the Americas is the extension of our current piece of the wealthy triad, NAFTA, southward into more of a free trade area for all, or at least most, of the Americas. However, certain U.S. presidential candidates (Ross Perot, Pat Buchanan, and Richard Gephardt), plus other vociferous critics of NAFTA (including labor union leaders), have significantly checked such progress. The loss of and subsequent inability to restore "fast-track authority"[9] to President Clinton has delayed the acceptance of Chile into NAFTA,[10] as domestic U.S. political pressures threaten to topple the U.S. position as the leader of the economic integration of the Americas. Meanwhile, Chile has chosen not to wait passively for acceptance, but rather to negotiate a number of trade agreements and linkages on its own, including one with Canada. Interestingly, *The Economist* notes that Canada is now seen by many "pan-American free trade" advocates as the North American nation most favorable to continued integration.[11] It is time for the United States to put aside political bickering and resume the leadership position it clearly established at the 1994 Miami Summit, when the motion to unite all of the Americas was brought to the floor as the U.S. Hemispheric Proposal. I make this strong statement because resuming integration would clearly benefit the growth prospects of many U.S. firms, and would eventually enhance the welfare of the vast majority of people in the Americas, including those in the United States. Thus, it is a strategy that links people with profits.

Meanwhile, economic integration in the Americas has not waited for the leaders of the United States to expand NAFTA southward. Rather, like Chile, the other South American nations have initiated their own bilateral and regional trade agreements. The most important of these, Mercosur, or "Common Market of the South," was created by four South American nations: Brazil, Argentina, Paraguay, and Uruguay. When it was implemented on January 1, 1995, it became the world's fourth largest trade bloc (after the European Union, NAFTA, and ASEAN). Mercosur contains 205 million inhabitants, the majority of whom (160 million) reside in Portuguese-speaking Brazil. Thus, Mercosur has two official languages, Spanish and Portuguese.[12]

Mercosur accounts for almost 60% of the total economic output of Latin America. In late 1996, Chile and Bolivia became associate members, further widening the scope of the alliance. Including these two associate members, Mercosur constitutes roughly two-thirds of the economic activity of Latin America. *The Economist* summarized (26 July 1997, p. 66) the tremendous progress Mercosur has made in integrating member economies in South America:

> Beyond a doubt Mercosur, the South American trade agreement, has made for closer relations among its members. International trade among Argentina, Brazil, Paraguay and Uruguay increased from $5 billion in 1991 to $16.9 billion in 1996, and cross-border investment is growing apace.

Even more significantly, if NAFTA expansion gets back on track, Chile is "on deck" as the likely next member. Thus, Chile can serve as a bridge between the two large trade groupings in the Americas: NAFTA in the north and Mercosur in the south. Linking the three NAFTA nations and the six Mercosur members and associate members would result in an integration of a great majority of the economic mass and business potential of the Americas.

The Americas macro-regional expansion might occur through the addition of nations to NAFTA, or via a merger of Mercosur and NAFTA, or by some other track. The actual mechanism is not as important as the forecast that the traditional triad power of North America will expand to include the other American economies. Thus, we expect (and hope!) that the emerging Americas macro-region will show significant integration by the year 2000.

Figure 2–1 shows the beginning steps of an extended triad, where an Americas trade bloc begins to form beyond the current NAFTA. By 2000 (or shortly after), I predict that first Chile, and then Argentina, should gain entrance into what is currently called NAFTA. I term this new entity "NAFTA &," to indicate that once these two nations join, our free trade area will extend beyond North America. Thus, we will enter the new century with a growing free trade area in the Americas that encompasses nearly half a billion people.

EXTENDING THE TRIAD

II. THE EVOLUTION OF AN INTEGRATED EUROPEAN ECONOMY

In contrast to the emerging Americas economy, a European macro-regional economy has been integrated and functioning for a number of years now. It traces its origin back decades, but the first large step toward unification occurred in 1950. The Schuman Declaration, which stated that "the gathering of the nations of Europe requires the elimination of the age-old opposition of France and Germany," recognized that Europe had been completely destroyed three times in 75 years by Franco-German wars. Six nations originally rallied to the concept of a united Europe when, on April 18, 1951, the Treaty of Paris was signed, setting up the European Coal and Steel Community. The six nations were France, the Federal Republic of Germany, Italy, Belgium, Luxembourg, and the Netherlands. This highly successful treaty resulted in a dramatic increase in coal and steel trade between these nations.

The Treaty of Paris was a significant first step toward European integration, but it provided economic integration in only two industries. In 1957, the Treaties of Rome were signed by the same six nations, setting up the European Economic Community (EEC), which established targets aimed at lowering tariff (import tax or duty) levels on most goods traded between these nations. Again, dramatic results were seen. Between 1958 and 1970, trade increased over sixfold within the EEC, and threefold between the EEC and the rest of the world. Also, average real GNP within the EEC rose by 70% during the same period. Europe's integration— movement toward free trade and a single market—allowed trade expansion to be a locomotive of overall economic growth.

The EEC sought to expand its membership by allowing any nation in Europe to apply for admission, provided that nation had in place democratic procedures and was committed to the same fundamental objectives and

Figure 2–1   THE "EXTENDED TRIAD" AND THE POPULOUS SOUTH
Projected Population (millions) in Year 2000

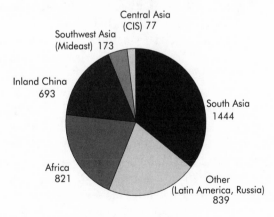

conditions established by the founding treaties. The first wave of EEC expansion occurred on January 1, 1973, when the United Kingdom, Ireland, and Denmark became members. Thus, the six-nation core at the heart of continental Europe expanded northwesterly to a group of nine. The 1980s saw a second round of expansion to the south, with Greece joining in 1981 and Spain and Portugal in 1986, bringing the total to twelve nations.

A new direction was taken by the EEC in the 1990s. On November 1, 1993, a treaty signed in Maastricht established the European Union (EU), transforming the EEC from a primarily economic community to one that hopes to coordinate foreign and security policy, defense, justice, and domestic affairs. Essentially, political union was begun with the formation of the EU. The Maastricht Treaty also began the process of establishing a common currency in Europe, the Euro. Of course, the path toward a European Economic and Monetary Union (EMU) has been rocky, but I forecast it will become fully established in the coming years.

Membership in the EU again was increased on January 1, 1994, with the addition of Sweden, Finland, and Austria. The inclusion of nations that were compelled to remain neutral during the Cold War highlights the new potential for business expansion unleashed by the Soviet Union's demise and dissolution. This round of expansion brought the total membership to 15 nations, where it currently stands, with a population of 360 million.

Other countries that have applied for membership in the past decade or so are:

1987: Turkey
1990: Cyprus and Malta
1992: Switzerland (its voters later rejected inclusion in a referendum)
1994: Poland and Hungary
1995: Bulgaria, Estonia, Latvia, Lithuania, Romania, and Slovakia
1996: Czech Republic and Slovenia

In July 1997, the EU placed six nations on the short list to begin negotiations: Estonia, the Czech Republic, Hungary, Poland, Slovenia, and Cyprus. Note that five out of the six are Central and Eastern European nations formerly coerced to join the Warsaw Pact rather than the open capitalist world. Thus, forty years of effort since the Treaty of Rome have led to the advanced stage of integration achieved by Europe, as opposed to the budding integration begun by America. Clearly, the EU is well on its way to becoming a macro-regional integrated area.

Around the year 2000, I expect that the most economically advanced nations in Central Europe will graduate from their current associate member status to become members of a broader European economic area. In Figure 2–1, I include Hungary, the Czech Republic, and Poland under the title "Central Europe 3." These three nations are the furthest along the path toward capitalism, having been the first to begin serious economic reforms and the dismantling of their respective state-dominated economies. Furthermore, the

European economic area in a de facto or business sense includes nations that opted to remain in the European Free Trade Area (EFTA), rather than join the EU. I include these small but quite wealthy and industrialized nations, Switzerland and Norway, in the European economic bloc, because they receive reciprocal trading privileges with the EU and are economically highly integrated with it. Interestingly, Figure 2–1 shows that the European bloc will have essentially the same population as the bloc that should be formed in the Americas by the year 2000. These two blocs will be very wealthy and growing focal points for business as the new century dawns. Yet both are predicted to grow even further in the succeeding decades, as we will see later in this chapter.

EXTENDING THE TRIAD

III. STEPS TOWARD INTEGRATION IN THE ASIA-PACIFIC REGION

East Asia shows signs of economic integration that go well beyond the very informal relationships dominated by Japan and Korea at the beginning of the 1990s. Since then, there has been tremendous momentum toward both East Asian integration and a wider integration of economies all along the borders of the Pacific. This momentum is highlighted by the success of APEC and ASEAN.

APEC, the Asia Pacific Economic Cooperation forum, was inaugurated in 1989 in Australia. Formed to advance open trade in the region, APEC grew from an original twelve members to eighteen economies on both sides of the Pacific by 1994. In 1995, APEC had a combined GDP of over U.S. $13 trillion, which represented approximately 55% of total world income and 46% of world trade.

In 1994, the same year as the adoption of the U.S. Hemispheric

APEC Member Economies

Australia	Malaysia
Brunei Darussalam	Mexico
Canada	New Zealand
Chile	Papua New Guinea
People's Republic of China	Republic of the Philippines
Hong Kong, China	Singapore
Indonesia	Chinese Taipei (Taiwan)
Japan	Thailand
Republic of Korea (South)	United States

Proposal by the leaders of the Americas economies, APEC leaders adopted the Declaration of Common Resolve at their meeting in Bogor, Indonesia. Of great significance to business, the leaders of the eighteen nations pledged to create "free and open trade and investment" in the Asia Pacific macro-region by the year 2020. APEC contains the three largest economies on earth—the United States, Japan, and China—as well as exciting up-and-comers such as Indonesia, Korea, Thailand, Mexico, and Chile. Thus, if APEC continues to make progress toward free trade and investment in the Pacific, no corporation can afford to ignore this evolution when forming its business strategy.

East Asian integration has been accelerated by the success of ASEAN, the Association of Southeast Asian Nations, which also forms a dynamic core of APEC. Five nations (Indonesia, Malaysia, Philippines, Singapore, and Thailand) signed the Bangkok Declaration in August 1967, formally establishing ASEAN. Brunei joined in 1984, and Vietnam became the seventh member in 1995. The admission of Vietnam to ASEAN shows the dynamic evolution toward a more open capitalist international business orientation in Southeast Asia, an orientation that has most business leaders quite excited. The telling irony is that "ASEAN was founded in 1967, primarily as a political group to counter Vietnamese communist aggression."[13]

Yoichi Funabashi details the success of ASEAN, which foreshadows its rising importance for business strategy (p. 166).

Beside its success of maintaining a unified position against Vietnamese expansion, ASEAN's greatest achievement has been economic growth and expanded trade, although it was not originally dedicated to economic integration. Since its inauguration, all of the ASEAN economies, with the exception of the Philippines, have enjoyed growth rates greater than 5% per year. In some cases these rates have approached or exceeded 10%. In 1992 ASEAN launched the ASEAN Free Trade Area (AFTA), which targeted tariff levels on selected manufacturing and service sectors.

With the inclusion of Vietnam, ASEAN has come full circle, and with a market of more than 420 million consumers (or potential employees) it is a new focal point for business leaders throughout the world. On July 24, 1997, Laos and Myanmar (Burma) were admitted to ASEAN during its thirtieth anniversary celebration, bringing its total membership to nine nations. The initial plan was to expand to ten members, but this was abandoned after Cambodia's tragic coup in July 1997. The eventual status of Myanmar and Cambodia, given their lack of democracy, should remain contentious issues. Indeed, the ASEAN attitude toward the inclusion of these two nations may be changing even as you read this book. As we enter the new century, the Asian part of the triad clearly extends well beyond (south of) Japan in the strategies of foresighted business leaders.

Figure 2–1 also shows my projection of the formation of a macroregional trading bloc in industrializing East Asia. Unlike the East Asian bloc in the traditional triad, this one incorporates developing countries and therefore swells to a very large population. Indeed, we see in Figure 2–1 that this bloc will be by far the most populous part of the extended triad. Japan is still the most wealthy anchor in this bloc. The other wealthy areas include Oceania (New Zealand and Australia) and the three remaining newly industrialized countries[14] (NICs: South Korea, Singapore, Taiwan). The East Asian bloc will become massive by the end of this century when two populous developing areas become essential members.

The first area includes the four recently industrializing countries (RICs): Indonesia, Malaysia, Thailand, and the Philippines. Despite their current financial troubles, I predict that by the year 2000, these key members of ASEAN will be major trading powers, and should continue their current steps toward integration both regionally and globally.

Second, while I include the coastal provinces of China, now including Hong Kong, in this emerging trade bloc, I do not include the inland provinces. This does not mean that I predict that the People's Republic of China will split into two separate nations. Politically, it will likely (but not definitely) remain united. Economically, however, China today contains basically two separate economies. The "Coastal China" economy is integrating closely into the global economy and becoming a trade powerhouse, as well as a beacon for foreign investment. The "Inland China" economy, however, has not opened up nearly as much to capitalism and thus to international business. As Ashoka Mody and Fang-Yi Wang put it in a detailed recent research study:[15]

Gains in industrial output were especially marked in the coastal region. . . . Five coastal provinces (Fujian, Guangdong, Jiangsu, Shandong, and Zhejiang) were at the center of the "miracle."

China's coastal provinces are already linked to Hong Kong in a cross-border region state, as Kenichi Ohmae describes in *The End of the Nation*

State.[16] Further evidence of this split in economic development is provided by the *Wall Street Journal,* which cites much higher rates of private home buying in the coastal region than inland.[17]

> In contrast to people in the prosperous coastal regions, few Chinese in poorer inland regions have saved enough to afford even the cheapest urban apartment. . . . A different picture is emerging along the prosperous coast. Three-quarters of the people own their own homes in the southern cities of Guangzhou and Shenzhen as well as in some cities in the eastern provinces of Zhejiang and Jiangsu, says Chen Xuebing, director of the State Council's Leading Group for Housing Reform Office in Beijing.

Thus, it is clear that already two distinct regional economies exist within China. Figure 2–1 continues to treat them as separate entities, as it seems clear that the de facto economic split will remain as we move into the new century. My forecast is that Coastal China will contain about 45% of China's total population, or a total of about 567 million people.

EXTENDING THE TRIAD:
THE REGIONS LEFT OUT

All three legs of the traditional triad have gained momentum and scale in their integration. The European bloc is expanding eastward and to a certain extent northward, with the potential to go much farther east and even south. The North American bloc has begun the process of expanding southward and should go well beyond Mexico, reaching the tip of South America by 2005, or 2010 at the latest. Likewise, an East Asian bloc has expanded beyond Japan and is now forming southward as far as Indonesia.

The final component of Figure 2–1 shows that even if the triad extends along all three dimensions, most of the world's people will remain outside this main network of international business as we enter the imminent new millennium. I term the areas that remain outside of the extended triad the "Populous South," because they are densely populated regions many of which are in or near the southern hemisphere. Africa is a prime example. So is South Asia, anchored by India with its huge population, and by the burgeoning populations of Pakistan and Bangladesh, each of which is forecast to exceed 200 million people by 2050. Figure 2–1 shows my expectation that even by the year 2000 much of Latin America, the various parts of the former Soviet Union, and Inland China will join Africa and South Asia in remaining outside the main network of international business—*the extended triad.*

FURTHER EXTENDING THE TRIAD: THE SHAPE OF BUSINESS IN 2010

Figure 2–2 depicts my forecast of the continuing evolution of the extended triad concept to the year 2010. A significant development is the further southward extension of a free trade bloc in the Americas. Indeed, I incorporate the current plans to form a truly hemispheric Free Trade Area of the Americas (FTAA) by 2010. This bloc would contain over 900 million people, with greater than half living in South and Central America. Quite an inducement to learn Spanish, as we will discuss later in the book.

A second major development is the formation of a Pan-European Free Trade Area (PEFTA) that itself will total nearly three-quarters of a billion people. The growth in population in this macro-region is largely due to the addition of the significant populations in Central Europe and the European republics of the former Soviet Union, such as the Baltics, Russia, and Ukraine. A number of leading scholars are quite bullish on the potential of this integrated European economy, including MIT professor and former business school dean Lester Thurow.[18]

A third significant development is the formation of a true East Asian Free Trade Area (EAFTA) by 2010, as detailed in Figure 2–2. Already the most populous part of the extended triad, this East Asian bloc sees further gains in population based on two key projections. I am assuming that Vietnam will graduate into the club of industrializing nations and become the fifth RIC. In addition, I assume Coastal China will rise to 47% of China's total population, because ambitious Chinese desiring a higher quality of life and involvement in the global economy will continue to migrate south and eastward to the coastal provinces from the inland regions. Already, estimates are that up to 100 million Chinese have migrated to the more open and de facto capitalist provinces along China's coast, most of them neglecting to inform or consult with the central government or other communist authorities before migrating.

Thus, significant population is added to the extended triad core of global business in the first decade of the new millennium. Due to this large expansion of the triad, the oft-neglected Populous South is projected to fall to 56% of total world population, from 66% in the year 2000. This will be largely a result of incorporating the remainder of Latin America into the Americas bloc, and the incorporation of parts of

Figure 2–2   THE "EXTENDED TRIAD" AND THE POPULOUS SOUTH
Projected Population (millions) in Year 2010

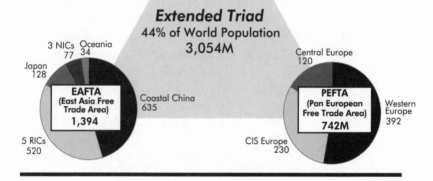

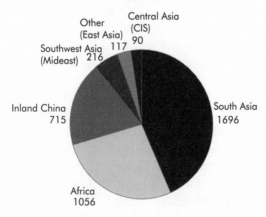

the former Soviet Union and the balance of Central or Eastern Europe into the European bloc.

COMPANY SPOTLIGHT
ABB Extends the Triad in Its Business Strategy

Asea Brown Boveri (ABB) is a European-based firm justly celebrated for its evolving global strategy. Indeed, its chairman, and, until recently, CEO, Percy Barnevik, is arguably Europe's leading business executive (*The Economist* termed him "Europe's most successful international manager" in its May 3, 1997 issue, and he is cited favorably in the *Harvard Business Review* quite frequently). If we examine ABB's strategy, we will see how it anticipates the contours and potential of our prediction for an "extended triad."

ABB's industry—heavy engineering, especially electric power generation, transmission, and distribution—is a key one in the emerging markets. These emerging or developing nations plan to do literally billions of dollars of investment spending to improve their infrastructure, and electricity is a big part of this as they increasingly become leading industrial nations and world manufacturing shares shift their way.

How has ABB anticipated an extended triad in its strategy? First, ABB was a pioneer in extending its base from Western Europe eastward (ABB evolved from a Swiss and Swedish merger in 1988), making massive foreign direct investments into Eastern Europe in search of skilled labor with lower wages, in order to remain globally competitive. The *Financial Times* reported (11 October 1996, p. 14) that ABB "bolstered its competitiveness and profitability by boldly shifting production to central and eastern European sites."

Second, its current strategy reflects or anticipates the likely extension of NAFTA southward into an Americas component of an extended triad. It is focusing on job expansion in Latin America, where it sees promising emerging markets, at the expense of further job cuts in Western Europe and North America. When he succeeded Mr. Barnevik as CEO in 1997, Goran Lindahl revealed these aspects of his strategy, observing that "growth prospects were particularly good in Latin America. . . . (*Financial Times,* 9 June 1997, p. 22).

Third, CEO Lindahl revealed in his strategy discussion the eventual focus on an extended East Asian leg of the triad, including China and Southeast Asia. He sees the likelihood of job creation in the large emerging economies of Asia, including India. The importance of this strategy was evident in late August 1997, when ABB's stock market price jumped on the news that it had won a contract involving China's massive Three Gorges Dam project. ABB was early to realize the potential of an "extended triad": in an interview with William Taylor in the *Harvard Business Review* (March–April 1991) Percy Barnevik pointed out that as early as 1991, ABB was the largest Western investor in Poland—and its strategy for growth in emerging markets appears prescient and highly successful.

While some companies are responding to the Asian financial crisis by scaling back operations, ABB has pursued a strategy of further expansion in the region. The devaluation of several Asian currencies has made it cheaper for firms to manufacture and export goods, a fact that ABB will take advantage of as it further shifts jobs and production from Europe to Asia. "Mr. Lindahl forecast that south-east Asia will recover from its problems like Mexico which is now 'booming again,'" reports London's *Financial Times*.[19] Confident that Asia will bounce back, ABB is poised to reap the benefits of this investment in the future.

THE MAJOR REGIONS OF THE GLOBAL ECONOMY IN 2025

Figure 2–3 summarizes my forecast for the macro-regional structure that may still underpin the global economy by the year 2025. This figure is similar to Figure 2–2, because most of the extension of the triad is expected to occur by 2010. It differs, however, in that it illustrates the result of the sizable divergence in population growth rates for the world's major regions. The first thing to note is that the population of the Populous South grows significantly, because this region contains nations that have the highest projected population growth rates on Earth. Thus, the Populous South rises back up to 58.5% of world population by 2025.

Second, note that the population of the European economic bloc is projected to remain completely flat or stagnant, a consequence of its aging demographic profile and projected low fertility rates. We will discuss this lack of population growth in Europe in Chapter 3. Third, the population of the Free Trade Area of the Americas is projected to rise beyond 1 billion people. This growth occurs in all major regions within the Americas, but is particularly apparent in Latin America. An important finding for business strategy grasps the potential link between people and profit growth: nearly two-thirds of the people in the Americas are forecast to reside south of the Rio Grande (i.e., in Latin America vs. the United States and Canada) by the year 2025.

Fourth, the East Asian Free Trade Area grows to over 1.5 billion

Figure 2–3 THE "EXTENDED TRIAD" AND THE POPULOUS SOUTH
Projected Population (millions) in Year 2025

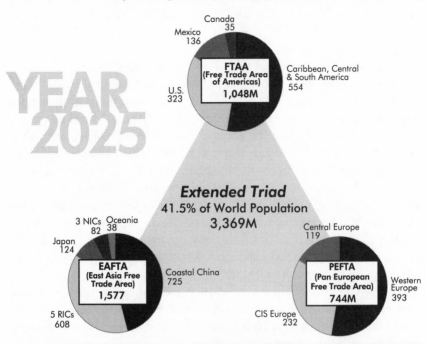

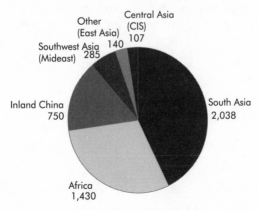

people. The population growth in this region occurs despite declining population in Japan and rather flat population projections in the other currently advanced nations. Therefore, we can attribute the future population growth in this region to the projected growing populations in the five recently industrializing countries, including Vietnam, and the migratory growth in population of Coastal China. For the sake of forecasting to 2025, I assume the coastal provinces will increase from 47% to 49% of China's total population.

Chapter 3 will show that the world's fastest population growth rates are in nations not even in our *vision* for a more "extended triad." These nations with rapidly growing populations are in our residual grouping, the Populous South: Africa, inland China, South Asia, Central Asia, and Southwest Asia including the Middle East. The Populous South is not targeted even in the future growth strategies being formulated today by the network of powerful firms in the triad. Recall our forecast that the Populous South regions' share of world population will shrink by 2010 from 66% to a still massive 56%— the shrinkage being due to the big extension of the triad that I foresee over the next decade. Then, I forecast the Populous South population to grow dramatically from 3.89 to 4.75 billion people between 2010 and 2025. Thus, its share of world population will rebound to nearly 60% by 2025.

We can hope that policies will change and that the nations and regions now in the Populous South will eventually gain greater access to what would then become a truly global network. Meanwhile, we hope to establish a potential link between growing populations and future profits: there are too many potential customers or employees in the currently neglected Populous South to be ignored by businesses that hope to grow and prosper well into the 21st century. It would be senseless to ignore roughly three out of every five humans forecast to inhabit our planet, which is why we now focus on the Populous South and its demographic dynamics in the next two chapters.

CHAPTER 3

THE POPULOUS SOUTH:

Will Markets for Growth or a Tragic Human Trap Emerge?

In Chapter 2, we showed the possibility of a great expansion of the traditional triad, that is, the set of three major trading and economic blocs that has dominated global business well into the 1990s. Although some analysts may consider this extension of the global business network overly optimistic, I have tried to portray it as the logical extension of current trends now evident in the three traditional trading blocs.

The first bloc, North America (NAFTA), should expand southward aggressively as we move into the 21st century, with the formation of a free trade area of the Americas (FTAA) by 2010, perhaps even as early as 2005. Secondly, the European Union is likely to expand eastward, not only to the nations of Central and Eastern Europe such as Hungary and Poland, but also into the major parts of the former Soviet Union, particularly Russia and Ukraine. Finally, but importantly for growing business, an East Asian trading bloc will develop that combines the wealth and technology of the more advanced nations in Northeast Asia (particularly Japan) with the dynamic and populous economies of ASEAN and increased economic links with "Greater China." Already, an informal "bamboo network" of Chinese and overseas Chinese capitalists is integrating a great deal of business in this East Asian region.[1]

The striking aspect of this analysis is that even with an optimistic expansion of the strongly networked economies dominating global business (i.e., the triad), only some of the nations on Earth will be included. More to the point, the nations that seem likely to continue to be left out of even an extended triad comprise well over half the world's people. This seems a two-sided tragedy: billions of people in these "left out" nations will experience great difficulty reaching their economic potential and raising their living standards; and businesses may miss out on more than half the potential customers and laborers in the world unless they globalize outside of even an expanded triad.

Thus, it is counterproductive for business to continue to ignore the nations outside of this expanded triad, because these already populous nations have the most rapidly rising populations. We saw in Chapter 2 that the triad may be extended greatly by the year 2010, but from that time onward, the share of world population captured within the triad will continually shrink because of much faster population growth in the nations that we currently forecast to remain outside of even a greatly extended triad. Indeed, this is a good time to look back at Figure 1–1 in Chapter 1, "The World According to Trade." Again, the striking fact here is that most of the economic activity in the mid-1990s is in the three blocs of the traditional triad, which are almost exclusively in the Northern Hemisphere.

Now we combine this picture with a very powerful insight: the babies are being born in a crescent that begins in the Southern Hemisphere in South Africa, bends up through Africa, North Africa, and the Middle East, into Southwest Asia, and then down into the Indian subcontinent across to Bangladesh. I have recently taken, somewhat tongue-in-cheek but actually quite descriptively, to calling this increasingly populous area of the world the "Modern-Day Fertile Crescent." Unlike the ancient Fertile Crescent (watered by the Nile, Tigris, and Euphrates rivers), which spanned from Egypt through Mesopotamia (current-day Iraq), this new one is named not for the ready availability of water and the fertility of the soil, but for the huge percentage of the world's babies being born here. There is a striking contrast between how small this region shows up on Figure 1–1's "The World According to Trade," (or on *any* map showing economic or technological magnitudes), and how large this area would be on a map that displays "The World According to Population," or even more starkly, "The World According to Births."

Figure 3–1 shows a rough sketch of my conception of a modern-day fertile crescent. It includes the larger or more populous nations in the regions of the world with the most rapid population growth: Africa, Southwest Asia (the Middle East), and South Asia. To illustrate the concentration of much of the world's births in this "new fertile crescent," the figure gives the total fertility rate (TFR) for each nation pictured. The TFR is the most often used measure of fertility and is defined as the average number of children that would be born alive to a woman during her lifetime, if she were to bear children at each age in accord with her nation's prevailing age-specific birth rates.

The map in Figure 3–1 makes it obvious why this region is both the

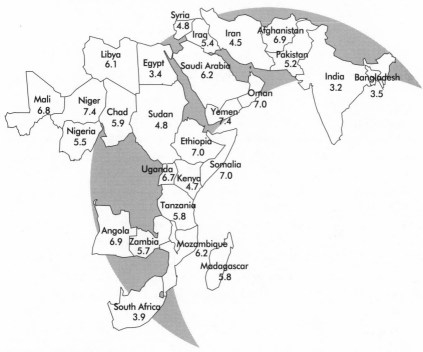

Figure 3–1 OUR MODERN-DAY FERTILE CRESCENT
Numbers inside each nation represent its total fertility rate (TFR).

Data Source: The World Bank

key part of our new concept the "Populous South" and the "Modern Day Fertile Crescent." The fertility rates in this area, ranging from *three to seven* live births per woman, contrast sharply with those of Europe, North America, and Japan, as these triad members all have total fertility rates *less than two.*

This chapter is devoted to showing two things. First, we will discuss the population or demographic dynamics of the region we term the Populous South, including explanations of how it became so densely populated and why its population continues to expand at a rate that dramatically outstrips the growth of triad nations. Second, we will portray some of the economic and business dynamics within the diverse subregions and nations of the Populous South. Although a disparate group of nations, they are linked by large and/or growing populations, lack of trading and telecommunications linkages, and abject poverty (arguably often a consequence of the first two characteristics). In Chapter 4, we will build a model to more deeply analyze the dynamic system, that is, the negative feedback loops that often result in hardship and tragedy in the Populous South. The goal will be to make explicit the linkages between poverty, population growth, environmental degradation, lack of foreign investment, lack of communications or transportation infrastructure, and the like.

POPULATION GROWTH RATES DECELERATE, PARTICULARLY IN THE TRIAD

Figure 3–2 shows the actual historical record and the projected growth of world population from 1975 to 2050, graphically illustrating why we term the many nations not included even in an extended triad the Populous South. We immediately note two very important trends. First, world population has grown dramatically since 1975 and is expected to continue to add billions of people as we move into the middle of the 21st century. Fortunately, at least for those of us worried about the fate of this planet and its environmental sustainability, the *rate* of growth has been decelerating and continued deceleration is projected by almost all analysts.

Second, the growth rates of world populations are not uniform across different regions or across groupings of nations based on their level of economic development. Figure 3–2 shows quite clearly that the developed or so-called advanced nations, which correspond quite closely to notions of the traditional triad, have accounted for just a small part of the popula-

**Figure 3–2   DEVELOPING REGIONS DRIVE
WORLD POPULATION GROWTH**

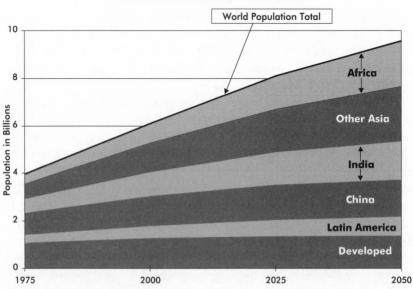

Data Source: World Bank, *World Population Projections*, 1994–1995.

tion growth since 1975. More significant for the purposes of business strategy is the indication that in the future, these advanced nations will count for even a smaller share of the world's increased numbers; indeed their share of global population growth will be minuscule.

Many insightful scholars, including Paul Kennedy,[2] have analyzed and highlighted a powerful key point of current world population growth: if 95% of population growth is occurring in the developing or lesser-developed nations, policymakers around the world should pay more attention to these nations, despite their current lack of economic wealth. One certainly cannot doubt the wisdom of this assertion. However, a central thrust of my book is that it is *business leaders* who need to become more aware of the developing nations outside the traditional triad, since that is where future growth opportunities will most likely reside.

Returning to the master spreadsheet highlighted in Chapter 1, we analyzed world population in the year 2030 as compared to the year 2000, as well as the developments during the 1990s. A startling fact emerged: only 2.6% of the world population growth in those first three decades of the 21st century will occur in the advanced economies! A full 97.4%, or a whopping 2.3 billion out of the total 2.36 billion world population growth in these upcoming 30 years, is projected to occur in the emerging or developing nations outside of the traditional triad (i.e., outside the 26 industrialized trading nations). Moreover, this ITN group will comprise a very small share of total population growth, despite the World Bank's forecasts of migration from poor countries into the advanced countries. Without accounting for such migration, if we just projected fertility and mortality rates within the countries, the advanced nations would constitute an even smaller share of world population growth than the minuscule share projected here.

Of course, no one can forecast future migration flows with any great degree of confidence. If the burgeoning populations of the developing or less-developed nations continue to lack infrastructure, economic opportunity, and other reflections of life in the more-advanced nations, there could be tremendous pressure of immigration flows (legal or illegal) into the advanced nations. Paul Kennedy gives a clear description of the possible pressures that could lead to, and result from, a mass flow of migrants attempting to leave the lesser-developed nations (what I term the Populous South) for the more economically advanced nations.[3]

Returning to the moderate immigration flows into advanced nations currently forecast by the World Bank, let us put the population growth projections into perspective. Each and every year during the 1990s, the world has added on net between 80 and 85 million people. This constitutes almost 230,000 additional human beings *each day,* as births far exceed deaths, causing net population to grow impressively. This means that each hour the world population total grows by over 9,500 people.

In the time it takes you to read this paragraph (roughly 37 seconds), the world will add about 100 people. The key point for business is that almost 95 of these people will reside in the nations of the developing world. Fewer than six (5.47% to be precise) of these 100 people will be living in the advanced nations. Thus, the world is facing a *demographic revolution,* one that suggests business had best look to emerging markets in developing nations for growth.

Why does such a small percentage of the *growth* occur in the advanced nations? After all, the advanced nations (the ITN) currently contain about one-sixth of the world's people, so why do they only constitute one-twentieth of the world population growth? The answer lies in the lower birth rates or lower relative fertility of these nations compared to the developing nations. Only in the developing nations is the birth rate so high that it far outstrips the mortality rate. Hence, populations grow rapidly in many developing nations, whereas in most advanced nations the population grows slowly, if at all, because the low fertility rates barely replace the current mortality. Indeed, some nations that are quite important in current business, such as Japan, Germany, Italy, and Spain (as well as Russia, Ukraine, and Romania), are projected by the World Bank to experience *declining* populations well into the 21st century. Furthermore, this very slow population growth in the triad, and in some cases even a decline in absolute populations, is projected despite the forecast of moderate immigration into these advanced nations.

A key element in the ITNs' very small forecast share of world population growth is that the 15 nations now in the European Union have a projected absolute decline in population after 2000, led downward by Germany, Italy, and Spain with their very low birth rates—fertility rates well below replacement level. Thus, the European Union falls from 6.6% of world population in 1994 to a projected share of only 4.33% in 2030. In other words, it falls from containing 1 out of every 15 of the world's people to a mere 1 in 23. This major demographic trend of our times seems to imply that being overly "Eurocentric" is not only "politically incorrect," it is also likely to stunt future business growth.

GLOBAL POPULATION SHARES
SHIFT SOUTHWARD

What will be the population trend between the years 2000 and 2030? On average, world population will grow about 78 million per year, or nearly

216,000 per day. That is almost 9,000 hourly, or 150 per minute, which means that every 40 seconds world population will increase by 100 persons. The crucial finding here is that 97.4% of these added 100 global citizens will reside in developing or emerging economies. This finding is tremendously significant for businesses contemplating the location of future potential customers or employees.

Figure 3–3 illustrates where in the developing world these 97 out of 100 net new global residents added on average every 40 seconds will be located. Knowing this distribution *can* help you design a time-phased, global business expansion. Fully 31 of them will be in Africa, which is one reason we focus on the population explosion projected for Africa in Chapter 4. Nearly nine will be in Latin America. This key area for demographic growth helps to explain why many business leaders are currently, and I think correctly, pushing for an extension of NAFTA southward (along lines portrayed in the preceding chapter) to facilitate their strategies for business expansion in the Americas. But these numbers are dwarfed by the 57 new citizens projected for Asia. Nearly half of these 57 people will be in the world's two massively populous nations: 17.6 in India and 10.4 in China. Obviously, in terms of population growth, Asia and Africa are set to dominate Europe and the Americas.

Figure 3–3   POPULATION GROWTH FROM 2000 TO 2030
(Roughly every 40 seconds, world population will grow by 100 people, distributed as shown here)

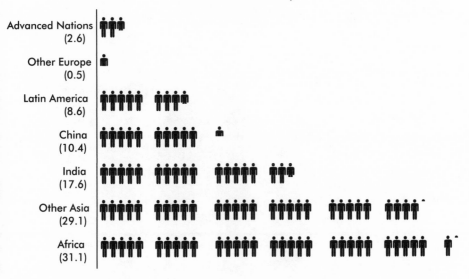

Source: Professor Jeff Rosensweig using World Bank, *World Population Projections.*

Figure 3–4 further helps us analyze the Southern Hemisphere's increase in population share. In 1990, Europe had 13.7% of world population (Europe is defined to include all of Russia), more than Africa's 11.9% share. These nearly equal shares represent a major shift from 1939, when Europe

Figure 3–4   WORLD POPULATION BY REGION

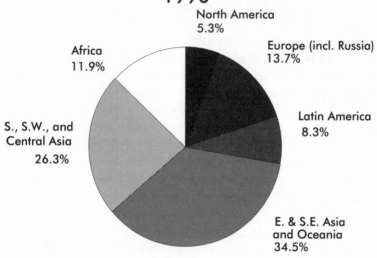

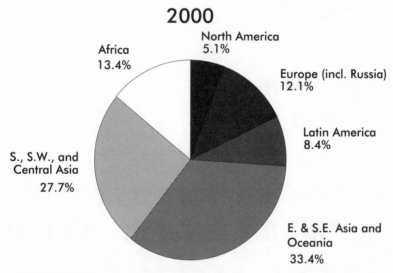

Source: World Bank, *World Population Projections*, 1994–1995.

was roughly three times as populous as Africa. The Second World War and the Holocaust, however, put a tragic brake on Europe's population. Meanwhile, Africa's population (and that of South Asia) has exploded during the second half of the 20th century.

Thus, any use of pre-World War II data would reveal an even greater relative decline of Europe vis-à-vis Africa and Asia. For our purposes, even a more conservative portrayal will clearly reveal the major trend: the world population mix is shifting toward the "Populous South" or "Fertile Crescent" region. As this region gains population, not only absolutely but in terms of its relative global share, some regions must be losing relative shares of the world population pie. This is evident even in the historically brief period of ten years illustrated in Figure 3–4, when clearly Europe, and to a lesser extent North America, lose share as Africa and South and Southwest Asia gain share.

However, one other very important region is losing relative population share. Figure 3–4 shows that in 1990 East Asia was the most populous region on Earth. A prime reason for its huge population is China, of course, since China is the world's most populous nation. Furthermore, East Asia contains the various populous nations of ASEAN, particularly Indonesia and Vietnam. A striking aspect of the two pies in Figure 3–4 is the recent relative *decline* of the population share held by East Asia. It is important for business executives to understand that in absolute terms the population of this region is still increasing. This population increase, combined with rapid economic growth in the region (as will be illustrated in Chapters 5 and 6), clearly shows that East Asia should be a major focal point for any business striving to go global. Nonetheless, when we analyze population trends, we see that this massive region is experiencing a declining share of global population.

At least in part due to its huge absolute population, dynamic forces have been unleashed in East Asia that are leading to its declining share of world population. Recall that the People's Republic of China, with roughly 1.25 billion people, constitutes more than 20% of total global population and is, therefore, the major population mass within this East Asia region. Given its already huge population and the eventual worry about feeding, let alone housing, such massive numbers of people, China in 1979 instituted its one-child policy.[4] Setting aside for the moment the social and ethical problems this policy has fostered, particularly with regard to female infanticide, we can say that it has put an effective brake on China's tremendous population growth.

I recommend to readers the book by Lester Brown of the Worldwatch Institute, entitled *Who Will Feed China?* Lester Brown represents the "environmental lobby," but he has a clear and useful global perspective.

The book provides an excellent analysis of China's earlier and current population momentum, its possible inability to feed the masses (or at least the huge cost to China, if population did continue to grow so fast), and the attendant policy changes. China's one-child policy has probably done more than any other single factor to help the world's population growth

Figure 3–5   WORLD POPULATION BY REGION
The Rise of the Southern Hemisphere

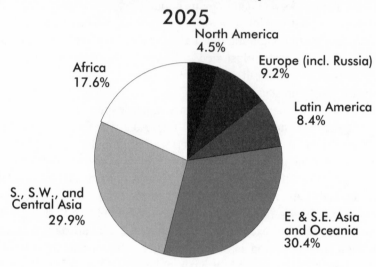

2025

North America 4.5%

Europe (incl. Russia) 9.2%

Latin America 8.4%

Africa 17.6%

S., S.W., and Central Asia 29.9%

E. & S.E. Asia and Oceania 30.4%

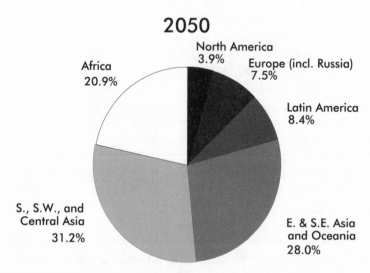

2050

North America 3.9%

Europe (incl. Russia) 7.5%

Latin America 8.4%

Africa 20.9%

S., S.W., and Central Asia 31.2%

E. & S.E. Asia and Oceania 28.0%

Source: World Bank, *World Population Projections*, 1994–1995.

decelerate. Without this deceleration, world population would have boomed and the planet would now be at an even greater risk than the considerable threat it currently faces from population growth pressure.

That China's one-child policy is having a globally significant effect is apparent in the pie charts shown in Figure 3–4 and Figure 3–5. Although China actually has a total fertility rate much closer to two than one child per woman (many people just pay the official penalty fee or otherwise circumvent the one-child limit), the policy and the costs of avoiding it lead to a significantly lower fertility rate in China than in the only other hugely populated nation, India. Thus, India and its region, South Asia, are growing in population relative to China and its region, East Asia. Finally, from the perspective of global sustainability, China compares very favorably to many other nations of the "Populous South," where fertility rates can reach as high as three times or more that of China currently.

REGIONAL DIFFERENCES IN FERTILITY DRIVE PROJECTED CHANGES IN WORLD POPULATION SHARES

Figure 3–6 summarizes the fertility assumptions that underlie the World Bank demographic model,[5] and thus the population projections used in this book. These projections assume a *convergence* of total fertility in the world's major regions. If we did not have a strong assumption—that fertility rates would ultimately move toward a convergence from their current widely divergent behavior—we would see an even more dramatic shift in world population toward Africa and South Asia. Indeed, some of the projections by the United Nations and other groups have Africa approaching one-quarter of world population by the year 2050, whereas our more conservative assumptions have Africa's share growing to just under 21%. Thus, our assumptions form a bias against the case we are trying to make: that world population shares will shift toward what we term the Populous South, particularly toward Africa and South and Southwest Asia, and away from Europe and North America and East Asia.

What specific assumptions regarding fertility convergence underlie the population projections? First, as we see in Figure 3–6, we assume somewhat rapid declines in fertility rate in some places that we project will gain absolute population share, particularly South Asia and Africa. In contrast, we assume that the very low fixed fertility rates now seen in nations in the industrial north will soon return upward to a replacement ratio of just over 2 on the total fertility rate scale. What do we mean by "replacement ratio"? First, recall the definition of the total fertility rate

Figure 3-6 GLOBAL POPULATION SHIFTS SOUTH

(Despite assuming "converging" fertility rates)

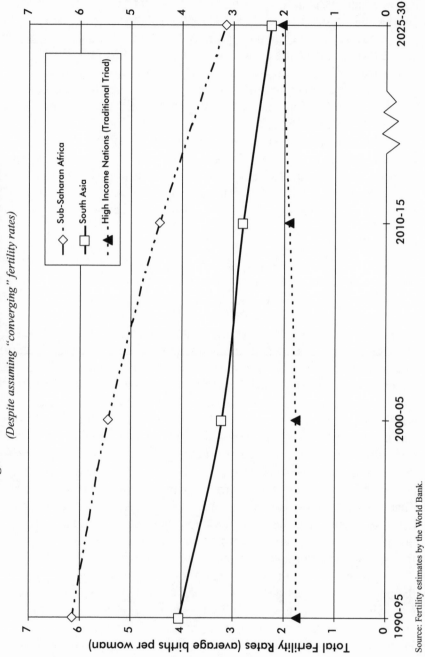

Source: Fertility estimates by the World Bank.

(TFR): the average number of children that would be born alive to a woman during her lifetime if she were to bear children in accord with her nation's prevailing birth rates. The reason we need a TFR of just over 2 to maintain population in the long run (i.e., achieve the replacement ratio) is that men obviously could not stand the pain of labor, so women must bear two children for each couple. Moreover, some women die before the end of their childbearing years; thus the average woman who does survive for the full childbearing period must give birth to just over 2 children in order to maintain the population. So, we can say that, if anything, these two assumptions add a strong bias against the "Populous South" case.

Figure 3–6 shows that because of the current large divergence in fertility rates, most of the world's births occur now in the Populous South. This divergence is causing a "population momentum" to build, so that 20 or 30 years from now, most of the women of childbearing age will be in the Populous South. Thus, even if fertility rates in Africa and South Asia eventually do diminish, as projected in Figure 3–6, their relative population share will continue to increase because of the great numbers of babies being born there *now:* these babies represent the women of childbearing age a generation from now.

As starkly divergent as the regional averages depicted in Figure 3–6 are, the fertility gap between individual nations is greater still. In Southwest Asia, for example, Afghanistan has a TFR of 6.9, while Yemen and Oman in Southwest Asia each have a TFR of over 7 babies. Further, the total fertility rate in Africa as a whole exceeds 6, averaging nearly 6.3 births per woman. Many African nations, such as Angola, Ethiopia, Mali, Niger, and Somalia have a TFR as high as roughly 7 births per woman. The salient point is that even if these high fertility rates come down to a range near 3 for Africa, and even if they decline toward a replacement rate of just over 2 for South Asia by the year 2025, the momentum will be such that world population will still shift dramatically toward these two main regions.

Figure 3–6 shows a convergence of fertility rates because we follow the World Bank in assuming that the high-income nations in the triad will raise their fertility rates back up to a replacement ratio of slightly over 2, from the current average of 1.75 babies per woman. This low current average masks the very low fertility in some nations in the triad, with rates as low as 1.2 babies per woman in major nations of the European Union such as Germany, Italy, and Spain. Europe is a region that is not only losing population dramatically in relative terms as seen in Figures 3–4 and 3–5, but is also at risk of absolute declines in population.

Europe now faces one of the sharpest demographic implosions in recent history. *The Economist* traced the implications of Europe's low fertility in an article entitled "Europe's Population Shrinking."[6]

As the rest of the world struggles to stop people breeding too fast, Europeans, it seems, are fading away. Central and Eastern Europe's population is shrinking because of drooping birth rates, climbing death rates, and emigration. But the rest of Europe—immigration apart—is losing people too.

In 1995, European Union's birth rate was the lowest in peace-time this century. . . . More Germans and Italians died than were born in 1995.

The most sluggish and reluctant breeders in the European Union, however, are those supposedly amorous Mediterraneans. Italians and Spaniards are making fewest babies of all, EU-wide. Their women, on average, now bear only 1.17 and 1.18 babies, respectively. Portuguese and Greek women are barely more creative. . . .

Central and Eastern Europe's shrinkage is still bigger. . . .

If people in the west refuse to breed as they once did, and easterners are prevented from doing so by the trauma of post-communism and by dire health services, only immigration will keep Europe's numbers level. . . .

Expect Europe to go on shrinking.

Furthermore, on Europe's eastern end, Russia's total fertility has collapsed along with its economy. Russia has slipped back to a new type of Third World ranking, and parents' individual economic prospects are so uncertain that they may fear bringing children into this world. A report in The *Wall Street Journal*[7] supports this startling demographic implosion: "Russia said its population in 1996's first nine months decreased by 350,000 people to 147.6 million, noting 14.5 deaths per 1,000 people exceeded the rate of 9.1 births, the latter down 4.9% from a year earlier because many Russians can't afford more children."

Japan also has a TFR well below replacement ratio—currently it is under 1.5. This has led to much recent commentary in Japan, and some forecasts extrapolate blindly from this and project huge declines in Japan's population. An article in the *International Herald Tribune* reports that: "a Japanese government projection now suggests that the population will fall by more than half over the next century. It is forecast to tumble to 55 million in 2100, from 125 million today. Reflecting the unease, a weekly magazine went even further and calculated that by the year 3000, if trends continue, the population will have dwindled to 45,000."[8]

The above numbers represent wild extrapolations more than reasoned analysis. However, this article shows that Japan is worried about current birth rates and resulting population trends:

> [There] is apprehension about the destabilizing effects of a smaller work force, declining land prices and a shrinking economy. [There] is worry that Japan will become a less important country, as its population drops to just one-quarter of America's soon after 2050, from two-thirds of America's a century ago.

As a result, certain regions in Japan are offering cash incentives to women who have more than two babies. The Japanese government is also considering substantial increases in child and maternity benefits. A major point in this book, both here and again in Chapter 6, is that analysts should not extrapolate blindly. Our forecasts incorporate an eventual rise in fertility in nations like Japan that are currently below the replacement fertility level, that is, a movement toward a more balanced position, as shown in Figure 3–6.

In other ways, also, the assumptions from the *World Bank Population Projections* that we employ here are, if anything, biased against the "demographic rise of the Populous South" case. These World Bank projections do not assume a cure for AIDS, which somewhat depresses the rapid growth of population in Africa. However, the projections *do* assume that public health measures will help to slow the proliferation of AIDS from current exponential rates.

Even our conservative forecasts are rich with implication, as they still show a dramatic increase in the total population share held by nations in the Populous South, particularly those in Africa. It is also clear that the nations that are experiencing offsetting declining shares are those of the traditional triad, particularly European nations and the recent industrial powerhouse, Japan. Even North America is projected to lose share of world population; however, at least North America gains population in absolute terms.

We cannot overemphasize that businesses looking to grow must incorporate in their strategies the relative demographic decline of Europe and Japan. Incredibly, those two key regions for business will experience *absolute* declines in population. The message of this chapter is that the incremental consumers of the 21st century will be located outside of the northern triad of wealthy nations that businesses have traditionally focused upon. To be sure, there will be billions more potential consumers a few decades from now, but almost all of them will live in the Fertile Crescent of the Populous South.

The final implication of our population forecasting model is that by the year 2050 more than half the world's population is projected to reside in just two major areas of the Populous South: Africa and the South, Central, and Southwest regions of Asia. This part of Asia includes the Islamic nations of the Middle East and Southwest Asia, as well as the Islamic republics of the former Soviet Union that now constitute Central Asia. The high fertility rates in these Islamic nations and their Islamic neighbor, Pakistan, may lead to a dramatic shift in world population shares along the lines of religious distribution as well. However, some populous Islamic nations, such as Indonesia, Bangladesh, and Iran, are already stressing family planning, even favoring contraceptive use, and have seen dramatic declines in total fertility rates.[9] On the other hand, Pakistan and Saudi Arabia have not instituted such policies, and continuing high fertility rates there imply large and fast-growing populations. Furthermore, Iran's population is still growing rapidly, due to the "population momentum" caused by its youthful age structure (many women in, or approaching, childbearing years), as the family-planning-induced decline in TFR is a recent event. Business should anticipate a likely shift in global religious distribution, and develop strategies that promote tolerance and respect for diversity.

By 2050, Figure 3–5 implies, Africa's share will approach 21% of the global population. Thus, Africa will have nearly three times Europe's population, a startling and crucial *reversal from 1939,* when European population was three times larger than its continental southern neighbor. It is not only "politically incorrect" to ignore Africa, it is also myopic in light of the demographic and economic trends portrayed in this book.

THE CURRENT STATE OF THE POPULOUS SOUTH: MASSIVE POTENTIAL OR BASKET CASE?

Given the huge absolute population increases foreseen for Africa and the regions of Asia spanning from the Middle East to Bangladesh, we will examine the current economic, international trade, and communications or information technology situation in some of the larger nations in the Populous South. These nations often lack infrastructure, particularly that of modern information and communication technologies. The lack of infrastructure, among other deterrents, leads these nations to partake in a disproportionately small amount of world trade, and to attract a disappointingly low share of global foreign investment flows. Much of this disparity was already highlighted in Chapter 1, and will be further highlighted in future chapters. Hence, we will just mention a few indicators of the general lack of current engagement of the Populous South in what is otherwise becoming a global business environment. I hope that when business leaders learn the central message of this chapter (the global demographic shift toward the Populous South), they will be motivated to explore potential linkages with many of the Populous South nations in order to expand their businesses.

Just how isolated is the Populous South now? Let us start by examining the five most populous nations in the heart of Africa (leaving out South Africa and the nations of North Africa that are slightly more integrated with the triad): Nigeria, Ethiopia, Democratic Republic of Congo (hereafter DR Congo, formerly Zaire), Tanzania, and Sudan. These five nations comprise nearly 5% of the world's people. Furthermore, by the year 2030, they are projected to comprise a full 7.35% share of world population. Importantly, these nations will account for more than 13% of the world's total population growth in the first three decades of the 21st century. Despite their increasing demographic importance, these nations are barely a blip on the radar screen of world trade. They constitute a negligible one-quarter of 1% of total world exports; and even this minor share is dominated by Nigeria's oil exports, not by job-creating manufacturing exports. Likewise, these five nations total a mere one-quarter of 1% of world GDP measured using market exchange rates. Even measuring using hypothetical purchasing power exchange rates to reflect the low value of their currencies, these nations still total less than 1% of world GDP. The picture is even more depressing when we look at information or communications infrastructure: these five nations in the heart of Africa have only one-ninth of 1% of the world's telephones, and they have yet to gain any noticeable share of Internet host computers. Certainly there is great and growing human potential in these five populous nations in the heart of Africa, but business has yet to significantly link up to this region. The region does have tremendous natural or mineral resources, as well as the potential of its teeming human resources, hence farsighted analysts join me in suggesting business leaders consider it in future strategies.

Investment guru Jim Rogers, the wildly successful first partner of George Soros in the Quantum Fund, literally motorcycled around the world, both for adventure and for fresh investment insights. His fascinating and at times prescient book, *Investment Biker,*[10] describes the current deplorable conditions in much of sub-Saharan Africa, especially the lack of working roads and phones, but it forecasts that Africa eventually will rise economically. Rogers predicts Africa will most likely surpass the former Soviet Union, a region he sees as chaotic, violent, and likely to fracture further. Rogers states (p. 258): "Even though neither they nor anyone else knows exactly where they are going, Africans are now on the right road for the first time in decades."

Rogers presents (pp. 274–275) his "bullish case for Africa," one I agree with and urge business leaders and aspiring entrepreneurs alike to heed:

> . . . the Africans will adopt either the Western model or the Chinese model, . . . allowing every kind of vigorous free-market activity. . . . As African problems get cleaned up, the entrepreneurs who already exist throughout Africa will be freed to develop real economies. Africa has huge natural resources. . . . Someday the world will be desperate for Africa's resources, especially as production in the former USSR falls apart.

Rogers concludes (p. 275): "What I know for certain is that big fortunes will be made on the African continent in the next twenty-five years." Thus, the five nations discussed here represent huge potential, despite their current alienation from the global business community.

Next, we consider the five populous Islamic nations that lie in an arc ranging from Northeast Africa through the Mideast and through South Asia: Pakistan, Bangladesh, Iran, Egypt, and Afghanistan (listed in descending order of population). These nations total nearly 7% of world population, and are projected to comprise almost 9% by 2030. Their high fertility rates imply that they, much like the nations in the heart of Africa, will account for more than 13% of total world population growth during the first three decades of the 21st century.

Despite their large and growing populations, these Islamic nations in the modern Fertile Crescent of the Populous South are not proportionately engaged in the current international business network. In fact, they total only three-quarters of 1% of world exports, and even this small share is dominated by Iran's oil exports. They also constitute only three-quarters of 1% of total world production, or GDP measured in market value terms. However, their very weak currencies and low prices domestically do mean that if we measure their GDP using the hypothetical PPP exchange rates that equalize purchasing power, these nations produce about 3% of world GDP. Of course, even a 3% share of world production is low in light of the fact that this region contains almost 7% of the world's people. Sadly, these nations lack communications infrastructure, as they contain only 1/70th of the world's phones for nearly 1/14th of the world's people. With regard to technology infrastructure, these nations have negligible shares of total world computing muscle and Internet hook-ups.

Indeed, the Populous South does seem very isolated when we examine the current infrastructure and economic indicators. We shall now turn to an in-depth discussion of one Populous South nation in order to explore the potential pitfalls and promises so many of these nations face as the new century begins. This nation, India, will become the most highly populated nation on Earth. India has recently adopted some useful economic reforms and is starting to exhibit healthy economic growth. However, it still has a very mixed record in creating the conditions necessary to attract the massive private foreign investment it will need to build up its infrastructure and gainfully employ its rapidly rising population. We project that India's economic reform will continue to be positive, albeit sporadic. Combining this progress with its impressive share of world demographic potential, these trends have inspired me to include India among the anticipated six great economies of the next century, which will be described in Chapter 6.

India currently contains just under 1/6th (16.3%) of the world's people. Despite its size, India provides less than 0.6% of world exports. Furthermore, India's GDP, measured using market exchange rates, barely exceeds 1% of the global total. The picture looks slightly brighter when one realizes that India's currency is very weak and its domestic prices are quite low; using PPP exchange rates to equalize purchasing power, we see that India produces 3.78% of total world GDP. Still, when 16% of the world's people account for less than 4% of world production, the poverty and low income that characterize most of India's living standards become obvious, despite the frequent rhetoric in the popular business press about India's "rising middle class." India suffers from a teledensity of less than 1/10 of the world's average, as India has 1/6 of the world's people, but only 1/65 of the world's total telephones. However, the number of telephones in India is beginning to rise rapidly. Thus, it is not unreasonable to say that the current lack of telephones throughout the world's Populous South is a great opportunity, *and not a threat,* for future business expansion. Particularly exciting is this simple but profound idea: the projected population growth is almost entirely in regions of the world that are dramatically lacking in communications infrastructure and thus underserved by "global" telecommunication firms currently. Obviously, from our vantage point at the dawn of a new millennium, we understand that it would be slow, wasteful, and anachronistic to start stringing tons of phone wire. Hence, we can anticipate a global boom in wireless communications, particularly telephony.

Not surprisingly, India has less than 1% of the world's total computing muscle, including host computers on the Internet. Despite its current paucity of Internet and general computer connections, widespread poverty, and the absence of even one phone in nearly three-fourths of its villages, India should figure prominently in farsighted business strategies. Consider that many businesses added a focus on Australia in the early 1990s. It is certainly true that Australia boasts a big and beautiful geographic base, not to mention kangaroos, koalas, and the Olympic games in the year 2000. However, Australia's *total* population in the early 1990s, 17 million, was less than the *annual growth* in India's population! Indeed, India adds nearly 18 million people annually, or roughly 48,000 daily. *This is 2,000 net new people each hour*—a dynamism that truly reflects huge growth opportunities! If you still don't think that India has sufficient future customers to warrant a serious look, just take a nap!

India's massive growth in literate, technically trained human resources (who are also potential future customers) justifies why *I* think, for example, that future business leaders need to focus less on countries like Ireland[11] and more on India, despite Ireland's wonderful attributes. Business investments in India (assuming India reforms its FDI policies), will allow that country to continue to progress economically and provide a massive platform for future expansion and prosperity. India, then, like so many nations of the emerging business world, will enter the 21st century poised on a knife-edge: it will either partner with global businesses to grow and prosper, or it will add many millions more poverty-stricken citizens.

**Figure 3–7   POPULOUS SOUTH:
WORLD'S DEMOGRAPHIC FOCAL POINTS**

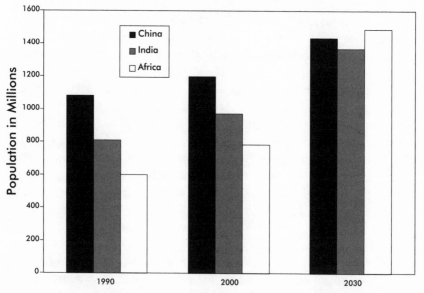

Source: World Bank, *World Population Projections*, 1994–1995.

Figure 3–7 makes explicit the lessons of this chapter. It presents a new triad for the 21st century that contains demographic focal points rather than the current industrial and trading powers. Africa's population is on such a steep exponential growth path that it will probably be the key demographic focal point as we move a few decades into the upcoming century. Further, India's population growth rate exceeds China's (because of China's one-child policy) to such an extent that India's population will catch China's gargantuan population by the fourth, or at the latest, the fifth decade of the new century. Why is this *original* model of a new, demographic triad for the 21st Century important to aspiring business leaders? Figure 3–7 shows us that by the year 2030, a time when many of today's young executives will still be working (particularly given the threat for the U.S. Social Security system implicit in the Chapter 7 analysis), these three demographic focal points are projected to contain nearly *1.5 billion* people apiece. We turn now to Chapter 4 and a model that attempts to explain the rapid exponential growth of population in the Populous South regions, particularly in Africa, but also in bordering Asian nations.

CHAPTER 4

THE CHALLENGE OF DEVELOPMENT:

Ending the South's Vicious Spiral

In Chapter 3, we examined a startling shift in world population shares, away from the wealthy triad and toward the nations of Africa, the Middle East, and South Asia. We saw that this already populous region, located largely in the southern hemisphere (hence we termed it the Populous South), will continue to gain a greater share of world population as it has the highest fertility rates in the world. Indeed, we pointed out that some nations in the Populous South have total fertility rates of seven live births per woman. This contrasts dramatically with most of the wealthy nations of the traditional triad, which have total fertility rates of less than two babies per woman.

In this chapter, you will learn *why* there is such a wide gap in total fertility rates across key world regions, and gain an understanding of why it may be quite rational for couples in the poor nations of the Populous South to desire six or seven babies. The high fertility in Africa and parts of Asia is not merely a matter of a lack of contraception; it has an underlying economic basis. We will examine a model that we term the "Surviving-Son Syndrome" or SSS model which, although simplified here, captures the essence of seemingly rational behavior that nonetheless leads to a population explosion and a poverty trap in this region. We will also explore a key concept termed the "demographic transition," which has occurred in East Asia and to a certain extent in parts of South Asia, such as India and Bangladesh, but has yet to extend westward into the remaining regions of the Populous South, such as the Middle East and Africa.

Recall that the forecasts in Chapter 3 relied upon an eventual convergence of fertility rates; otherwise Africa and South Asia would have even greater increases in world population share than displayed there. Essentially, the World Bank model we employed in Chapter 3 assumed that the demographic transition to lower fertility rates experienced in East Asia and parts of South Asia will eventually expand into the remaining areas of the world. If it does not, the world's population, already rising significantly, will truly explode. The implications for the global environment and for natural resource depletion are not pretty.

The central question of this chapter is: *Can we build a dynamic model to explain the system underlying the population explosion and poverty of the Populous South—the area of the world often left out of business strategies for the emerging global economy, despite its ever-increasing share of world population?* Such a model must be able to help us understand why intelligent couples in Africa and parts of Asia, particularly Southwest Asia, average six or seven babies each.

THE "PPE" VICIOUS CIRCLE: A KEY MODEL AND EXAMPLE OF SYSTEMS THINKING

Figure 4–1 portrays essential elements and dynamic linkages that constitute, in part, the explanatory model which we will build in this chapter. The figure illustrates an ever-widening vicious spiral. It is a key example of "systems thinking," that is, the attempt to understand a phenomenon more fully by first understanding the underlying dynamic system that may be driving the phenomenon and other related behaviors.

Business leaders, in recent years, have realized that they can profitably improve their organizations by applying key tenets of systems thinking. The justly popular book by Peter Senge of MIT's Sloan School of Management, *The Fifth Discipline: The Art and Practice of the Learning Organization,*[1] highlighted for many executives the benefits of applying systems thinking. Senge defines systems thinking and points to its eventual use in facilitating needed change (p. 7): "Systems thinking is a conceptual framework, a body of knowledge and tools that has been developed over the past fifty years, to make the full patterns clearer, and to help us see how to change them effectively."

Senge sees systems thinking as the "fifth discipline" that integrates the others (such as "building a shared vision" and "team learning") in order to form effective learning organizations. Systems thinking enables us to see underlying forces and their dynamic linkages. Understanding such linkages is usually a critical ingredient in successful change. Senge

Figure 4–1 PPE: THE VICIOUS SPIRAL OF POVERTY, POPULATION EXPLOSION, AND ENVIRONMENTAL DEGRADATION

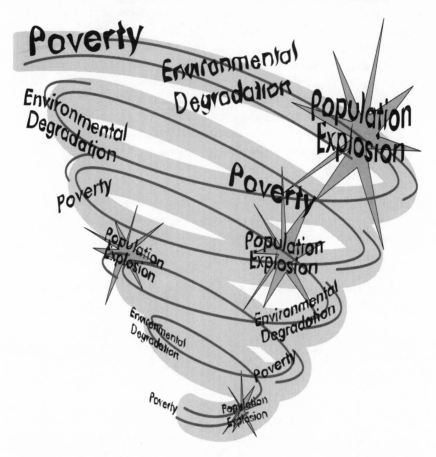

points out (p. 73) that, "The practice of systems thinking starts with understanding a simple concept called "feedback" that shows how actions can reinforce or counteract (balance) each other." He then elaborates, stating that, "Reality is made up of circles but we see straight lines." In other words, it is often best to avoid linear thinking, the tendency to look for unidirectional causality.

Senge defines two types of feedback, reinforcing and balancing (p. 79). We will mainly consider reinforcing feedback processes in this book.

Reinforcing (or amplifying) feedback processes are the engines of growth. Whenever you are in a situation where things are growing, you can be sure that reinforcing feedback is at work. Reinforcing feedback can also generate accelerating decline . . .

Reinforcing feedback processes can spiral in two possible directions, yielding two types of dynamic models (each to be applied later in this book):

> Some reinforcing (amplifying) processes are "vicious cycles," in which things start off badly and grow worse. . . . But there's nothing inherently bad about reinforcing loops. There are also "virtuous cycles"—processes that reinforce in desired directions. For instance, physical exercise can lead to a reinforcing spiral; you feel better, thus you exercise more, thus you're rewarded by feeling better and exercise still more. (p. 81)

A key theme of our book, foreshadowed in the Preface, is that the world approaches the 21st century poised on a knife-edge. It is easy to imagine either a pessimistic or an optimistic scenario unfolding for the billions of residents of the Populous South. A *catalyst* is needed to ensure that the whole world becomes part of a prosperous, open and capitalist, global economy. Without such a catalyst, a massively populous portion of the world may remain mired in the deepening vicious circle portrayed in Figure 4–1.

Figure 4–1 summarizes what is probably the world's most significant vicious circle model: the spiraling reciprocal influences between ever-burgeoning poverty, population growth, and environmental destruction in many nations of the Populous South. Termed the "PPE vicious circle" by many scholars, including Paul Kennedy of Yale, this model derives its name from the dynamic linkages between poverty, population, and the environment. Until recently, I thought the "deficit/debt/debt-servicing vicious spiral" to be described in Chapter 7 was the most crucial vicious circle model. However, researching the present chapter has convinced me that the PPE circle is potentially the most vicious of all: poverty feeds a population explosion because parents desire many children as family-supporting laborers; the population explosion pressures and degrades the natural environment through deforestation and depletion of many other natural resources; this in turn engenders further poverty, and so on.

Despite the recent and highly encouraging economic development in many parts of the world (highlighted later in Chapter 5), the lack of progress in certain nations (e.g., Congo, Afghanistan, Haiti) currently enmeshed in the PPE vicious spiral sounds a clear and cautionary tragic note. The vicious interplay between poverty and population explosion is summarized by the United Nations Development Programme (UNDP) in its *Human Development Report 1997:* "Between 1987 and 1993 the number of people with incomes of less than $1 a day increased by almost

Figure 4-2 GENDER BIAS LEADS TO THE PPE VICIOUS SPIRAL

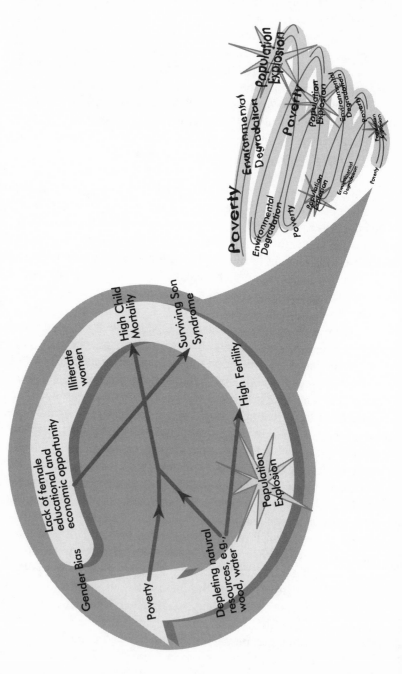

100 million to 1.3 billion—and the number appears to be still growing in every region except Southeast Asia and the Pacific."[2] The report highlights the negative linkages of massive poverty and population with the natural environment (p. 32):

> Continued environmental deterioration is a source of continued impoverishment. . . . Today nearly half a billion poor people in developing countries live in ecologically fragile regions. Thus poor people suffer most from deterioration in the environment— because of the threat to their livelihoods, but also because of aggravated health risks from pollution.
>
> Environmental threats around the world stem from degradation of local ecosystems and of the global system. The water supply per capita in developing countries today is only a third of what it was in 1970. . . . In the developing world some 8–10 million acres of forest land are lost every year.
>
> In Sub-Saharan Africa 65 million hectares of productive land have become desert in the past 50 years. Salinization damages 25% of the irrigated land in Central Asia and 20% in Pakistan.
>
> . . . In the industrial world air pollution is devastating Europe's forests, causing economic losses of $35 billion a year.

Figure 4–2 shows more fundamental forces or behaviors that are posited to drive the PPE vicious spiral. This figure illustrates my own simplified version[3] of a dynamic model that captures the essence of the system of behavior and linkages driving the current PPE vicious cycle in large parts of the Populous South. This dynamic model is supported by many (but by no means all) scholars of economic development. We shall examine each of the linkages in further detail.

Crucial to understanding the model and explaining important current trends are the cultural attitudes toward women in much of the Populous South. Many, arguably most, of these African and Asian nations display a clear *gender bias,* favoring males over females.[4] This lack of empowerment of females, and at times denial of even basic rights, is a critical feature driving the PPE vicious spiral. Indeed, we see it as largely igniting the vicious spiral pictured in Figure 4–2.

This gender bias leads to a lack of educational and economic opportunities for girls and women in these countries. Illustrating my earlier point about the inadequacy of linear thinking in most cases, it is hard to say whether educational or economic handicapping comes first. Perhaps it is the lack of education that harms economic opportunities, particularly in this "age of the knowledge worker." Conversely, it may be that parents perceive a lack of economic opportunity for women, due to bias in the labor market, and so invest less in educating their daughters. In this case, the parents invest scarce resources in the education of their sons, because favoritism toward males in the labor market boosts the relative private investment return of such biased educational choices. Both directions of causality are quite possible, thus illustrating a vicious spiral once again.

Figure 4–3 illustrates quantitatively the gender bias in education and the resulting plight of women in much of the Populous South. Unlike the nations of the extended triad, where recent improvements have led to near equal educational opportunity, the three regions representing the Populous South in the graph display two shocking or tragic outcomes. First, note the low overall average level of education for both genders. Second, note the gender bias or clear disparity in average years of education invested in male vs. female human capital formation. For example, we see in Figure 4–3 that Africa averages just less than one year of formal schooling for girls, while South Asia barely exceeds this depressingly low level of female education.

Think about what it actually means to receive not even two years of formal education. Parents and teachers know that it is usually in second or third grade that our children truly begin to master reading and writing.

Figure 4–3   DISPARITY IN HUMAN CAPITAL FORMATION: EDUCATIONAL INVESTMENT BY WORLD REGION AND GENDER

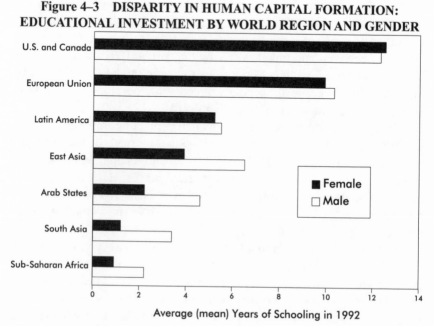

Average (mean) Years of Schooling in 1992

Data Source: UNDP, *Human Development Report,* 1994.

Figure 4-4 SURVIVING-SON SYNDROME
(Girls Often Lack Basic Educational Opportunity)

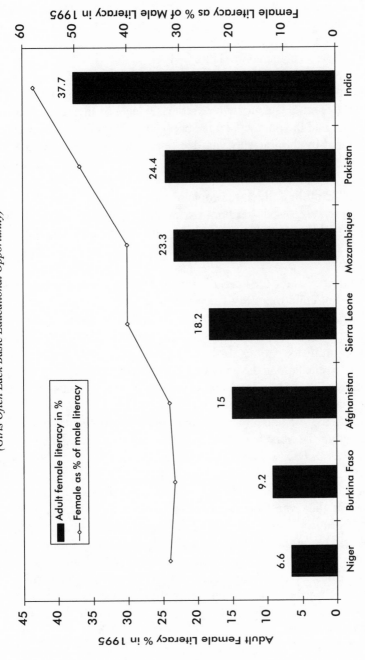

Data Source: World Bank, *World Development Indicators*, 1997.

Thus, the average schooling level of roughly one year for girls in Africa or South Asia results in many illiterate adult women in these regions. This crucial linkage for our overall model is made explicit in Figure 4–2. However, the truly sad extent of the problem plaguing many Populous South nations is depicted in Figure 4–4.

Figure 4–4 reveals two unsettling portrayals: (1) the shockingly low percentage of adult females who have had the opportunity to achieve what, in this case, is actually a rather basic level of literacy (see the left-hand scale and the numbers on the bars); and (2) the huge bias or disparity captured by the line showing that female literacy rates are often less than half the percentage of adult male literacy (see the right-hand scale).[5] More aggregate data clinches this chilling point: Developing nations contain 872 million illiterate people over age 14; and an astounding 64% of the illiterates, or 557 million, are women.[6] Literacy rates that include barely one-third of adult women throughout most of the Populous South are both a cause and a consequence of the PPE vicious spiral, as shown in Figure 4–2.

We next examine the link in Figure 4–2 between illiterate mothers and high rates of child mortality, often combined with desperate poverty and lack of resources, particularly a deadly lack of clean water. Indeed, so many infants (under one year of age) or children (under five years of age) are dying in many nations of the Populous South that we should take a moment to reflect upon the individual human tragedies that are aggregated into, but can never be adequately expressed by, national statistics. Figure 4–5 reveals that infant mortality can exceed 15% of live births of babies in some nations, including Afghanistan and Liberia. Correspondingly, or exacerbating the very human dimensions of this tragic system, *roughly one-quarter of babies die before age five* in many nations of Africa and in certain nations of Asia, such as Afghanistan.

Further, Figure 4–5 illustrates a crucial linkage that becomes explicit in the overall model portrayed in Figure 4–2. High rates of infant mortality seem linked to high rates of fertility. In nations such as Liberia or Afghanistan, dreadfully high levels of infant and child mortality (see left-hand scale) seem clearly connected with elevated fertility rates, approaching seven babies per woman (see right-hand scale). The figure also supports the notion of a *linkage* between high child mortality and high fertility; India, for example, now has much lower rates of mortality and fertility than the other nations pictured. Perhaps the most practical way to illustrate this hypothesized linkage is by focusing on a key part of the overall model that I term the "Surviving-Son Syndrome."

Figure 4-5 THE VICIOUS CIRCLE OF HIGH MORTALITY AND HIGH FERTILITY

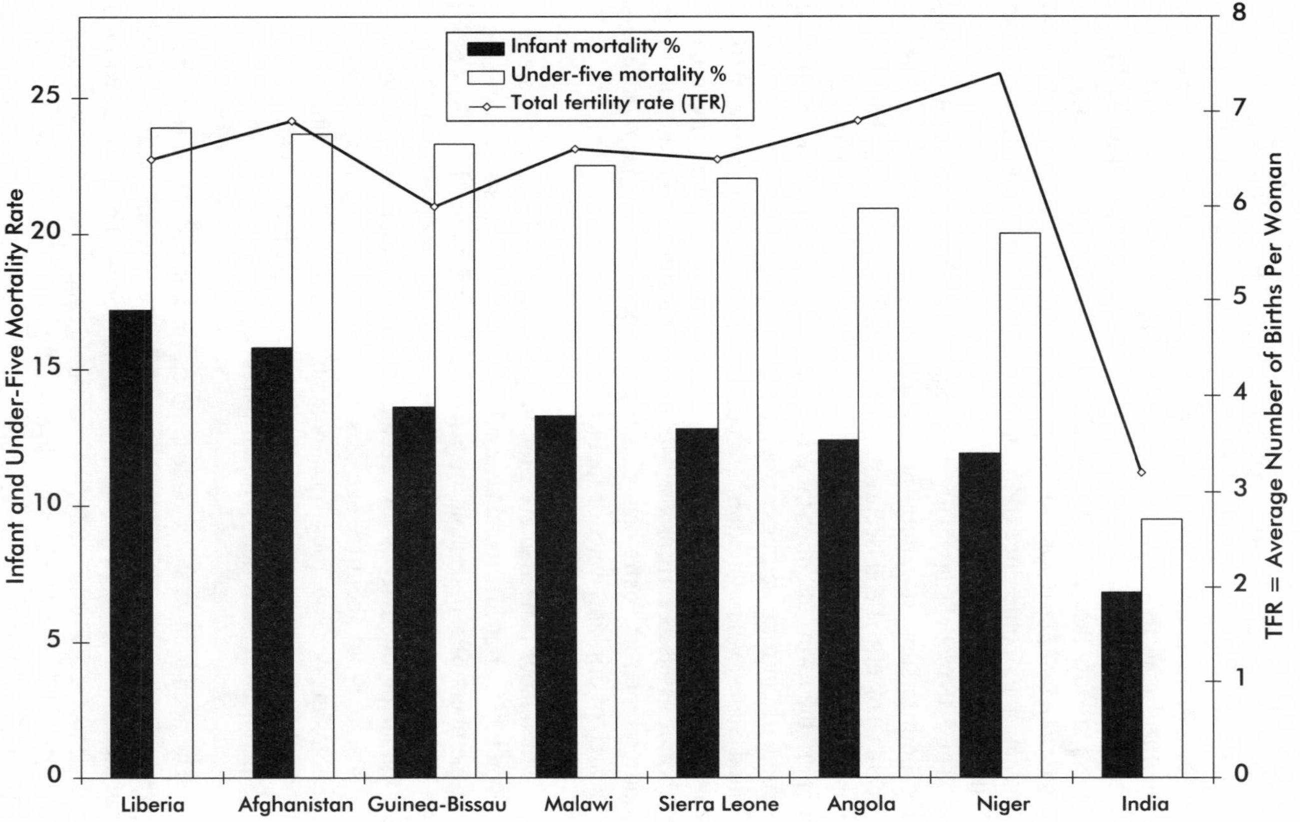

Data Source: World Bank, *World Development Indicators*, 1997.

95

THE SURVIVING-SON SYNDROME

The Surviving-Son Syndrome (SSS) is a term which I use to denote a set of culturally based practices that contribute mightily to the PPE vicious circle. Although not all scholars would agree to every aspect of the model as I conceive it and portray it below, most would support major parts of it. For example, see the major survey article written by Partha Dasgupta for the *Journal of Economic Literature*[7] or the book *Population and Development*[8] prepared by The World Bank for the 1994 International Conference on Population and Development, held in Cairo, Egypt.

The SSS model starts with the notion that parents demand large families, both to support cultural norms and for explicit economic reasons. Lacking solvent social security systems, parents perceive that if they manage to live to old age, they must depend on a surviving child to support them. In addition, they recognize that children can be useful, particularly in rural settings, as added labor for the family. Unlike in the United States, where children are considered financial liabilities until at least the age of 21, in some very poor nations children are seen as economic assets as early as age five or six.[9] Dasgupta points out that these children represent "extra hands" that can help out on the farm or be sent in search of drinking water or fuel (p. 1895).

> Much labor is needed even for simple tasks. . . . [With no] water on tap . . . nor fuel wood near at hand when the forests recede . . . members of a household may have to spend as much as 5 to 6 hours a day fetching water and collecting fodder and wood. . . . Labor productivity is low because environmental resources are scarce. From about the age of six years, children in poor households in poor countries mind their siblings and domestic animals, fetch water, and collect fuel wood, dung, and fodder. Children are then needed as workers by their parents.

The need to have at least one child survive, in order to care for aging parents, leads to very high birth rates because of the simple, but depressing, fact that in some poor nations, more than one-quarter of kids will *not* survive to age 5. Furthermore, the seemingly excessive fertility problem is exacerbated by the gender bias discussed earlier. The lack of economic opportunity for females necessitates having not just a child, but a *son* survive, hence our term "Surviving-Son Syndrome" (SSS). The result? Two distressing alternatives: (1) female infanticide, a horrible but too frequent practice in many poor nations, particularly in Asia, or (2) fertility rates as high as six or seven babies per couple, which, as Dasgupta points out (p. 1894), is actually a very rational decision by parents who are intuitively intelligent. Sadly, the *system* is such that individually intelligent decisions lead to a collectively tragic outcome—the vicious spiraling of population explosion, poverty, and environmental degradation.

The current situation in much of Africa and Southwest Asia is bleak, with the huge fertility fostered by the SSS bringing about a population explosion (thus explaining the trends shown in Chapter 3). The resulting environmental degradation and resource depletion (illustrated in Figure 4–1 and Figure 4–2) show their effects in many areas. For example, Figure 4–2 displays resource depletion and environmental damage as one bridge linking population explosion to poverty. It also helps explain high child mortality—as the environment becomes increasingly poor and unhealthy—and high fertility, as parents need added family laborers to search further for increasingly scarce fuel wood or water.

Deforestation provides another clear example. The World Bank[10] reports that during the 1980s the following nations lost *at least* 3% of their forests *each year* on average, for ten years: Armenia, Bangladesh, Costa Rica, Haiti, Jamaica, Pakistan, Philippines, Thailand, and Uzbekistan. The cumulative effects of 3% declines per year for ten years translate to large-scale destruction. Sadly, in most cases, similar rates of deforestation and environmental degradation are continuing in the 1990s. Furthermore, other areas of Asia, the Caribbean Basin, and sub-Saharan Africa are also suffering glaring losses of forested land (nearly 1% yearly). Deforestation also leads to numerous other environmental problems, such as global warming and species extinction. The loss of biodiversity due to species extinction has serious implications for both individuals and businesses. It is slightly heartening to note, however, that a few pharmaceutical companies are taking financial steps to preserve rain forests, in hopes of reaping economic benefits from otherwise lost-forever drugs or treatments.

Massive poverty is an inevitable outcome of the dynamic model or negatively reinforcing system portrayed in this chapter. Further, widespread poverty, particularly when combined with an exploding population, makes it even less likely that there will be enough resources to adequately feed and educate all children. Thus, this "negative feedback loop" continues and, along with the culturally determined gender bias, exacerbates the lack of educational opportunities for girls, as well as the high rates of infant and child mortality.

What is killing so many babies and children? Usually it is not some complex or expensive-to-cure disease, but rather, simple dehydration due to diarrhea.[11] The lack of access to clean or safe water explains this major cause of childhood death, as it leads to a tragic dilemma for the mother: the baby becomes dehydrated from diarrhea, but the only available water is dirty and contaminated. Contrast this with the situation in the United States, where most parents would call their pediatricians, who would instruct them to give the child Pedialyte, a refrigerated electrolyte therapy. Obviously, Africa has a dearth of pediatricians,[12] let alone refrigerators or Pedialyte! Indeed the same bacteria-laden dirty water the mother tries to use to rehydrate her child started off the tragic process in the first place. Anne Platt, in an article titled "Water-borne Killers," details the issue.[13]

> Water-borne pathogens and pollution kill 25 million people every year. . . . In 1993, the most recent year for which data were available, there were more than 1.8 billion cases of diarrhea worldwide, predominantly in sub-Saharan Africa. Every year, diarrhea alone kills nearly 3 million children under age 5.

Figure 4–6 shows the astonishing lack of access to clean or safe drinking water. In this case, "access" is not even defined as running water in the home, but rather as availability within roughly *three hours* of walking distance (each way!) to collect it in a water jug or urn. The figure links the startling low percentage of population with access to safe water to a tragic consequence: Frequent premature death in many Populous South nations, often due to drinking polluted or unsafe water, is clearly related to the abysmally low life expectancies in these nations. One cannot help but shudder when pondering the dreadful conditions that result in *life expectancies of less than forty years* in some African nations, as depicted in Figure 4–6. Many of us in the United States, when we turn forty, think with some justification that our best days are ahead of us. Imagine living in a nation where turning forty means that you have exceeded the normal span of life—that you are living on borrowed time! Contrast this with Japan, where women have a life expectancy of 83 years. In other words, citizens of some of the nations pictured in Figure 4–6 have average life expectancies *less than half* of what is obviously humanly possible in a wealthy nation such as Japan.[14]

The above situation, as tragic and depressing as it is, points to potential catalysts or ways to start breaking the current vicious spiral. Needed are public health measures to provide clean water sources and to educate often illiterate mothers to filter water through fabric or whatever rudimentary filters can be obtained. The depth and profundity of this problem have prompted me to direct my own volunteer efforts primarily toward CARE and the Carter Presidential Center of Emory University. Both of these nongovernmental organizations have "child survival" programs focused

Figure 4–6 LACK OF CLEAN WATER SHORTENS LIFE EXPECTANCY

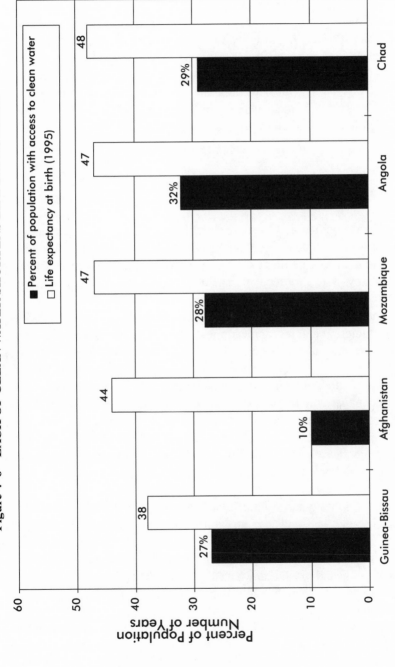

■ Percent of population with access to clean water
□ Life expectancy at birth (1995)

Percent of Population
Number of Years

Guinea-Bissau: 27%, 38
Afghanistan: 10%, 44
Mozambique: 28%, 47
Angola: 32%, 47
Chad: 29%, 48

Data Source: World Bank, *World Development Indicators*, 1997.
Note: Women in Japan have a life expectancy of 83 years.

on Africa and the poor regions of Asia as key elements of their work toward *sustainable development* in these populous regions.

Nations that have been able to build up public health systems, particularly through providing access to clean water, have been able to reduce their infant and child mortality rates significantly during the past few decades.[15] Further, by spreading information on public health measures, these nations have been able to *convince* parents that their babies are likely to survive. This is critical in breaking the vicious spiral of population, since parents will not reduce very high fertility rates until they are less fearful of losing children to disease and death.

EDUCATING GIRLS AND EMPOWERING WOMEN

Solving the population/poverty problem also requires a greater empowerment of women in developing nations of the Populous South. In societies where women have neither educational nor economic opportunity, parents desire many more children (or, tragically, engage in female infanticide) in order to secure their retirements, as only surviving *sons* are expected to have the economic power eventually to support their parents. Indeed, many studies, including some important ones performed at the World Bank when current U.S. Deputy Treasury Secretary Larry Summers was its chief economist, show that the world can reap a very high *financial* return, as well as human return, by investing in more primary education for women, particularly in Africa, but also in South and Southwest Asia.[16] Furthermore, recent studies show that the catch phrase of the 1974 World Population Conference in Bucharest, "Development is the best contraceptive," embodies useful insight. The World Bank's *Population and Development* book summarizes recent evidence (p. 53):

> That schooling has a powerful effect on reproductive behavior is undisputed. . . . [There are] differences of two to five births between women with no education and those with ten or more years of schooling. . . . Large percentages of women with no schooling and low literacy have been identified as a serious obstacle to fertility decline in Sub-Saharan African countries where the demand for children is still high. . . . Fertility declines have been most rapid in the countries that have adopted multisectoral approaches in population and balanced family planning with investments in girls' education, child health, and improvements in women's status, property rights, and so forth.

THE DEMOGRAPHIC TRANSITION:

BREAKING THE VICIOUS CIRCLE OF
HIGH MORTALITY AND FERTILITY

On a hopeful note, recent evidence is accumulating that many nations are significantly reducing fertility, and world population growth is decelerating as a result. Indeed, the evidence shows that many nations are beginning or are completing the famous process that demographers refer to as the *"demographic transition."* The theory behind this transition is that low or falling mortality rates will eventually lead to lower fertility. However, the transition to lower fertility usually occurs after a time lag, a delayed response during which population can grow sharply. This transition was first observed in France and Sweden early in the 18th century. Similar behavior then spread through Western Europe, and later was also observed in North America. The World Bank, in *Population and Development,* describes the demographic transition in Europe.

> Prior to the onset of this process, population grows very slowly because high death rates offset the high birth rates characteristic of preindustrial societies. . . . In Europe, the demographic transition got underway at about the time of the Industrial Revolution, which gradually brought improved living conditions, followed by advances in public health and medical technology, which together resulted in declining mortality. Initially birth rates remained steady or even increased, but eventually the social, economic, and cultural changes occurring at the time also brought declines in fertility. It was this lag between the onset of declines in fertility and mortality that accelerated population growth during the demographic transitions of European countries.[17]

More recently, a demographic transition has been achieved in East Asia and appears to be progressing throughout Latin America and probably South Asia as well. The results seen in Figure 4–7 provide more updated evidence supporting and extending the World Bank's conclusion in *Population and Development* (1994, p. 25):

> Developing countries vary considerably with regard to where they are in the demographic transition. Some have nearly completed the transition (notably, China and several other Asian countries), others are in the midst of it, with fertility at intermediate levels (several Latin American countries), and some have yet to start (much of sub-Saharan Africa).

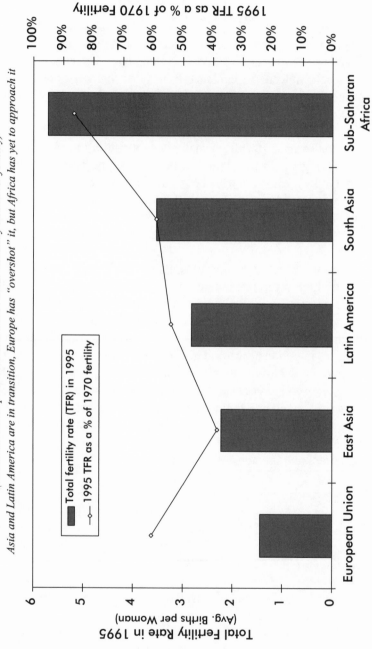

Figure 4-7 THE DEMOGRAPHIC TRANSITION

(Economic development leads to lower child mortality and lower fertility)

Asia and Latin America are in transition, Europe has "overshot" it, but Africa has yet to approach it

1995 TFR as a % of 1970 Fertility

100%
90%
80%
70%
60%
50%
40%
30%
20%
10%
0%

Total fertility rate (TFR) in 1995
1995 TFR as a % of 1970 fertility

Sub-Saharan Africa
South Asia
Latin America
East Asia
European Union

Total Fertility Rate in 1995
(Avg. Births per Woman)

6
5
4
3
2
1
0

Data Source: World Bank, *World Development Indicators*, 1997.

102

Figure 4–7 illustrates the widely divergent positions with regard to the demographic transition that different regions of the world have achieved. Europe has even overshot the transition: the bar graph shows that it has reduced fertility (TFR) well below 2, that is, below the population replacement level. East Asia is now close to completing the transition: the bar graph shows its total fertility is declining toward only 2 births per woman, whereas the line graph (see right-hand scale) shows the huge transition East Asia has made, as its TFR is now less than half what it was as late as 1970.

Meanwhile, Figure 4–7 also shows that, as the World Bank indicated, Latin America is right in the midst of a very impressive demographic transition toward much lower fertility. In addition, and highly significant for the deceleration of the whole world's potentially explosive population growth, the huge populations of South Asia seem to be following the path toward lower fertility. This reduced fertility in such populous nations as India and Bangladesh, if it continues, represents a hopeful sign that the world's PPE vicious spiral can be slowed or even stopped. In other words, sometime in the 21st century we *can* end up on the "virtuous" or prosperous side of the world's current perch on a knife-edge. However, the data for sub-Saharan Africa displayed in Figure 4–7 should temper any euphoric optimism, as we see this region has barely begun to reduce its fertility along the lines of the demographic transition; indeed at a TFR near 6, it still has almost 90% of its 1970 fertility rates.

There are clear examples of countries in each region that exhibit the demographic transition discussed here and summarized in Figure 4–7. We will illustrate this by contrasting national total fertility or infant mortality rates in 1970 with those of 1995.[18] First, the overshooting decline of fertility in Europe is exemplified by Spain, where fertility (TFR) declined from 2.8 to a mere 1.2 births per average woman. Likewise, Italy's fertility halved from 2.4 to 1.2 babies, following a steep fall in its infant mortality rate (from 30 to 7 babies per thousand). East Asia has key nations clearly completing the demographic transition, as China has had its TFR fall (or be pushed, via the one-child policy) dramatically from 5.8 to 1.9. This steep fall is a major world trend, helping the rate of world population growth both decelerate and shift in distribution away from East Asia. The other populous East Asian nation, Indonesia, has also shown a demographic transition, by slightly more than halving both its infant mortality (to 5% of births) and its fertility rates (to 2.7 live births).

Similarly, key Latin American nations do appear right in the midst of the demographic transition. The demographically dominant nation in South America, Brazil, has cut both its infant mortality (to 4.4%) and its total fertility (to 2.4 live births per average woman), by more than half since 1970. Mexico has seen similar massive declines to an infant mortality of 1 out of 30 babies (from 1 out of 14 in 1970), and to a TFR of 3 births per average woman (versus 6.5 in 1970).

South Asia seems the likely next candidate to complete the demographic transition, as two of its three populous nations are well along the process. India has reduced its TFR from 5.8 to 3.2, no doubt aided by its halving of its infant mortality rate to 6.8% of babies dying by age one year. Impressively, Bangladesh is right in the transition; its infant mortality rate has fallen from 14% to 8% of babies. This greater chance of survival, combined with population policies allowing a greater availability of contraception, has contributed to a dramatic halving of Bangladesh's TFR, from a massive 7 to a more manageable 3.5. However, Pakistan is not as far along: its TFR has declined only by one-quarter, from 7 to 5.2; the high fertility may be partly attributable to its high infant mortality (9% of babies die by age one year, but still, this is better than the 14.2% in 1970).

Substantiating the overall message of Figure 4–7, sub-Saharan Africa has large nations that continue to exhibit high fertility rates, albeit slightly diminished since 1970: Nigeria's TFR has declined to 5.5, South Africa's to 3.9, and Kenya's to 4.7 (from a whopping 8.1, declining as its infant mortality thankfully has declined). However, Niger's TFR actually rose to 7.4, and Ethiopia's and Somalia's are also very high, at 7.

Finally, Southwest Asia (the Middle East or Arabic Gulf states) is at the stage of burgeoning population brought on by mortality declines not yet matched by a transition to a lower fertility. Indeed Oman and Yemen have TFRs exceeding 7. Saudi Arabia's exceeds 6 despite a huge drop in infant mortality, while Iraq's TFR is still a hefty 5.4.

The main point, for our purposes, is that some quite populous parts of the world (notably, those that are suffering from the most vicious spiraling of the PPE system), exhibit little or no evidence of entering a demographic transition. These regions still need a combination of economic development and public health measures to lower their abysmally high rates of infant and child mortality. If this major and humane goal can be achieved, then public information measures can help to quickly spread the word that more babies can be expected to survive to adulthood. This, in turn, would provide a possible solution to the high TFRs, because right now parents *choose* the very high fertility that is a key element both of the surviving-son syndrome and of the resulting PPE vicious spiral.

One key element of the model employed in this chapter is that the high fertility exhibited in much of the Populous South is mostly caused by the economic choices of parents living in systems where rational individual choices lead to dismal outcomes in the aggregate. Before conditions change enough so that parents will not choose to have such high fertility, birth control availability (contraception) is not really a significant answer to high fertility and the current population explosion.[19] However, it could be part of the answer *after* parents' choice sets change.

REASONS FOR OPTIMISM:
SUCCESSFUL CASES AROUND THE GLOBE

Are there reasons for optimism? Can we identify successful cases that provide proof that poor nations now caught in the PPE death spiral can end up on the positive side of the knife edge? Fortunately, the answer is "yes." Our analysis of the data in the World Bank's *World Development Indicators 1997* yields many examples of nations that have undergone a demographic transition; they have reduced their infant and child mortality dramatically in the past few decades, while subsequently reducing fertility and generating the type of rapid per capita economic growth that is leading many of their citizens out of poverty. In a recent article in the *American Economic Review*,[20] Obed Galor and David Weil build a theoretical model which employs a "positive feedback loop" that illustrates a virtuous circle linking per capita income growth and a decline in fertility. A key aspect of their model and this chapter is the reduced "gender gap" as women's relative wages rise, causing the fertility decline.

Table 4–1 lists a number of nations that have successfully combined economic development and a demographic transition. The table details both fertility and infant mortality rates for each nation in 1995 compared to 1970. Tremendous progress toward a global demographic transition has clearly been achieved this past quarter-century. In each example chosen here, we see dramatic declines in infant mortality and related steep declines in total fertility rates. Importantly, the fifth column in the table shows that these nations' demographic transitions have been linked with substantial economic development, measured as average annual growth in real GNP per capita, during the same 1970–1995 quarter-century of progress. Also of significance, note that the twelve examples listed in Table 4–1 come from various regions of the Earth. The first two are in sub-Saharan Africa, the next two are in North Africa, the fifth is South American, the sixth is South Asian, and the remaining six are East Asian.

Recall that Figure 4–7 clearly demonstrates that, in aggregate, sub-Saharan Africa is not close to the kind of fertility declines needed to

Table 4–1   A More Virtuous Circle
Examples Linking Economic Development and Demographic Transitions

	Infant Mortality (Deaths by Age 1 Year per 1,000 Live Births)		Total Fertility Rate (Average Number of Live Births per Woman)		Economic Growth per Capita*
	1970	1995	1970	1995	1970 to 1995
Botswana	95	56	6.9	4.4	7.3%
Kenya	102	58	8.1	4.7	1.0%
Tunisia	121	39	6.4	2.9	2.3%
Morocco	128	55	7.0	3.4	1.8%
Chile	77	12	4.0	2.3	1.8%
India	137	68	5.8	3.2	2.4%
Singapore	20	4	3.1	1.7	5.7%
Hong Kong	19	5	3.3	1.2	5.7%
South Korea	46	10	4.3	1.8	10.0%
Thailand	73	35	5.5	1.8	5.2%
Indonesia	118	51	5.5	2.7	4.7%
China	69	34	5.8	1.9	6.9%

*Annual average growth in real GNP per capita, 1970 to 1995.
Data source: World Bank, *World Development Indicators* 1997, pp. 6–12.

succeed in a demographic transition. However, Table 4–1 indicates some hope for the future; it shows two examples or models of a successful start in sub-Saharan Africa. To be fair, we should not push this point too far because Botswana, the clear example of success, has a small population and tremendous diamond reserves. The table's other sub-Saharan African nation, Kenya, is included because it is beginning to exhibit a much needed demographic transition. However, Kenya's economic development over this period leaves much to be desired; indeed Chapter 5 will reveal that its per capita economic growth record in the shorter period commencing in 1982 is even more dismal.

The other national examples in Table 4–1 serve as instructive models. Tunisia and Morocco prove that North Africa is economically and demographically distinct (more prosperous) from sub-Saharan Africa. North Africa is likely to develop further close links with the expanding pan-European free trade area portrayed in our second chapter. Indeed, plans point toward an eventual free trade area spanning both sides of the Mediterranean.

Chile's story is also quite instructive. It has completed a very successful demographic transition; it achieved a tremendous drop in infant mortality (spurred by economic development) which also led to a decline in fertility to a sustainable level. Now that it combines a transition to democracy with the demographic and economic development transitions highlighted in Table 4-1, Chile serves as a useful model for other Latin American nations which represent key emerging markets for business (e.g., Brazil, Mexico, Argentina). The next chapter will build upon this theme of Chile as a success model for Latin America.

The data support the notion that India is right in the middle of a demographic transition and is making steady, if not rapid, economic progress. India will comprise over *one billion* people before the imminent new century dawns, so its ability to complete its demographic and business developmental transitions is an open question of global significance. Chapter 6 will detail long-run forecasts for India's economy under both optimistic and pessimistic scenarios.

Finally, the clear success of the bulk of East Asia in achieving both rapid economic growth and a demographic transition is shown by the bottom half of Table 4-1. The six nations included here were chosen as representative, as they comprise three of the "Little Dragons" (NICs, as discussed in Chapter 1) and three of the much more populous, recently industrializing countries (RICs, or big emerging nations). Notable is China's amazingly rapid economic growth and demographic transition in the past quarter-century. The one-child policy, and the opening toward limited capitalism and more free markets commencing in 1979, clearly had significant impacts in China. Given that China now contains nearly 1.25 billion people, its transition, in which fertility rates were cut by *two-thirds,* has major global implications and is a prime contributor to the recent deceleration of world population growth. A continuation of this decelerating pattern worldwide is necessary to avoid the environmental nightmare of the PPE vicious circle described in this chapter.

The important lesson in this section is that useful policies such as public health measures, freedom for women to pursue careers and for girls to receive formal education, and an opening to capitalism (particularly to foreign investment) have led to clear success stories. It is crucial for our future strategies that these successes can be found in various populous regions, not just in East Asia. However, East Asia has been shown in this chapter to be leading the recent demographic transition, while the next chapter will show that it also leads in terms of economic growth during the past few decades.

Singapore is probably the most extreme example of East Asia's successful transition. Singapore illustrates a virtuous circle system, making good use of catalysts such as public health measures, universal education for girls as well as boys, governmental policies that motivate high savings rates and attract (job-creating and technology-transferring) foreign direct investment. Singapore has drastically curtailed poverty and has protected its environment by reversing its population spiral. It now has a sustainable birth rate, critical for such a geographically constrained island nation. Parents are able to invest more in each child's health, nutrition, and education. I can best support my claim that Singapore exemplifies a demographic virtuous circle by comparing changes in infant mortality rates.

Table 4–1 shows that Singapore's infant mortality declined by 80% and is now only four deaths per 1000 babies. Incredibly, this formerly poor (and still poor in natural resource, but not human capital) nation now matches Sweden and Japan for the lowest infant mortality rates on Earth. Sadly, the infant mortality rates in the United States are now twice Singapore's or Japan's rate. In fact, the infant mortality rates in rural parts of the U.S. South often exceed *four times* Singapore's rate.[21] Singapore provides ample evidence that nations can develop, that good policies and effort can turn vicious spirals into virtuous circles, and that new markets *can* emerge. For example, the United States now exports more to tiny Singapore than to France!

We can now see that successful models do exist, and that it is possible to break the PPE vicious circle and turn from rapid population growth to rapid economic growth. We have portrayed both vicious and virtuous circles in examining various nations' systems of economic and demographic linkages. The world enters the 21st century poised on the brink; appropriate policy and investment choices are needed to break the momentum of the population/poverty/environmental degradation vicious spiral detailed here. The World Bank highlights the stakes in the Executive Summary of *Population and Development* (1994, pp. 3–4):

> Population momentum can be reduced by investments to increase educational opportunities, to expand reproductive health and family planning information and services, and to reduce maternal and child mortality. The *timing* of these investments is critical to offsetting momentum. Slowing population growth sooner rather than later could reduce future global population size by 2 billion–3 billion when global population finally stabilizes at the end of the next century. Delaying such investments will only add to the ultimate costs of poverty reduction.

Fortunately, large parts of the developing world *are* achieving substantial economic progress, as we will identify in the next chapter.

Worthwhile policies are moderating population growth, improving citizens' lives, and enabling these nations to emerge as big markets for business. The next chapter will detail economic development trends, and describe nations in which growing incomes enable many to leave widespread poverty behind. We will demonstrate that some large developing nations will see a massive influx of citizens into a middle class, or at least a lower middle class, implying a gain of purchasing power that should make them the next frontier for business growth.

FIRM SPOTLIGHT
Breaking the PPE Vicious Circle:
The Coca-Cola Company Spurs Economic Growth in Africa

While the presence of the Coca-Cola Company in Africa dates back as far as a bottler agreement in 1938, recent massive investments highlight the company's commitment to reach nearly every African throughout the continent. Coca-Cola already enjoys greater than an 80% market share in Africa, but intends to double its recent volume there by the year 2000. Such ambitious plans require strong financial backing. Indeed, Zimbabwe, Mozambique, South Africa, and Tanzania are just four of the African nations in which Coca-Cola invested more than $600 million in the period 1995–1997. In February 1997, the company announced it would invest an additional $220 million in South Africa over the next five to seven years, to further enhance its bottling operations there. By purchasing coolers, equipment, and support systems, Coca-Cola expects its sales there to double as its beverages become even more readily available.

The expansion in Africa is spurring new economic growth there, as Coca-Cola's leadership has always stressed the need to develop the local industry rather than source materials from abroad. The result of this effort is the stimulation of dormant or nonexistent local industries, producing at, or moving towards, world class standards. According to Peter Lawson, Business Development Manager of the Coca-Cola Company, "Coca-Cola will not compromise its worldwide standards of quality, so we work closely with local suppliers and operations to develop and maintain the same high quality of inputs and products that our customers and consumers will find anywhere else in the world."

The result? New industries are popping up all around Coca-Cola bottling operations. For example, glass, crates, crowns, and sugar are just some of the items needed to produce and sell Coca-Cola. The company estimates that every one job it creates directly produces another eight to ten jobs as a result of local economy growth. In addition, existing suppliers produce more efficiently as best practice procedures are brought on board. Coca-Cola obviously gains as its costs are driven lower, while the local citizens gain jobs, entrepreneurial opportunities, and a higher quality of life.

Clearly, large corporations have a great opportunity to affect emerging economies and markets in a positive way. Ultimately, investment in the local economy can help stem the outflow of hard currency, build up foreign reserves, and end the flight of capital that severely depresses so many African nations. This chapter has highlighted the need to break the PPE vicious circle, and the role of the Coca-Cola Company in Africa is an excellent example of the good that corporations can do while pursuing further growth and profitability.

PART II

THE POTENTIAL OF MORE GLOBAL ECONOMIC PROGRESS

CHAPTER 5

TOMORROW'S CUSTOMERS:

The Middle Class Goes Global

W e have now arrived at a major turning point in this book. The preceding chapter's discussion of the vast extent of poverty, the risks of overpopulation, and environmental degradation on this Earth may have left you with a gloomy feeling. It is time for some good news, and even some models of success that should point the way to a more prosperous future for the billions of poor people discussed in the preceding two chapters.

We will now examine the generally impressive, yet mixed, record of economic growth in the largest nations of the economically developing or economically lesser-developed world. After the last two chapters you may well be asking yourself: "Is this author fixated on population? When are we going to start talking about dollars and purchasing power again?" Here we begin to formalize the link between people and profits, turning our attention to the increases in production around the world that lead to increased incomes. Increased incomes, in turn, lead to increased purchasing power. Increased purchasing power implies a growing demand for the goods and services provided by global business.

In this chapter, I must assume yet another burden of proof: to show that the ever-increasing billions of people in the developing world are gaining, or will likely gain, *significant purchasing power.* Gains in productivity and living standards are needed to justify my strategic claim that business should add a focus on the developing world. This claim is based on trends, shown in the preceding chapters, indicating that almost all the world's population growth will be in developing nations. The question before us is: *Can we show that much of the world's population lives in nations that, although relatively poor today, are, or could be, experienc-*

ing enough economic growth that they can be considered the emerging markets for expanding business?

The recent performance of many developing nations surely justifies the claim that they are, in the currently fashionable term, "emerging markets." I will present evidence to show that emerging markets are a reality, and that the phrase is not just a euphemism for what we used to call "least-developed countries" or even "basket cases." When economists talk about economic development, they consider a complex range of improvements in living standards. However, I will follow the usual practice of trying to proxy for overall economic development by studying the growth, or lack thereof, in the gross domestic product (GDP) of a nation or region. Of course, the entire discussion in this chapter will use *real* GDP, that is, GDP in constant dollar terms, so that we capture real volume changes and not just those due to inflating prices.

An important distinction is the one between growth in total real GDP and the related, but potentially crucially different, change in real GDP *per capita*. Consider the case of South Africa or Ethiopia. Reflecting rapid population growth, total GDP in recent decades increased, but output (hence income) per person declined. In this case, growth in total GDP masks what is actually a decline in living standards. There is no doubt that the pie is getting slightly larger, but with many more mouths to feed, the only slightly larger pie means smaller slices for each individual. An examination of changes in GDP per capita provides a refined picture of the economic development, or lack thereof, in such a case.

The data trends presented here are here critical in that they help us answer a major question underlying this book: *Are populous developing nations truly* emerging *as markets—that is, are they likely future markets for globally oriented firms?* If in fact there are large or populous regions of this world where standards of living are rising rapidly and consistently, then the major thesis of this book will be supported: those hoping to prosper in the upcoming century had best start forming a strategy now to grow in a pattern consistent with an *emerging global economy.* Clearly, the firms that establish a more global presence focused on these rising markets today will be at a distinct competitive advantage.

MARKETS EMERGE FOR U.S. FIRMS OUTSIDE THE TRADITIONAL TRIAD

Figure 5–1 highlights a key trend that supports the claim that the developing world truly contains big emerging markets. I decomposed total U.S. exports in a unique way, in order to test the hypothesis that there are big markets for

U.S. businesses emerging outside of the powerful nations of the "traditional triad." To test this hypothesis, I divided total U.S. exports into two categories. The first category is the total of U.S. exports to the other six nations in the Group of 7 (G-7). The G-7 comprises seven of the world's largest and most advanced economies, those nations whose leaders gather for annual summit meetings. This group reflects 20th century economic power: Japan, the United States, Canada, Germany, France, Italy, and Great Britain. Thus, this category measures U.S. exports to our six partners in the G-7. (*We* are the seventh member, and in trade, as in other aspects of life, it doesn't really count if you do it with yourself—you need a partner.)

The second category in Figure 5–1 measures total U.S. exports to all the nations of the world outside of the G-7. Measuring U.S. exports to 200 or so nations against U.S. exports to a mere six of the G-7 may seem an unfair comparison. However, even with the far greater number of nations in the non-G-7 total, as late as the mid-1980s the G-7 partners constituted a more significant total market for U.S. exports than the rest of the world combined. This is probably why most global strategists as late as the early 1990s advised U.S. firms to concentrate on all three legs of the traditional triad in pursuing international markets.[1]

Figure 5–1   U.S. MERCHANDISE EXPORTS SHOW RAPID GROWTH IN MARKETS OUTSIDE THE G-7

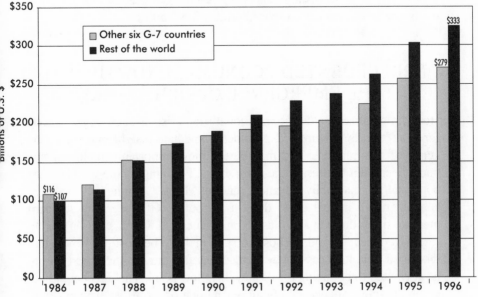

Data Source: U.S. Department of Commerce, *Survey of Current Business,* March 1998.

Figure 5–1 provides clear confirmation for our hypothesis that there are markets emerging for U.S. firms outside of the traditional triad. Significantly, U.S. exports to non-G-7 nations have more than tripled in just one decade, from 1986 to 1996. This represents "real money" for U.S. business, as these exports reached one-third of a trillion dollars in 1996 and are still growing. Furthermore, this includes only merchandise exports, so the tally would be even higher if service exports were included. The two important trends to notice are the rapid exponential growth in our exports to the emerging markets, and the related or secondary trend that these U.S. exports recently surpassed and now clearly exceed exports to our G-7 partners.

What is important, however, is that this secondary trend is *not* a result of stagnant export growth to our G-7 partners. A closer look shows that U.S. exports to our six G-7 partners have gone from under $120 billion in 1986 to nearly $280 billion in 1996. In other words, our exports to the G-7 grew almost two and a half times in a mere decade. Thus, U.S. exports to the G-7 continue to grow strongly. That they are being outstripped by our exports to the rest of the world is not due to any stagnancy in our traditional export markets, but rather, is a reflection of the very rapid growth of new markets for U.S. exports.

Conclusively, there truly are huge markets for U.S. products emerging in the developing world. Again, this provides further confirmation of the trend identified in the introduction to this book: Globalization is not mere rhetoric, it is a deepening reality representing a leading-edge growth sector for U.S. firms or U.S.-based production facilities.

UNPRECEDENTED ECONOMIC GROWTH LEADS TO THE EMERGENCE OF NEW MARKETS

How did nations outside the traditional triad arise as such large markets for U.S. exports? Figure 5–2 provides immediate insight into the emergence of new markets, and may be the most important graphic in this book, because it buttresses the main thesis. Focusing on the world's most populous or financially advanced nations, I have graphed the average annual growth in real gross domestic product (GDP, i.e., the standard measure of production and thus income generated within a nation) for an extensive recent period. I chose to start in 1982 because the world had recovered from its recession by then, so any fast growth uncovered cannot be attributed to bouncing off of a cyclical low point. The data behind the graph provide evidence satisfying our burden of proof: we have recently witnessed an unprecedented, significant period of rapid economic development in major populous regions of the world. Particularly, but not exclusively, in Asia, this economic development has been so impressive that it justifies the recent widespread use of the new, more optimistic phrase, "emerging markets" to describe the less-developed nations.

A key aspect of Figure 5–2 is the shading or patterning of the different bars. Look carefully at the solid black bars. You may think that they represent the "fastest-growing nations," because there are so many of them in the fastest growth positions. However, a closer inspection shows that the solid bars all represent *Asian* nations. Clearly, the past few decades have been ones of breathtaking economic development in Asia.

Note, however, one diagonally shaded bar among the Asian nations—a bar for the South American nation, Chile. Apparently, rapid economic growth can be achieved even *outside* of Asia. This is an important point in the debate regarding the sources of the unprecedented economic growth seen in the last decade or so. Some commentators think that the diverging pattern of growth seen around the world, where some nations, particularly in Asia, have grown very rapidly and others have grown barely at all, is mainly attributable to cultural differences. This argument would hold that the relatively rapid Asian growth is due to aspects of Asian culture such as their reliance on family or community, and their respect for hard work, savings, and education. Indeed, some commentators chalk up most of the differences in economic growth rates, as portrayed in Figure 5–2, to the idea that Asian nations have a culture that lives up to certain Confucian ideals which have spurred economic development.

The other side of the debate, peopled more by macroeconomists than sociologists, holds that while culture of course plays an important role in economic development (or the lack thereof), most of the observed variations in growth rates can be attributed to differing national economic policies. The nations most likely to experience rapid economic growth are those that: (1) welcome foreign investment and open up to the competition implied by international trade; (2) have tax systems that encourage entrepreneurial activity and savings along with concomitant investment (rather than favoring consumption); and (3) focus on investments in at least primary education and training for almost all citizens (who constitute both present and/or future workers).

The items I have just mentioned are the major components of what is often termed the "East Asian model of economic development." Despite East Asia's current troubles, I believe that reports of the demise of this model are premature. However, it is clear that by allowing "crony capitalism" instead of free and open markets, some nations diverted from the model and crisis ensued. In a major study, the World Bank examined eight

Figure 5–2 REAL GDP GROWTH RATES DIVERGE: LOW GROWTH IN ADVANCED NATIONS

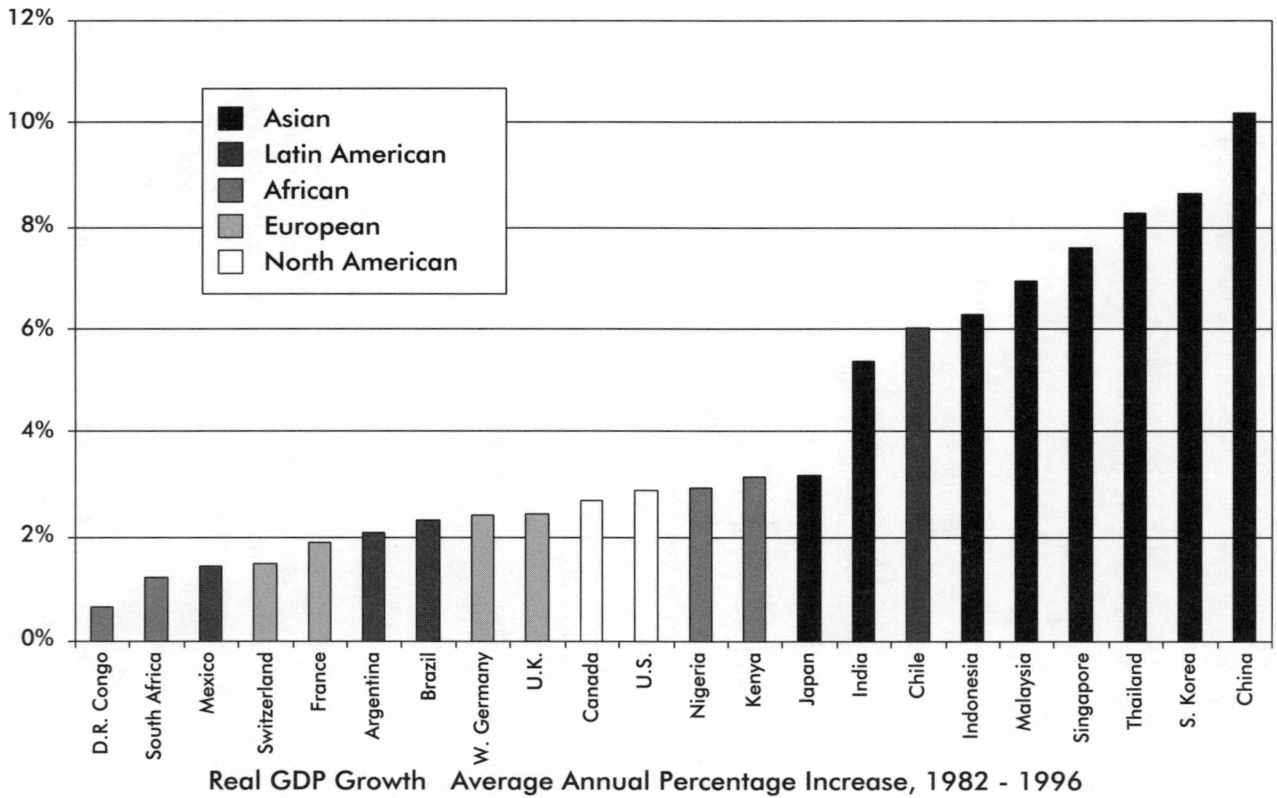
12%
10%
8%
6%
4%
2%
0%
Asian
Latin American
African
European
North American
D.R. Congo
South Africa
Mexico
Switzerland
France
Argentina
Brazil
W. Germany
U.K.
Canada
U.S.
Nigeria
Kenya
Japan
India
Chile
Indonesia
Malaysia
Singapore
Thailand
S. Korea
China
Real GDP Growth Average Annual Percentage Increase, 1982 - 1996

Data Source: IMF.

high-performing Asian economies (HPAEs): Japan and the four NICs or "Little Tigers" along with Indonesia, Malaysia, and Thailand. All have achieved striking growth. "Since 1960 the HPAEs have grown more than twice as fast as the rest of East Asia, roughly three times as fast as Latin America and South Asia, and twenty-five times faster than sub-Saharan Africa. They also slightly outperformed the industrial economies and the oil-rich Middle East–North Africa region."[2] The World Bank summarizes this development:

> What caused East Asia's success? In large measure the HPAEs achieved high growth by getting the basics right. Private domestic investment and rapidly growing human capital were the principal engines of growth. High levels of domestic financial savings sustained the HPAEs' high investment levels. Agriculture, while declining in relative importance, experienced rapid growth and productivity improvement. Population growth rates declined more rapidly in the HPAEs than in other parts of the developing world. And some of these economies also got a head start because they had a better-educated labor force and a more effective system of public administration. In this sense there is little that is "miraculous" about the HPAEs' superior record of growth; it is largely due to superior accumulation of physical and human capital.
>
> Fundamentally sound development policy was a major ingredient in achieving rapid growth. Macroeconomic management was unusually good and macroeconomic performance unusually stable, providing the essential framework for private investment. Policies to increase the integrity of the banking system, and to make it more accessible to nontraditional savers, raised the levels of financial savings. Education policies that focused on primary and secondary schools generated rapid increases in labor force skills. Agricultural policies stressed productivity and did not tax the rural economy excessively. All the HPAEs kept price distortions within reasonable bounds and were open to foreign ideas and technology.

Similarly, Joseph E. Stiglitz, the World Bank research director who chaired President Clinton's Council of Economic Advisors, found that the governments' *policy choices* proved crucial[3]:

> No single policy ensured success, nor did the absence of any single ingredient ensure failure. There was a nexus of policies, varying from country to country, sharing the common themes that we have

emphasized: governments intervened actively in the market, but used, complemented, regulated, and indeed created markets, rather than supplanted them. Governments created an environment in which markets could thrive. Governments promoted exports, education, and technology; encouraged cooperation between government and industry and between firms and their workers; and at the same time encouraged competition. (p. 174)

No doubt the willingness and capability to adopt these astute policies are enhanced by aspects of the Asian culture. However, a critical point here is that with similar, and in my mind good, governmental policies, nations outside of Asia can also achieve healthy rates of economic development. This is why the example of Chile is significant, because it shows that rapid economic growth can be sustained even in nations outside of Asia. Thus, the important question becomes: Did Chile adopt most of the economic policies discussed above and often termed the East Asian model of development?

In fact, Chile adopted just such a set of policies following a financial crisis in the early 1980s. Like many East Asian nations, Chile at that time had an authoritarian government.[4] My mission here is not to debate the political legitimacy behind various policies, given my own presumption in favor of democracy, but to examine the actual trends in economic development. However, I must note that a debate currently rages whether authoritarian rule, at least in the initial stages of attempted economic development, can permit some nations to move more quickly toward an economic growth path by allowing a consistent set of economic policies to be implemented and sustained. Chile's authoritarian government, following the financial crisis, was able to apply a consistent set of policies that welcomed foreign investment and encouraged entrepreneurial activity as well as savings and investment. More recently, Chile has increased freedom, even privatizing social security. This last item has helped create a pool of savings or capital that can be borrowed by entrepreneurs to help grow new businesses in Chile. Thus, it is an idea that is deservedly being studied in the United States.

We will discuss some of the brewing problems of U.S. debt accumulation more fully in Chapter 7; here let us note that the privatization of social security is just one example where we could learn from our Latin American neighbors, if we could only stop telling them how to do things better, that is, "our way." Figure 5–2 shows that Chile's economy has grown at a rate more than double that of the United States over the past fourteen years. Perhaps we could learn something from the "bottom up" geographically speaking, rather than always lecturing "top down."

Largely as a result of improved communication flow and information technology, people in the other major nations of Latin America are well aware of the rise in Chilean living standards. These citizens now understand that compared to their nations, Chile has achieved much more rapid economic development over the past fourteen years, as a result of policies very different from those that their own nations pursued. New governments in each of the other large nations of Latin America (Brazil, Mexico, and Argentina) have been elected on a promise to pursue more free market policies and economic reforms that welcome foreign investment and provide incentives for savings and investment. Thus, we might modify the name given to this set of policies and term it the "East Asian or *Chilean* model of development."

These policy reforms, inspired (or even mandated upon politicians) by the recent record of sharply diverging economic growth portrayed in Figure 5–2, are very encouraging. We saw before that Brazil is a demographic anchor of Latin America. If Brazil can continue to reform its economy and adopt policies in the Chilean mode, then a new era may be dawning in Latin America: an era in which huge populations (190 million forecast for 2010 in Brazil alone) will achieve rapidly increasing standards of living as a result of vigorous economic growth. In other words, if a successful model of economic development can spread, and huge masses of people can follow the pattern established in East Asia, then rapid improvements in their standard of living will enable them to "march into the middle class." They will have enough discretionary income that they can finally become, collectively, big emerging markets for goods and services.

The brilliant record of economic growth seen in large parts of the developing world, plus the ability of modern information and communication technology to help share the lessons of such growth—the idea that open and capitalistic economic policies do work—are grounds for optimism that such growth can become more widespread as we move into the new century. This chapter is entitled "Tomorrow's Customers" to show that economic growth can lead to significant enough increases in living standards that the middle class—that is, people with purchasing power—can eventually and truly "go global." We will return to the subject of the middle class in developing regions in the last part of this chapter. First, however, we must analyze in more detail the record of diverging economic growth, as this will enable us to forecast the future location of potential customers. This analysis is crucial for those endeavoring to position themselves and their firms to prosper in the emerging global economy.

Note in Figure 5–2 that all the major economies of the traditional triad have experienced decent, but rather moribund, growth over the past 14 years. Because I did not want to prejudice the story toward showing stagnant growth in the traditional triad, I used 1982 as the starting date to exclude the 1981 big recession in the United States and slow growth in the traditional triad. In the fourteen-year period studied here, the United States gets the benefit of the rapid growth years of the "Reagan Boom," without the earlier recession. Still, we see that the major economies of Europe and North America could not achieve even 3% annual growth. And Japan, the miracle economy up to the late 1980s, suffered its "post-bubble" recession in the 1990s; and thus we see that its real GDP growth rate, although exceeding that of Europe, still pales by comparison to other Asian nations.

Figure 5–2 shows the world's largest economies and most populous nations, as well as some successful models of economic development. Singapore, Malaysia, and Chile, nations that represent successful models, welcomed foreign investment and experienced rapid economic development. It is quite literally true that many Asian and even African nations are sending missions to Singapore to study its success. In a similar vein, Chile serves as a model for Latin America.

Given the current financial troubles in Asia, why do I keep referring to the unprecedented growth in Asia and how it has led to significant economic development? Note that East Asia's rapid rate of economic growth was sustained for many years, indeed for a full 14 years in the time period graphed here. Healthy levels of growth sustained over time lead to large *cumulative growth* as the "joys of compound growth" increasingly kick in. Let me illustrate this important technical point. Do you recall going to the bank with your savings account passbook as a child? The teller would stamp the new savings balance in your passbook, and you would enjoy seeing your limited wealth grow by the addition of interest. What fascinated us as kids was the *compounding of interest,* that wonderful idea that over time we got "interest on our interest" and that the dollar amount of the quarterly interest additions to our savings stamped in by the teller would grow. For example, say our grandparents gave us $1,000 and we used it to establish a bank account. At 4% annual interest compounded quarterly, after the first quarter that $1,000 was increased by 1%, or $10. Amazingly to us kids, after the next quarter we earned a further 1%, but this same rate applied to our now augmented balance of $1,010 meant we received slightly more than $10 in interest. In successive quarters we continued to receive a 1% return on our total bank balance of increasingly more than $1,000, that is, we were also receiving *interest on our prior interest* receipts. This was exciting, but frankly, it still seemed to take forever for us to double our money.

Why did it take so long to grow our bank accounts? Because the interest rate was fairly low. This same insight applies to economic growth in the United States or in Europe. Sure, our economies are growing, but at rates so slow that it would take decades for them to double. But what if our interest or growth rate was 8% annually? Then growth would be 2%, not 1%, per quarter. Even after one quarter we would have $20 of interest, and in each succeeding quarter we would receive the higher 2% quarterly rate on this higher total of interest already paid. The compounding would proceed much more rapidly and we would accumulate a tidy sum much more quickly. This same mathematical logic also applies to nations that experience rapid economic growth: the growth compounds much more quickly, accumulating into a much larger total economic size.

Note that the major economies of East Asia sustained roughly 8% economic growth annually for the entire time period of the study. Indeed, China has experienced an even more rapid rate of economic growth. What are the consequences of growing 8% or 9% a year for many years, particularly compared to the consequences of growing only 2% or 3% annually?

Here it is time to share with you one of the few truly practical and interesting tools or tricks of basic finance. A rule has been discovered that allows us to very easily calculate how many years it will take something to double. In finance, that "something" is usually wealth or another financial dimension. But this rule also applies to macroeconomic magnitudes such as GDP, and in fact, to any magnitude that is growing, such as the volume of wood in a tree or the amount of waste in a landfill. Importantly, it also applies to population growth. This "Rule of 72," known to readers who work in finance, holds that, to a rough approximation, we can divide the percentage growth rate of any variable into the number 72 and the result (or quotient) will give us the number of years it will take the variable to double.

We are fortunate that 72 is the number that works, as it is readily divisible by so many whole numbers (its neighbors, 71 and 73, are each prime numbers and thus not neatly divisible).

If a magnitude grows by 2%, be it an interest rate on a financial magnitude or population or economic growth, it will double in 36 years. Likewise, 3 and 4 divide in neatly, producing a doubling in 24 or 18 years, respectively. In addition, 6, 8, 9, and 12 all divide neatly into 72. If a country can grow its economy (real GDP) at 6% a year, as Chile and Indonesia have (and India has come close to achieving), then it will take a mere 12 years to double the economy. More dramatically, if a nation can grow at 8% a year, as many major East Asian nations have, the economy can double in a mere 9 years.

A nation that can somehow achieve 12% annual real growth can double in just 6 years. China has nearly achieved this in recent years. Indeed, for more than a decade it has been growing at over 10%, so it has been *doubling every 7 years!* This shows that China is truly a big and a rapidly emerging market, because, even though the mainland Chinese started out poor, doubling the economy every 7 years means that their aggregate purchasing power is rising to a level that no business leader can afford to ignore. China has achieved over 9% annual growth, on average, since it really opened to the world and began economic reforms in 1979. The math works beautifully here, as 9% growth means a doubling every 8 years. Doubling in 8 years, then doubling again in the succeeding 8 years means that in 16 years at 9% growth, an economy *quadruples* in size. And in fact China's economy in 1995 was more than four times its size in 1979. It was a poor nation in 1979, but with over a billion people being fed, sheltered, and clothed, it clearly had a relatively large economy even then. Quadruple it and we begin to see that the term "big emerging market" is more than a euphemism; in China's case, it tells us a lot about the future of business. Amazingly, by 2002 China's economy may be eight times its magnitude in 1978: it has the potential to double three separate times in 24 years!

What of other populous nations in Asia? Even if nations such as India or Indonesia grow at "only" 5% or 6% per annum (versus the faster rates seen earlier in China, South Korea, and Thailand), this growth would be much faster than that in the traditional triad, and over time would accumulate into a significant record of economic development. Recall that even at 6% a year, a nation doubles its economy every 12 years, and at slightly over 5%, every 14 years. In other words, in well less than three decades, these populous nations can also see a quadrupling of the size of their economies. Take a relatively poor but still significantly sized economy, quadruple it in a few decades, and once again we see support for the notion of big emerging markets. Tomorrow's customers are likely to be found in these populous and growing nations, not just in East Asia but also in South Asia and Latin America.

In contrast to the quadrupling of China in the past decade and a half, and the quadrupling of, for example, an Indonesian or Indian economy in two dozen years or a bit more, note that major European nations and the United States have been growing between 2% and 3% annually. At these rates, it takes at least 25 years to double an economy, and more than 50 years for a quadrupling (70 years for those growing at 2% a year). Of course, western Europe is already relatively rich, so smart global firms should retain some focus on this very wealthy market.

A fine example of a major U.S. firm that is impressively growing its business in the wealthy, albeit slowly growing, markets of Europe is General Electric. An article in *Fortune*[5] shows that in 1995, GE's operating profit in Europe.

jumped 59%, to $1.41 billion, while operating profit in Asia declined 10% to $585 million. GE's European managers celebrated by thumbing their noses at Asiaphiles dismissing Europe as a place to do business. "Asia makes the headlines," cracked one GE Europe executive. "Europe makes the money."

The article goes on to make the point that there is still a great deal of wealth in Europe, comparing the $10.6 trillion of bank assets in the EU plus Switzerland and Norway in 1994 to the U.S. total of $4.3 trillion of commercial bank assets. The article concludes that GE's leaders

> know they must continue to push GE Europe to beat Asia's highly publicized growth rate. More important, they must drive the company relentlessly toward saturation of Europe's rich, if mature, market.

Clearly, General Electric understands the arguments made in this chapter, because even as the firm grows its business in Europe, it is also making large investments in the rapidly emerging markets of Asia, particularly China and Indonesia.

AFRICA AND THE POPULOUS SOUTH: THE EFFECT OF THE "LOST DECADE" AND RAPIDLY RISING POPULATIONS ON ECONOMIC DEVELOPMENT

The preceding two chapters pointed out that Africa is, and will remain, the most rapidly growing region in terms of the world's population pie. Thus, Africa's human resources are too large and growing too quickly to ignore. Indeed, the Rule of 72 applies here too: with population growth rates of 3% in many African nations, populations will double in parts of Africa within the next 25 years. Within the next 50 years, some nations could see a quadrupling of their population and thereby move up dramatically in the world population rankings.

Many economists summarize the decade commencing with the Latin American debt crisis that began in Mexico in 1982 (but then also spread to debtor nations in Africa) as "the lost decade." It was in that year that the process of economic development, which had been boosting production and income in Africa and Latin America, came to an abrupt halt. Meanwhile, economic growth continued at a rapid pace in Asia even after 1982, leading to the notion that Africa and most of Latin America "lost out" on this opportunity for continued economic development, as shown clearly by the diverging growth rates seen in these countries.

Am I being too dismal regarding Africa's recent economic development, when I claim that it lost out on economic growth in the last 14 or so years? After all, Figure 5–2 shows that two of the largest African economies, Nigeria and Kenya, grew at rates slightly faster than the United States and the main European economies. Of course, in this figure, Africa presents a mixed bag: Nigeria and Kenya grew at roughly 3%, but the populous nations of South Africa and D.R. Congo grew at less than half that rate. Figure 5–3 both supports "the lost decade" notion *and* provides new details about the location of tomorrow's customers, the emerging middle class. Here we look at the value of national output (thus national income) measured as real GDP, divided by population, each year. This reveals GDP per capita, which most economists use as a proxy for relative standards of living.

Note that growth in output per person (per capita GDP) will differ markedly from growth of total GDP *only* in nations that are experiencing rapid population changes. For example, consider the United Kingdom and Japan. The populations of both nations are growing very slowly, hence their total output growth translates into nearly equivalent growth per person, as seen by comparing Figure 5–2 to 5–3. The same can be said for most of the nations of East Asia, as they are now experiencing less rapid population growth. However, for those nations that still have fairly rapid population growth, such as Malaysia and Indonesia, there is a significant difference between their per capita and total growth rates. Nevertheless, the total income growth rate was so impressive in East Asia that even nations experiencing rapid population growth achieved a per person income growth of slightly over 4% a year. Using the Rule of 72, 4% growth a year means a doubling in per person output, or standard of living, in just 18 years. Thus, even in those East Asian nations which exhibit relatively slower growth of per capita income, standards of living have increased rapidly enough to imply huge new entrants into the ranks of the middle class in recent and prospective decades. The same holds for Chile, with a per capita growth rate of over 4% a year.

But note that Figure 5–3 sheds light on the truly tragic nature of the "lost decade" in Africa. Kenya exhibits just about the most rapid population growth on Earth, averaging over 3.5% per year. Sadly, while it may be growing its economic pie in total by 3% per year, it also has over 3.5% more mouths to feed each year. Thus, the amount of income available per person or the output per person is actually declining, as seen in Figure 5–3. Of the four large African nations studied here, only Nigeria has experienced an increased per capita output over the past 14 years. Nigeria's

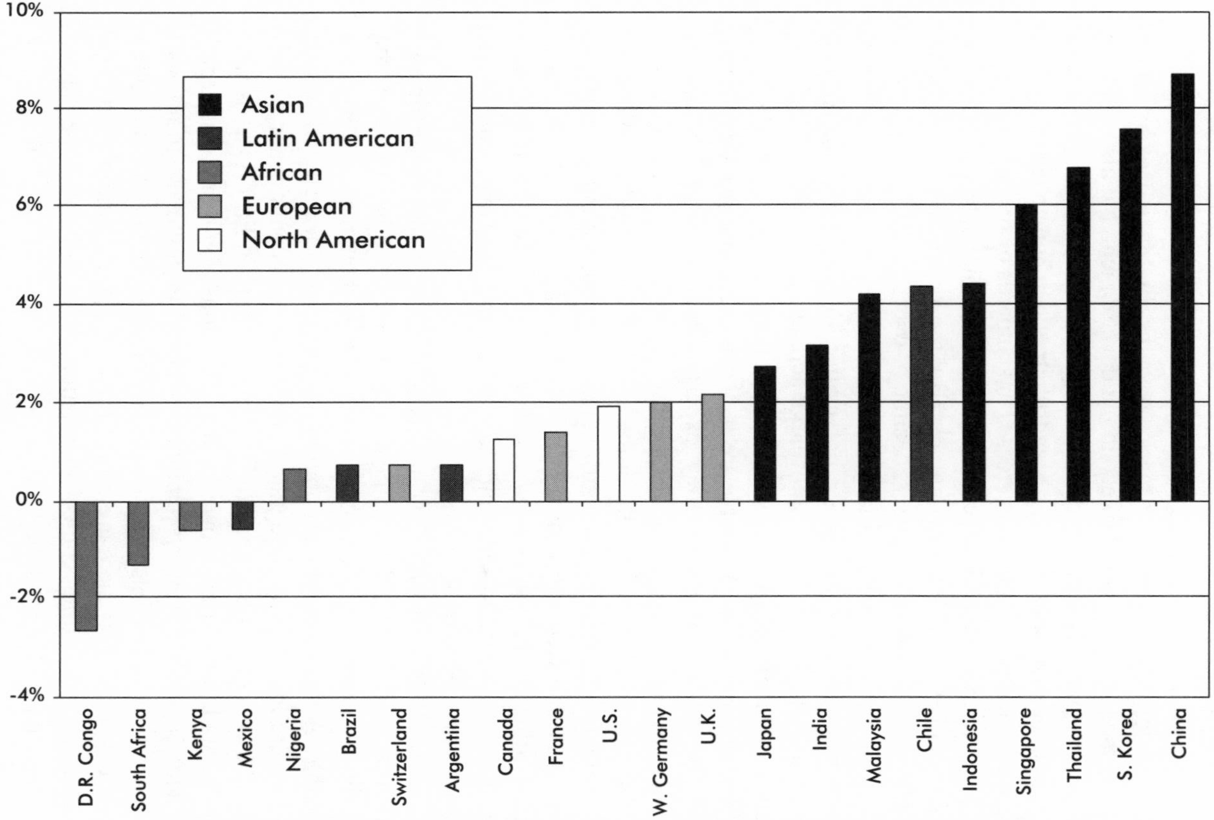
10%
8%
6%
4%
2%
0%
-2%
-4%
Asian
Latin American
African
European
North American
D.R. Congo
South Africa
Kenya
Mexico
Nigeria
Brazil
Switzerland
Argentina
Canada
France
U.S.
W. Germany
U.K.
Japan
India
Malaysia
Chile
Indonesia
Singapore
Thailand
S. Korea
China
Per Capita Real GDP Growth   Average Annual Percentage Increase, 1982 - 1996

Data Source: IMF.

economic growth is similar to Kenya's, but it has slower population growth. But even in Nigeria we see very slow growth of productivity and, thus, living standards.

Populous nations in Africa, notably D.R. Congo and South Africa, as well as major nations of Latin America, specifically Mexico, experienced not only the lost opportunity of economic development, but also absolute declines in standards of living over the 14 years through 1996. In the case of some African nations, this has been truly tragic in human terms, as they have seen roughly 2% annual decreases in standards of living.

Why is a 2% annual decline so catastrophic in human terms? After all, 2% does not sound like a large number. But the key point is the *cumulative* effect of the rate of decline. A decline of over 2% per year, as in D.R. Congo for 14 years, means a large cumulative decline in both economy and living standard. This would not matter so much if these African nations had started at a position of large economic surplus, but unfortunately a vast majority of the residents were living in abject poverty when the "lost decade" began. If people are at a level of income that allows them barely to subsist, and then they experience cumulating 2% annual declines, they can fall to a level that represents potential starvation and an inability to maintain their health or the health of their children. When we talk about declining living standards here, we are not talking about giving up the boat, the second car, or the annual vacation; we are talking about making difficult choices as to who eats or who receives even the most basic levels of education and health care. Obviously, the lamentable trends portrayed here need to be reversed.

One of the main reasons I wrote this book was to highlight the diverging nature of economic development and, as discussed in Chapter 1, the very limited extent of globalization to date. Throughout the book, we have seen that Africa and other populous areas in or near the Southern Hemisphere have neither integrated into the world economy nor experienced the economic development seen increasingly in East Asia, as well as in the traditional triad. However, the "Populous South" nations represent such large and growing populations that it is inhumane in a social sense and unwise in a business sense to ignore their plight. A major point of this chapter is that there are now models of rapid economic development showing the policy choices that nations need to favor if they are to have any hope of attracting foreign investment. Foreign investment is crucial, because it supplies needed capital and transfers modern technologies, both of which are required to move poor nations onto the path of economic development.

The tragic conditions seen in some of the nations of the Populous South can only be solved with *both* of two necessary actions. First, the nations must choose for themselves to adopt the more open-market, capitalist policies that led not just East Asian nations, but also Chile, to move from economic stagnation to economic growth. Second, business leaders must then recognize that if these nations do adopt such open policies, investing in them will not only help the reformed nations grow, but also contribute to their firms' future growth by helping create "tomorrow's customers." This joint action could greatly expand the pool of middle-class people, that is, those with enough purchasing power to become customers, by spreading income and wealth creation more globally, and in particular, to the regions that will contain almost all of the world population growth. Fortunately, the success of Botswana, although it is a small nation, shows that development *can* take root in sub-Saharan Africa.

THE MIDDLE CLASS GOES GLOBAL, OR DOES IT?

Numerous euphoric reports on television and articles in popular business publications have appeared over the past couple of years touting the growth of a global middle class. The reports or articles often have titles such as "The Emergence of the New Global Middle Class," or "India's 300 Million Middle-Class Consumers," or "Time to Pursue the Nearly 1 Billion Middle-Class People in Emerging Markets." My worry is that journalists, motivated to gain market share for their publications, are issuing ever more dramatic reports, seemingly oblivious to any actual data.

This chapter has shown that we can reasonably predict the emergence of a vast new middle class in developing nations as we move into the 21st century. Already, economic growth in East Asia and in some regions of South Asia and South America has been rapid and sustained enough to create tens of millions of new middle-class consumers. However, claims of hundreds of millions of new middle-class people in separate nations or regions around the globe are wildly premature. Thus, my intent here is to dampen some of the current euphoria while not letting the essential truth become obscured: a new middle class is in the process of emerging globally.

Figure 5–4 is my attempt to graphically portray the current reality, and future potential, of an emerging, more global middle class.[6] Each person or body pictured represents 10 million people who are middle class or more affluent. I came up with a new term for such people: people with purchasing power (PWPP). These are the people with enough discretionary income to buy the consumer products of global firms that go beyond the bare necessities of life. Not only can they buy Coca-Cola,[7] but, crucially, they can buy mobile telephones or perhaps even computers and printers. Thus, companies such as Motorola, Nokia, Ericsson, Hewlett-Packard, Intel, Microsoft, and the like are targeting their future expansion on just such an emerging, more global population of PWPP.

An important innovation in this graph is separate categories for what it means to be middle class in three distinct regions of the world. In the wealthy regions of the traditional triad middle class requires: an income of at least $4,000 a month, or $48,000 annually. Based on this definition, we can see in the figure that there are hundreds of millions of PWPP in each of the three legs of the traditional triad: North America, the Far East, and especially Western Europe, which has a more equal income distribution than North America and thus a larger middle class.

Next, we define a threshold for middle class in regions that have already emerged beyond the widespread poverty seen in less developed nations. We call this second grouping the *emerging regions*. In these regions, a middle-class status can be achieved with an income of about $1,200 a month, or $14,400 per year. Based on this threshold, tens of millions of people are achieving middle-class status in the emerging regions, notably in Eastern Europe and the former Soviet Union, but also in South America and even, to a certain extent, the Middle East.

Finally, we consider the middle class in the traditionally poor regions of the Populous South. The exaggerated claims of the popular media are usually the result of inadequately characterizing the middle class in this region. While these euphorically portrayed middle-class people do have, for the most part, high incomes within their own societies, they are well below what we term middle class within the wealthier societies of the traditional triad. In the Populous South regions, a family achieves a very good *relative* status on even $600 a month. Hence, we count them as part of the global middle class if they have incomes of at least $7,200 a year. This may seem too low to be truly middle class or to be a target for American multinational companies, but we must recall the differing purchasing power of currencies around the world. Housing, food, and personal services can be extremely cheap in dollar terms in poor regions. Thus, for people in weak-currency nations who earn over $7,200 a year, the necessities are so cheap that even this level of income can provide enough discretionary income for them to be "middle class enough" to be customers of global consumer product firms.

The most important point here is that there are tens of millions of middle-class people emerging in South Asia and Africa, but one should not put the cart before the horse. After all, the total is in the tens, not in the hundreds, of millions. Secondly, even our realistic Populous South middle class are people in the income range of $600 to $1,000 per month, a far cry from the triad's figure of $4,000 or more per month. It is important to

Figure 5–4 TOMORROW'S CUSTOMERS
The Middle Class Goes Global

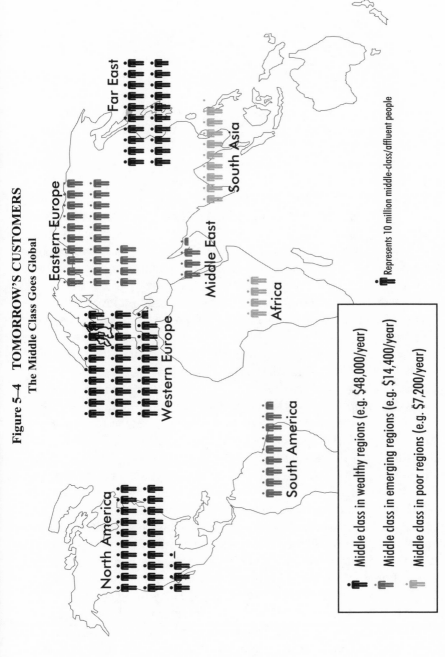

Data Source: *Business Week.*

realize that we self-described "middle-class" people in the United States have living standards way beyond what is available to so-called middle-class people throughout the developing world. Thus, it is a serious miscalculation of current business prospects to say there are hundreds of millions of people in areas such as South Asia with purchasing powers even remotely approaching our own.[8]

With this caveat in mind, there is still reason for great optimism. Even at this very lowered notion of middle-class purchasing power relevant in the Populous South, there are tens of millions of people who can purchase products such as Coca-Cola, basic medicines, and probably soon, even a first telephone. On top of that, the numbers are being augmented daily as the process of economic development continues and broadens. To apply these lessons to your own firm, first consider the nature of your business. If you want to sell an expensive Porsche, you will find a very limited market in the emerging nations of South Asia or Africa. Even with tens of millions of so-called middle-class people, only a very few among the elite classes can afford a Porsche. On the other hand, if you want to sell a soft drink, there will be many who have enough discretionary income for that. Furthermore, as economic growth proceeds, the magic of compounding growth increasingly kicks in, and more people rise to a level of discretionary income that allows them to buy a first phone,[9] and later a computer and a basic printer.

The conclusion of the foregoing analysis is that until the 1990s, the wealthier definitions of middle class implied that the vast majority of persons with significant purchasing power were in the nations of the traditional triad, lending some support to the fashionable notions of global strategy that indicated a need to focus on the three regions of that triad. However, in the last decade or so, rapid economic growth in many, but not all, parts of the developing world has led to the emergence of tens of millions of people who we term lower-middle-class; people who are becoming customers for some, but not yet all, industries.

Most important, in this chapter we have provided solid evidence that there is an unprecedented depth and expanding breadth of economic growth unfolding throughout the developing world. Economic growth is likely to spread more widely during the next decade, because nations in Eastern Europe, Africa, and South America are learning lessons about the benefits of free markets from models such as Hong Kong and Chile. The implications of this growth are profound. For even though I have gone to pains to debunk the myth that there are currently hundreds of millions of middle-class people (according to our own income standard) scattered in the developing world, we have also seen that compounded rapid growth can lead over time to doubling or even quadrupling of income per capita, that is, standards of living. Even poor people will move to a "quasi-poor" status upon doubling their income, and into a lower middle-class status after quadrupling their income. Such eventual quadrupling, or even greater multiplication, of incomes is forecast in many populous nations of the developing world, as the lessons and processes of economic development extend well into the 21st century.

Figure 5–5 summarizes the mix of PWPP across the developing versus the developed, that is the traditional triad, nations. It provides a rough summary of the important message of this chapter: if not currently, then surely by "tomorrow" (where tomorrow could still be a couple of decades into the future), business will find its new customers increasingly in the developing nations outside the traditional triad. Figure 5–5 shows the increasing importance over time of the emerging markets for most businesses, especially for industries that do not rely on selling luxuries to very wealthy people.

Figure 5–5 relies on a forecast that economic growth can be sustained for decades in many nations of the developing world. Recall from Figures 5–2 and 5–3 that rapid economic growth was achieved in East Asia and in nations such as Chile and India in the recent 14-year period. *Did this rapid growth in nations such as South Korea and Singapore occur only during this period?* In other words, did I cheat by selecting this limited period, or can we find evidence that the growth has been sustained for many decades? The evidence is that some East Asian nations have achieved economic growth of 8% or 9% for more than 30 years now. For example, despite its recent crisis, South Korea has grown at nearly *9% annually in real terms since 1960.* Applying the Rule of 72, we can see that the economy of South Korea has not merely quadrupled during this time period, but that within 25 years, it grew to 8 times the size of its economy in 1960, and after 34 years, it had grown to more than 16 times its size in 1960. If you start out poor, say with an average annual income of $1,000, but you increase your total real income sixteenfold, not only are you no longer poor, but you are probably middle class.[10] Similar rates of growth have been sustained in Southeast Asian nations such as Taiwan and Singapore.

The sustained record of economic growth seen in large parts of the developing world, plus the wonderful trend of positive lessons being diffused around the world by modern communication technology—and taken seriously by policymakers everywhere—has led the World Bank and other astute observers to forecast widespread economic development as we look forward from this point. The World Bank forecasts[11] that East Asia will return to growth of over 7% annually and that South Asia will approach 6% annually. More generally, the great news is that the forecast for Latin America and Africa, as well as Eastern Europe, implies that these

Figure 5–5   TOMORROW'S CUSTOMERS
The Emergence of Developing Markets
(Shares of World Middle-Class Market)

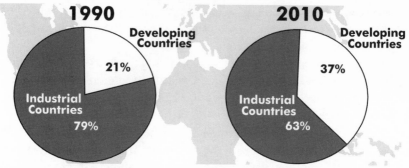

Data Source: Professor Jeff Rosensweig, derived from *Institute for the Future* and *World Bank* data.

regions will learn the lessons shown in the early parts of this chapter and adopt policies that will put them on solid (over 4%) growth paths. Even if they only grow 4% annually, and not at East Asian growth rates (i.e., even if the "Confucius matters" arguments mentioned above pertain to Asian culture), we can safely predict the rise of customers in the Populous South. Recall that even 4% annual growth implies a doubling of total economic size in 18 years and a quadrupling in 36 years.

However, such growth is not rapid enough to reach all members of a growing population that has, as a starting point, many people living in poverty. So I fear that, even with optimistic projections of economic development, widespread and often abject poverty will continue in the nations of the Populous South. Sadly, the absolute number of persons in poverty will probably rise in the nations that are experiencing rapid population growth, even as economic development also increases these nations' numbers of people with significant purchasing power. To be sure, economic reforms that lead to more entrepreneurial capitalism and that open economies to international trade and attract foreign investment will not, by themselves, cure all poverty in the short, or even the medium, term. However, this strategy is still the best hope for the people of the Populous South. The evidence clearly shows that such open capitalist policies lead to dramatically higher economic growth, and it is only with a rapidly growing overall economic pie that these nations can have any hope of feeding and educating their significantly increasing populations. A detailed recent World Bank study[12] shows that, for a sample of nations in sub-Saharan Africa, the ones that are reforming macroeconomic policy experience more rapid economic growth and are better able to contain poverty, even if such growth is a long way from solving the ubiquitous and serious nature of poverty in Africa:

> The evidence . . . demonstrates the poverty was more likely to decline in those that improved their macroeconomic balances than in those that did not. The critical factor is economic growth: the economy grew more rapidly and poverty declined faster in countries that improved macroeconomic balances. . . . But the findings also highlighted three causes for policy concern. First, many African governments have yet to display a real commitment to macroeconomic reform; second, the poorest of the poor have not benefited from recent growth in some countries; and, third, the prospects for the poor are not rosy unless there is more investment in human capital and better targeting of social spending. (p. 39)

Policy reforms (toward open and capitalist economic policies) are crucial, for the World Bank study concludes (p. 40): "The most striking finding, however, is the systematic link between policy implementation and outcomes for the poor—*effective reform programs are associated with reduced overall poverty, inadequate ones with worsening poverty.*"[13]

Let us turn to the important implications of Figure 5–5. The left-hand pie chart shows that as late as 1990, a vast majority of the world's people with purchasing power (PWPP) lived in the advanced nations of the traditional triad. Interestingly, we see once again that the 80/20 split we showed in Chapter 1 is indicative of current global inequality. However, the second pie chart in Figure 5–5 is the key one for business leaders and strategists. It shows that in a mere 20 years, the proportion of the world's PWPP that resides in the developing nations will rise dramatically. We see that developing regions are forecast to contain roughly 3 out of every 8 PWPP.[14] Contrast this with the situation in 1990, when businesses focusing on the traditional triad captured 4 out of 5 potential customers with effective purchasing power, and ignored only 1.

The key strategic point I want to make in this chapter is that ignoring the developing world will have increasing costs, whereas adding a focus on it will increasingly help ensure not just survival, but prosperity in the 21st century. To ignore 3 out of 8 potential customers would lead to competitive ruin in many industries. Business prospers and executives are rewarded not for maintaining the status quo, but for growing. This chapter has portrayed the exciting record of rapid economic growth in significant portions of the developing world over the last few decades, and the likelihood and business implications of a continuation, probably even more globally widespread, of economic development well into the 21st century.

Executives who heed these lessons and focus on the emerging markets will prosper in the new millennium.

Interestingly, the rapid economic growth or significant economic development in large parts of the emerging, previously poor, developing

Figure 5–6   GLOBAL MANUFACTURING
Developing Beyond the 80/20 Split

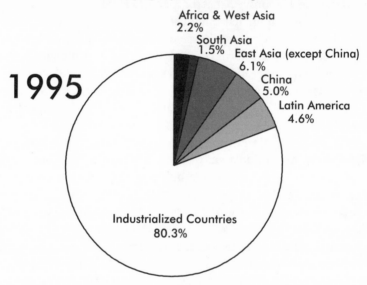

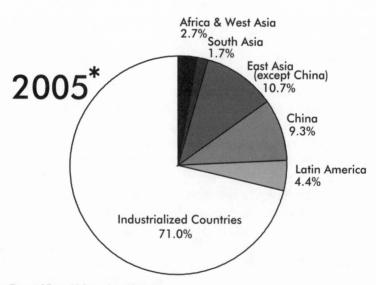

Source: *Financial Times*, 27 September 1996 p. 16.
*Baseline projection by UNIDO.

world means we may finally be "overcoming the 80/20 inequality." We just saw that instead of the usual 80/20 split, developing nations may rise to contain 37%—not just 21%, as in 1990—of the world's people with purchasing power. This is linked with, or partly driven by, a shifting of global manufacturing toward developing regions, particularly in East Asia. Figure 5–6 highlights this striking trend.

The ubiquitous 80/20 split we discussed in Chapter 1 is seen in Figure 5–6 to hold for global manufacturing shares even as late as 1995. However, present trends allow the United Nations Industrial Development Organization to make the baseline projection for 2005 pictured here. The industrial countries are forecast to fall, relatively, to a 71% share of global manufacturing, as the developing world finally moves beyond a 20% share, to almost 30%. The increased share for developing nations reflects the movement of global manufacturing sourcing toward Asia, particularly to East Asia. China is a key part of this enhanced share for East Asia, but so is Southeast Asia. This foreshadows our next chapter, where we show trends suggesting that for business it is already "mid-morning in the Asian Century."

The present chapter dispelled the current euphoria by pointing out that there are not hundreds of millions of middle-class people (especially if one uses our rather wealthy popular notions of middle class) currently in, for example, India or South America. However, a process of development is now underway that should lead to hundreds of millions of at least lower-middle-class customers emerging throughout the developing world in the coming decade. This book's main goal is to help you build your own personal and business strategy to prosper in this emerging wealthier global economy. Thus we turn in the next chapter to helping you focus your strategy by analyzing and forecasting the emergence of six massive or great regional economies into the 21st century.

INDUSTRY SPOTLIGHT ON U.S. HOSPITALITY
The International Travel and Tourism Industry

The global spread of capitalism, with the attendant rise in freedom and in economic development worldwide, is opening up tremendous business opportunities for U.S. firms catering to the international travel and tourism industry. When foreigners visit the United States, their expenditures count as U.S. service exports of travel or tourism.

Travel and tourism service exports represent one of the healthiest trends in the U.S. international balance of payments accounts. The travel and tourism industry data are separated into earnings on *passenger fares*— from foreigners using U.S. transportation firms' services and on *travel* overall expenditures (excluding fares) for such items as hotels, restaurants, and entertainment. The data indicate that the United States can prosper in this booming industry. Combining U.S. service exports of both travel and passenger fares, as reported by the U.S. Commerce Department in its *Survey of Current Business,* we can illustrate the tremendous growth trend in this important U.S. industry. U.S. exports of such travel services to foreigners set a new record high in 1997, with receipts exceeding $96 billion! The growth is dramatic, as the 1997 total far more than quadrupled the $22.2 billion total receipts in 1985. Of course, part of the reason for the dramatic rise is the decline of the U.S. dollar's exchange rate from its peak level in 1985. The depreciation or decline of the dollar's value has made the United States a relative bargain for foreign travelers, helping boost our travel exports in the past decade. However, there is another factor at work which augurs well for the continued growth of the U.S. international travel industry.

Foreign travel is a clear example of what economists term a "luxury," that is, a product which is in much greater demand when incomes rise, and in lesser demand when incomes fall. In other words, foreign travel has a very high "income elasticity"; the demand for it stretches in direct relationship to the changes in people's real income. My own past research indicates that foreign travel may have an elasticity as high as 2, meaning that for a certain percentage rise in real incomes, real spending on foreign travel will rise twice as much. For example, if real incomes grow 5%, people will more than proportionately increase their spending (by about 10%) on the luxury of foreign travel. Conversely, if incomes fall, people will look to a luxury such as foreign travel as an area ripe for cutting back spending.

The upshot of this is the tremendous growth in foreign travel that we argue is a consequence of the rapidly rising real incomes seen increasingly throughout the world, as detailed in this chapter. Thus, U.S. exports of travel and tourism services have grown dramatically in the past decades as rapid economic development spreads to much of the world. Looking back 18 years and comparing 1978 data to 1996 allows us to isolate the influence of rising incomes worldwide, as the U.S. dollar was low or cheap in 1978 as well as in 1996. Thus, changes in tourism can be ascribed to changes in foreigners' purchasing power, rather than to a dramatic change in relative prices within the United States caused by exchange rates.

Interestingly, we find that total U.S. travel and tourism export receipts increased more than tenfold in this 18-year span. Of course, there was some inflation during this period. However, prices in the United States as measured by our Consumer Price Index (CPI) "only" rose by 105%, that is the price level just more than doubled. Considering that our receipts on travel and tourism increased by 10.3 times, we can deflate this by the rise in the price level and we find that even in real—that is, inflation-adjusted—terms our travel and tourism exports rose more than fivefold. This is a tremendous increase in less than two decades, far outstripping the growth of most U.S. industries.

I argue that one reason U.S. travel exports are rising so dramatically is that economic development is spreading around the globe, leading to a rise of global purchasing power as portrayed in this chapter. The rise of people with purchasing power, even in emerging or nontraditional markets, fuels the demand for luxury products such as foreign travel, including travel from other continents to the United States.

Importantly, our analysis of the data reveals that nontraditional markets are emerging for the U.S. travel industry. During the 1990s, U.S. international travel receipts have risen strongly; they increased 55% in the short interval from 1990 to 1996. A noteworthy finding is that much of this growth came from areas beyond the traditional markets of Canada, Western Europe, and Australia. These traditional markets did provide steady growth of tourist spending in the United States, rising from nearly $28 billion to nearly $40 billion. However, the growth of receipts from these traditional advanced markets was far outstripped by the growth in U.S. travel exports to emerging regions such as Asia, Latin America, and Africa. Travel exports to regions outside of Canada, Western Europe, and Australia have boomed since 1990, rising from just over $30 billion to over $51 billion, a rise of 70%. These markets now comprise nearly 57% of total U.S. travel export receipts, up from 52% in 1990.

A recent article in the *Wall Street Journal* (25 July 1997, p. A9) exemplifies the newfound ability of big emerging markets to provide tourists with purchasing power as customers for the U.S. travel industry. The article, entitled "Brazilian Tourists Flock to U.S., But Strong *Real* Could Backfire," points out that Brazilian tourists, backed by the strength of their currency (the *real*), now are big customers for the U.S. travel and leisure industry. As Brazil's economy (and especially its currency) have strengthened, Brazilians have become high-end travelers. For example, "In Miami, Brazilians have passed the Canadians and Germans as the top-spending foreign visitors, pumping in $730 million in 1996. In New York, Brazilian shoppers spend an average of $75 a day; only the Japanese beat them—by a mere $1."

The United States is already the world's premier exporter of services, with travel (including passenger fares) being our largest service industry, and our booming service exports have led to a large U.S. trade surplus on services. My forecast is that total U.S. export receipts from foreigners for travel in the U.S. and passenger fares will exceed $100 billion before the turn of the century. A variety of U.S. firms stand to benefit greatly from the continued surge of the U.S. international travel industry, a surge fueled by the rapid economic development progressing worldwide. Increasingly, residents of diverse foreign nations can afford the luxury of a trip to the United States, and the continuation of this trend will benefit a wide variety of firms in the States. Airlines such as Delta, United, and American come to mind, as do travel firms such as Carlson. Further, a wide variety of firms in the hotel and even in the gaming industry stand to prosper if they adopt a strategy aimed to attract foreign visitors. Resorts and entertainment firms, such as Disney, also stand to continue prospering. Airline travel internationally continues to boom, to the great benefit of Boeing. Finally, the next time you stand in a long line behind many international visitors at a major U. S. tourist attraction, just remember that these visitors represent exports from the United States. Indeed, they represent such a fast-growing export that the international travel industry is contributing mightily to a trade surplus on services that is the brightest trend in our entire international economic account. Instead of resenting them for causing long lines, please welcome our visitors and urge them to return with their compatriots. They are spurring growth in an industry that is generating tremendous exports and many jobs for the U.S. economy—the international travel and tourism industry.

CHAPTER 6

STRATEGIC FOCUS:

The Six Great Economies of the 21st Century

To prosper in the intensely competitive emerging global economy, firms will need to focus on the identification of *core competencies*. They must determine which products to sell, that is, what industry to specialize in. Once the core competence has been identified, firms can gain economies of scale by selling only their core products on a more global basis. The Coca-Cola Company, for example, decided a number of years ago to get out of the movie business (Columbia Pictures) in order to concentrate on its core business of beverages. Since sharpening its focus, The Coca-Cola Company's stock price has increased dramatically, and the firm has been able to expand its beverage business world-wide.

A second aspect of strategic focus is the timing of *geographic expansion*. This book argues for a much more inclusive global view of business opportunity, and the preceding five chapters have highlighted parts of the world that business must focus on to be a truly global player. One such area is the Americas. Chapter 2 summarized the major regional economy that is developing there. Then, Chapter 5 gave the example of Chile as a model for rapid and successful economic development throughout Latin America that will eventually boost the entire Americas economy. Second, the continuing development of a much wider pan-European economy, as well as an economy comprising "Greater Europe," was examined in Chapter 2. Thirdly, Japan, despite some "post-bubble" financial difficulties in the early 1990s, is forecast to remain one of the world's major economies.

Now we go beyond the traditional triad of the Americas, Europe, and Japan, to build an original model that will provide focal points for the 21st

141

century. Chapter 5 indicated the importance of the dynamic growth that China has exhibited for nearly two decades now. This growth is unprecedented in history, in terms of speed, duration, and that country's massive demographic scale. Already, China seems well on its way to becoming one of the great economies, and in some people's forecast, *the* great economy of the 21st century. However, it would be wrong to focus solely upon China and ignore other populous developing regions that could very well lead to profitable business growth well into the next century. The two regions that come to mind most clearly after reading the preceding chapters are India and the nine Southeast Asian nations linked in ASEAN. We shall examine both in detail below.

Our original model will help business add a geographic focus for expansion. Establishing a global presence is an ultimate goal; however, only a few firms are blessed with the financial resources to "go global" all at once. Here we will try to show the economies that firms in most, but not all, industries should engage, in order to begin their quest. A first step is to ask what will be the great or largest "national" economies of the 21st century. We will then expand beyond this preliminary model of the great national economies, to recognize the increasing prominence of regionally integrated economies, as discussed in Chapter 2.

BUILDING THE MODEL:
I. USING PPP EXCHANGE RATES TO COMPARE NATIONS' GDP

Recall once again that economists measure the size of an economy by its real (inflation-adjusted) gross domestic product (GDP). An important point is that we must start with national GDPs, which are reported in local currencies, and then convert or translate them to a common standard in order to make comparisons. Following the usual practice worldwide, we will convert all these local-currency-denominated GDP totals into the equivalent total in U.S. dollars. This does not add any bias because the *relative* rankings would be exactly the same if we chose to convert every GDP into Japanese yen or German marks or even Mexican pesos.

An important decision that does affect relative rankings, however, is what exchange rates to use to convert these GDP totals from local currency to U.S. dollars. Recall from our extensive discussion in Chapter 1 that the two main choices are: (1) exchange rates given every day in the foreign exchange *market;* or (2) the hypothetical exchange rates (PPP) that would *equalize the purchasing power* of a currency such as the U.S.

dollar no matter where globally one made purchases. Although it may seem intuitively pleasing to use exchange rates given by the market, recall that these are volatile, often changing by numerous percentage points on a bit of news or even a speculative whim. Furthermore, because of various impediments to completely free trade, such as transportation costs and import tariffs, purchasing power is not equalized worldwide and market exchange rates often do not tell us very much about the relative purchasing power of a currency as we move around the globe. The classic illustration of the failure of market exchange rates to equalize prices around the world when converting to a common currency is *The Economist*'s annual study of the Big Mac.

The brilliance of *The Economist* analysis, although often done tongue-in-cheek, is that the Big Mac is seen as the perfectly standard product. The identical product sells for vastly different prices in terms of a common currency standard, and so we see that market exchange rates do not equalize purchasing power around the world. For example, the same Big Mac is very cheap in China, but much more expensive in Denmark and Switzerland. This difference cannot be easily arbitraged away (arbitrage being that very useful and key aspect of finance that can be summarized by the dictum: "buy low, sell high"). I have often tried to figure out how to buy Big Macs for the equivalent of $1 in China and sell them for the equivalent of $4 or $5 in wealthy nations of western continental Europe. (However, a Big Mac transported from China to Europe will be too soggy to taste like that typical standard product anymore.) I have even thought that all this modern communications technology that claims to make the world smaller *must* offer a solution. But the last time I tried to fax a Big Mac, I realized that this is just one price difference that even modern technology will not allow us to arbitrage away.

The crucial notion here is that perhaps it is best to compare the standards of living of various nations by asking what their currencies can actually purchase within those nations. Using market exchange rates may give us some misleading results. For example, converting local currency incomes into U.S. dollars using a market exchange rate will yield annual per capita incomes of only a few hundred dollars a year for many nations. Many of us no doubt have wondered, "How can these poor people possibly live on only a few hundred dollars a year?" We cannot conceive of even surviving on $1 a day, let alone enjoying life or prospering. *Within* their own economies, however, people in some very poor nations find that the local currency stretches a bit in terms of buying the necessities of life. They can buy much more than if they had to convert to "hard" currencies on the foreign exchange market and buy things in the United States, or in relatively expensive Japan or Europe.[1] Thus, it is helpful for business purposes to use a method that reveals something about the relative standard of living or purchasing power of people within their own economy.

For the reasons cited above, most international comparisons of markets and standards of living around the globe use calculated hypothetical rates that are called "PPP exchange rates." These are rates that yield "purchasing power parity"—making the buying power of anyone's currency the same, no matter where you might travel and exchange your own nation's money into the host country's currency. For example, the PPP exchange rate between the United States and India is not necessarily the rate given by the volatile foreign exchange market at any moment in time. Rather, it would be the exchange rate that would let me purchase the same basket of goods and services if I spent my $100 in the United States or traveled to India and converted that $100 into Indian rupees.

I have engaged in this lengthy description in order to justify the now standard practice of comparing nations by converting into a common currency using the hypothetical PPP exchange rate. This rate equates purchasing power of a currency no matter where one travels and converts that currency into local currency. The World Bank has conducted extensive and detailed research into purchasing power exchange rates and uses them to provide estimates of each nation's GDP in the common standard of the U.S. dollar. Thus, our model begins with calculated GDPs in U.S. dollar terms, converted using PPP exchange rates, as presented in the *World Bank Development Indicators 1997* or *World Bank Atlas 1997*.

BUILDING THE MODEL:
II. THE IMPACT OF DIMINISHING RETURNS

A key aspect of model building is the interpretation of trends underlying the data. That is, are the models based purely on previous results, or are those results subject to some further analysis? In our case, the predictive value of our model is enhanced by the fact that we do not blindly and optimistically forecast the future to mirror the past. For example, even after recovery from current economic woes, we do not predict that East Asian nations will return to the extremely rapid growth in real GDP that the past two decades have seen (portrayed in the previous chapter). With regard to economic development, expecting high growth rates to be sustained indefinitely into the future would be wildly speculative. Rather, our model takes into account diminishing returns, and decelerating economic growth rates. An excellent discussion that presciently debunked the East Asian Economic "Miracle" and highlighted the impact of diminishing returns is offered by renowned MIT Professor Paul Krugman, in an article in *Foreign Affairs*.[2]

Krugman dismisses the notion that rapid economic growth in East Asia has been a miracle. Instead, he cites the solid economic reasons behind this growth. Notably, he mentions the huge increase in the factors of production (inputs) that have led to the increased output (real GDP). In other words, if you save a tremendous share of your income in order to invest in the latest capital goods, and likewise invest in a huge amount of training and education for your people, then by bringing these better trained workers together with the latest vintages of machinery and other forms of physical capital, you should expect a great increase in production. Krugman points out that just such a transformation was seen in East Asia, and that rapid economic growth should be no surprise given the tremendous focus on savings, investment, education, and training.

A key concept of economic analysis is the "law of diminishing returns." When you are thirsty, if you drink one large lemonade, you may feel truly satisfied. The second one will probably even yield you some benefit. By the third lemonade, you are probably feeling the effect of diminishing returns, as this one provides much less satisfaction than either of the first two. By your fourth large lemonade, not only may the benefits, or what economists term "returns," be diminished, they may be negligible, as you now need to search the area for available facilities. The law of diminishing returns holds in most situations in any economy, and Paul Krugman highlights its importance in regard to savings and investment.

If we take what were poor rice farmers in a Southeast Asian nation and give them some equipment, their productivity, measured as output per hour, can rise dramatically. If we bring them out of subsistence farming altogether and into a modern factory with a machine or computer to work on, we can see a further great increase in their productivity. Give them a more modern and technologically sophisticated machine and we can boost their productivity further. However, diminishing returns will eventually set in: giving a worker two machines when each requires a person's full attention would boost the worker's productivity minimally, if at all. The only advantage is that if one machine gets jammed, the worker can quickly switch to the second.

Krugman shows that this basic insight of economics even holds for something that is near and dear to the heart of all of us professors: spending on education. Give someone enough education to make her literate, and her productivity leaps. Give her some technical education or training, and her productivity continues to increase. Give her a college education, and it has been documented that her productivity and therefore her potential income are greatly enhanced. Send her off to get a Ph.D., and we can hope that this increases her productivity, although I am sure the parents of many of us who stayed in universities for at least a decade in order to complete our doctorates harbor serious doubts. Further increase educational investment spending for such people to hang around universities and do some postdoctorate studies, and one may legitimately begin to wonder if this is boosting the production of society. In any event, Krugman's point is that the first major investments in modern capital—be it physical capital such as machinery or information technology equipment, or the human capital that is enhanced by education and training— are likely to rapidly boost production.[3] Further increments will increase production, but with diminishing impacts.

Why is this so important? In the early stages of economic development, a serious program to boost savings and thus physical investment, combined with more investment in human skills through education and training, is likely to lead to rapid economic growth. This type of dynamic economic development has been seen in East Asia, as described in the preceding chapter. However, it would be dangerous to extrapolate these rapid growth rates, which occur in the early stages of successful economic development, for many more decades into the future. Give some fish hunters fishing poles, and productivity will increase. Likewise, give some of them a fishing boat and some big nets, and they can catch even more fish.[4] However, at some point when there is in place a large trawler staffed by industrial robots with huge nets spread across the ocean, it will be hard to achieve further productivity growth, as we will have hit the wall of diminishing returns.

My forecast as illustrated in this chapter incorporates the essential insight of Krugman's article. Even after Asia recovers, I do not just extrapolate wildly by projecting the rapid growth rates experienced through 1996 in East Asia into the future. Instead, I build into my forecast the likely pattern of *deceleration* of these growth rates, as diminishing returns increasingly set in. Crucially, however, we see tremendous potential areas of further productivity improvement throughout Asia. Such potential gains will be enhanced by reforms spurred by the recent financial crisis in East Asia.

All recent analyses reveal that developing Asian nations are not nearly at the level of productivity of the United States. Although many of them have provided workers with increasing levels of modern equipment and training, all Asian developing nations can continue such a process for decades before they reach, for example, Japan's level of reliance on industrial robots or the education level seen in the United States and Europe. The key point is that China will not grow at double-digit rates forever, nor will the "tiger" nations of East Asia return to consistent growth at 8% or 9%, but there is no reason to assume that these nations will slow down to the rather moribund long-term growth rates seen in the traditional triad. *My ultimate point is that the emerging great economies do not need to grow 10% a year to gain increasing prominence. Growth at the level of 5% or 6% annually is sufficient for these emerging Asian nations to gain increasing prominence well into the 21st century,* given that the nations of the traditional triad are growing on average at less than 3% a year. Finally, 5% or 6% growth a year in East Asian economies is possible for many years into the future, given the much faster rates of growth recently seen in the dynamic economies of East Asia and the likelihood that (thanks to their high savings rates) they will continue to attract massive foreign investment as well as continue to increase their own investments in modern machinery, greatly needed infrastructure, and further training of their vast potential labor pools.

Further, there are examples of East Asian nations attempting to address the important lessons of the "Krugman critique" regarding the need to boost the *efficiency* (output per units of input) of their economies, rather than pile up more physical and human capital through savings and investment and education. Indeed, the *Wall Street Journal* reported in a major article that: "Just three months after Mr. Krugman's article was published, Singapore quietly formed a task force to examine ways to improve total factor productivity."[5]

BUILDING THE MODEL:
III. THE OPTIMISTIC SCENARIO

Note that Figure 6–1 is labeled an optimistic scenario. By that I do not mean "wildly extrapolative"; again, my forecasts take account of the crucial insight presented in Paul Krugman's celebrated *Foreign Affairs* article. Even in this optimistic scenario, I assume a *deceleration* of the past rapid rates of growth in Asia, as diminishing returns increasingly set in over time and begin to constrain rapid economic growth. All I mean by

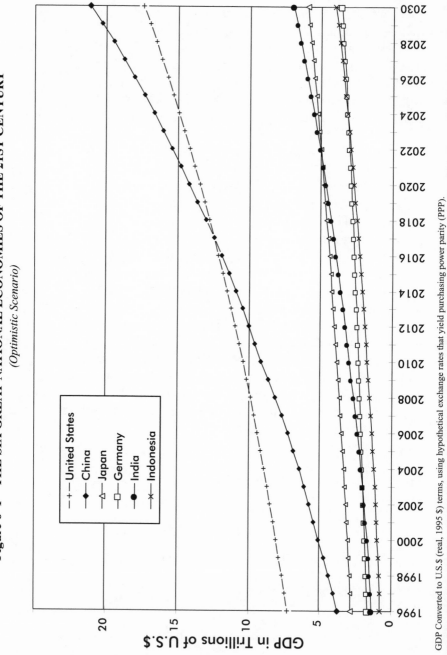

Figure 6–1 THE SIX GREAT NATIONAL ECONOMIES OF THE 21ST CENTURY
(Optimistic Scenario)

GDP Converted to U.S.$ (real, 1995 $) terms, using hypothetical exchange rates that yield purchasing power parity (PPP).

"optimistic" is that India and China will continue, perhaps shakily, on their current paths of economic reform toward more open markets and more capitalistic practices. The main assumption is that they will continue to accept foreign investment by globally oriented capitalist firms. "Optimistic" for ASEAN implies that member nations will successfully implement the reforms urged upon them in 1998.

In a more pessimistic scenario, China and India might close their doors to world trade or to capitalism. However, given the economic success of their steps toward reform in the past few years and the increasing sophistication of their people, who now have tasted success and can learn more about it by watching CNN International or reading about it on the Internet, this guardedly optimistic scenario is the most likely one. It is not an extrapolative forecast and not a wildly optimistic one, but a likely one, if we simply approach the world with any sense of optimism in the ability of people to learn from recent past experience.

BUILDING THE MODEL:
IV. THE PESSIMISTIC SCENARIO

Of course, it is easy to imagine a more pessimistic scenario for the big emerging markets. India seems to be a nation of great human resources, often held back by government instability and overregulation. I characterize India's economic policies as usually "taking two steps forward, then one step back." Even this would allow for growth in my optimistic scenario, as shown in Figures 6–1 and 6–3. Only if China and Indonesia, as well as India, start taking "one step forward, then two steps back" from more free market capitalism do we need to base plans on my pessimistic scenario seen in Figure 6–2.

Although, as I conceded at the outset of this book, I remain an optimist and therefore favor the optimistic scenarios discussed below, the recent Asian crisis reveals that the pessimistic scenarios are quite relevant. You should consider the sensitivity of your business's growth strategy to the differing growth trends embodied in these optimistic and pessimistic scenarios. No one can foretell the future of something as complex as the global economy with certainty, hence I recommend testing strategic plans against both scenarios.[6]

The need at least to consider the possibility of a pessimistic scenario ultimately ensuing is shown by the many risks inherent in emerging markets. Indeed, the dean of Yale's School of Management, Jeffrey Garten, titled his recent article in the *Harvard Business Review,* "Troubles Ahead in Emerging Markets."[7] Garten discusses many significant risks, including the powerful threats posed to the recent market-opening economic reforms in many of his "Big 10" emerging markets, such as Mexico. Further, he makes it clear that political risks are key factors in doing business in such big emerging markets as China, Indonesia, and even democratic yet rather bureaucratic India. Ultimately, Garten shows that a slowing or even reversal of market-opening economic reform in many big emerging nations is one possible scenario.

In order to help executives build their strategies for the 21st century, I will present both pessimistic and optimistic scenarios below. I do hope, however, that engaging the people and new leaders of the BEM can help them unlock their huge potential. A win-win global strategy can perhaps increase the odds that the optimistic scenario *will* ultimately prevail.

THE SIX GREAT NATIONAL ECONOMIES MODEL

By forecasting the magnitude of the national economies that we have focused upon in this book, it will become clear that a few nations will likely move into or remain in the top-league table for economic size. Of course, readers should realize that all the numbers that follow are just my attempts at creating the most relevant scenarios. The forecasts in this chapter do result from some rather uncertain stargazing, as I make projections all the way through the year 2030.

Why project so far? Despite the added uncertainty this contributes, the year 2030 represents the time when most U.S. baby boomers will be retired. By that time, business had better be engaged in nations with young and growing populations, in order to find plentiful labor supplies. In addition, the U.S. financial system will be at risk (this will be discussed in Chapter 7) because of all the Social Security payments to retired baby boomers. This confirms the central message of this book: the need to diversify through a time-phased global strategy. This time-phased strategy should incorporate forecast scenarios through 2030, given current demographic, financial, and economic trends.

Figure 6–1 presents the promised initial step of our model. Going beyond the traditional triad, we compiled data for numerous national economies to identify those that are forecast to be the largest a few decades into the 21st century. Not surprisingly, the anchors of the traditional triad, the United States, Germany,[8] and Japan, remain three of the great national economies of the next century. Indeed, each of them is anticipated to grow to impressive economic magnitudes. Even though a major theme of this book is the need to look beyond the traditional triad, its continuing importance is illustrated in Figure 6–1. Having said that, the innovation that no doubt catches your eye in Figure 6–1 is the identification of future great national economies that extend well beyond the traditional triad.

HOT SPOTS: EMERGING GREAT NATIONAL ECONOMIES
I. CHINA

Not surprisingly, given what has come before in this book, we see China as one of the next great national economies. By 2030, its real GDP (in PPP terms) should surpass $20 trillion in U.S. dollars, a truly massive economy. Indeed, my own calculations agree with many analysts' forecasts: China will one day surpass the United States to become the world's largest national economy.

A great debate has raged in the last few years regarding China's growing economy. Interestingly, this debate is not about *whether* China will surpass the United States, but *when* this will happen, and it often hinges on the topic discussed above—the proper way to convert China's national currency into a common standard such as the U.S. dollar. Almost everyone agrees that we should use some purchasing power exchange rate, because China's currency appears undervalued by its market exchange rate. The Chinese government has exerted more than a little influence over China's market exchange rate, keeping this rate very low, as this has the effect of making China's products relatively cheap on world markets. This has been a major factor in the unprecedented export growth achieved by China over the last decade or two.

Significant for business now, China's economy had already risen to a large total by the mid-1990s, using *any* of the various exchange rate estimates that would yield purchasing power parity (PPP) between the United States and China. The rise since 1980 has been dramatic on any measure. Even if China's tremendous growth becomes more moderate or decelerates, it will continue to move up in the standings of great national economies. Again, the question is not *whether* China will become the largest national economy, but merely *when*. My own forecast is not as wildly optimistic as some prognostications. I use the term "wildly" because a few commentators think that China will move into first place in the early years of the new century. This is highly unlikely, as their estimates usually just extrapolate some of China's recent tremendous growth rates, in an overly optimistic manner.

Two excellent sources address this controversy in some depth. One is *China in the World Economy,* by Nicholas Lardy. This book is rightly considered an authoritative source on China's recent economic development and the future issues that this tremendous development entails.[9] In his first chapter, Lardy cites the various estimates for China's GDP converted using purchasing power exchange rates. He concludes very forcefully that, while of course China's economy appears much larger when using purchasing power exchange rates than when converting the yuan at the very low value the foreign exchange market places on it, some of the estimates of its economy's current size may be seriously inflated. Lardy shows that it is not yet anywhere near the size of the U.S. economy; indeed, in 1994 it was only approaching the size of the Japanese economy (currently less than half that of the United States in PPP terms).

Recent World Bank estimates indicate that Lardy was correct in stating that many estimates of China's economy in PPP terms are too high. The World Bank itself has been considering lowering its own earlier estimates.[10] For the purposes of this chapter, I used the latest PPP estimates from the World Bank's *World Development Indicators 1997.* This estimate, $2,920 income per capita in 1995 (using 1995 dollars), is consistent with the various estimates now produced by leading and reputable sources.

A second excellent source is the article "China as Next Superpower?" by Martin Wolf, in the *Financial Times.*[11] Wolf agrees with Lardy that there is great uncertainty as to the actual size of China's economy. He explains why China's economy is not nearly as powerful as some overly generous estimates would lead one to believe. In particular, he makes the important point that the economy may look large when measured using purchasing power exchange rates, but that in per capita terms, China is still dwarfed by the United States and, indeed, by Japan and most of Europe. Further, China's economy still looks relatively poor if we convert Chinese income to dollars using market, not PPP, exchange rates. Its low purchasing power in actual market terms somewhat diminishes China's current economic power.

In truth, the power of China's economy lies somewhere in the middle. A large total economy does yield a certain amount of power, but the still rather small per capita income shows the limited standard of living or purchasing power of most mainland Chinese. The conclusion is that, measured by purchasing power exchange rates, China obviously has a fairly large total economy; however, China will not soon surpass the United States as the world's most powerful economy. That convergence, if it is to occur at all, is still decades away.

HOT SPOTS: EMERGING GREAT NATIONAL ECONOMIES

II. INDIA

Many business leaders are eager to invest in China, citing its huge population base. But how many business executives realize that by the middle of the upcoming century, as was pointed out in Chapter 3, India will probably have a larger population than China? Actually, even now, India is approaching one billion people. This is currently well below China's total, but it is much closer to China than to the third place nation in the population league, the United States. In fact, India's population is more than three times that of any other nation on Earth, except for China. This might be considered insignificant if India's economy was poor and stagnating. However, as we saw in the preceding chapter, India finally seems to have launched itself upon an impressive growth path of economic development. Although not nearly as rapid as the recent growth in China or some East Asian nations, India's steady 5% or 6% growth in GDP is accumulating to such an extent that living standards in India are progressing noticeably. India is approaching income levels where even hundreds of millions of new consumers may be available to global corporations early in the next century.

India's economy is currently slightly smaller than Germany's, even when one considers India's GDP converted at purchasing power terms rather than the low market value of its currency. Clearly, India has a long way to go, but I predict that it is likely one day to surpass not only Germany, but also Japan, to become the world's third largest national economy. How could India, now rather poor, surpass the wealthy Japanese economy in total GDP? This is where the role of population base becomes critical.

Recall from Chapter 3 that Japan has a stagnating population; indeed, it will decline below 120 million by the year 2030. In sharp contrast, India is adding roughly 17 million people a year and will, after a couple of decades in the 21st century, have a population more than ten times that of Japan. If India's current growth in productivity (i.e., output per worker) continues, then also by 2020 or so, it should reach at least one-tenth of the average output per Japanese worker. If India can reach one-tenth of

Japanese productivity levels, it will have a larger total economy than Japan, because its population will exceed Japan's by more than ten times. It is not difficult to imagine that given more educational opportunity and more modern physical capital to work with over the next few decades, Indian workers can easily reach one-tenth of the productivity level of even highly productive Japanese workers. Thus, India can surpass Japan in total economic size if it continues on its present path of economic growth. If India's government stopped meddling in the affairs of privatization and free enterprise, capitalism could lead to an economic boom that would astound many people. One point of this book is to make sure such a boom does not astound you, but rather, that you begin to prepare now by adding India as a key strategic focus for future business expansion.

HOT SPOTS:
EMERGING GREAT NATIONAL ECONOMIES
III. INDONESIA

Most business leaders I speak to are aware of the potential of Indonesia, although many completely miss the boat on this big emerging nation. To me, it is hard to miss Indonesia as it contains 200 million people (fourth highest population on Earth!) spread over 17,000 islands. Two hundred million people spread over many thousands of islands should thrill anyone involved in the communications business. Consider the potential Indonesia offers for the mobile telephony industry. Particularly important here is the fact that Indonesia's 200 million people are not living in abject poverty. Rather, as we saw in the preceding chapter, Indonesia preceded its current crisis with a healthy economic growth rate stretching back for three decades. Endowed as it is with plentiful natural resources and with fairly well-educated people, Indonesia, if it reforms, should recover to become an economic force in the 21st century.

Although Indonesia starts below the other five nations in our model, as seen in Figure 6–1, its economy experienced fast growth into 1997. If it can return to healthy economic growth, Indonesia in this optimistic scenario will ultimately surpass Germany and move into fifth position among the world's largest national economies (using PPP, not Indonesia's sharply depreciated market exchange rate). Again, my optimistic scenario depends on the economy of Indonesia resuming growth at a faster rate than the economy of Germany. However, even this optimistic scenario realistically builds in the type of eventual deceleration that Paul Krugman has pointed out is likely to occur. Indonesia has vast untapped human resources, unlike Germany, which is already at a stage of very high output levels per worker.

Indeed, Germany would suffer diminishing returns if it tried to add even more physical capital or education per worker. In contrast to Germany, or any nation in the wealthy triad for that matter, I predict that Indonesia can grow at relatively fast growth rates for decades before suffering significant diminishing returns. Interestingly, my arguments have been confirmed in a statement by Indonesian Coordinating Minister for Trade and Industry Hartarto, who effused that "if we [continue] liberalizing our economy, and maintaining 7 percent growth for the next 25 years, then by the year 2018, based on PPP, Indonesia [will] belong to the 'Big Five': the USA, Japan, China, India, and Indonesia."[12]

I agree with Minister Hartarto's forecast, with two important caveats. First, I still see Germany as one of the "Big Six" economies well into the upcoming century. Second, although I do think Indonesia can one day surpass Germany, at least with GDP measured by PPP exchange rates, I think that the year 2018 is too soon for this occurrence. It is overly optimistic to think that Indonesia can maintain 7% growth for the next 25 years. Obviously, Minister Hartarto's forecast does not take into account the "Krugman critique" explained earlier in this chapter, which warned that you cannot extrapolate fast growth forever, as diminishing returns will set in. Recall that my own forecasts in this chapter do not just extrapolate past high growth rates, rather they build in some deceleration. However, the important point is one of agreement: even with decelerated (albeit healthy) growth for many decades—a very realistic projection—Indonesia can at least become one of the "Big Six" national economies in the world, underpinning the need to extend our focus beyond the traditional triad. Of course, if Indonesia does not successfully reform, in this pessimistic scenario, it will not move into the top tier.

THE SEVENTH GREAT NATIONAL ECONOMY?

If we decided to expand our GDP-based great national economies model to include seven countries, some major studies[13] indicate that Korea might be up there by the year 2020. However, my own forecasts show that France will still be in the running to remain in the top seven, because Asian economies such as Korea and Thailand are experiencing growing pains and even after recovery, will likely decelerate from their past rapid growth paths. Thus, forecasts that Korea or Thailand will pass France, or even Britain or Italy, in the next two decades are premature. However, their past growth and recent reforms suggest that these emerging economies of East Asia could be powers to be reckoned with within three, if not two, decades.

Russia, too, is hailed by some as a potential great national economy. Indeed, optimists regarding Russia's prospects invested heavily in its stock market[14] during 1996 and 1997, leading to dramatically soaring stock prices. I did not take part in this investment surge, however, as I found Russia's stock market explosion inconsistent with its economic and demographic implosion during this decade. When I present my Six Great Economies model, executives sometimes ask how I can omit Russia and its massive natural and human resources. I answer that the natural resources, especially timber and energy sources, are plentiful, but the lack of infrastructure makes access costly. And although I have great respect for the human resources of Russia, a lot of its human capital has emigrated to the United States, Israel, and Western Europe.

Finally, when asked if consumer firms can afford to ignore the "vast" population of Russia, I point out that they often ignore Indonesia and Pakistan. These two nations are also rich in resources, but unlike Russia, they have growing populations. When setting priorities for future global expansion, executives would benefit from these World Bank forecasts for population in year 2010: Indonesia—235 million, Pakistan—190 million, Russia—145 million. Brazil, Bangladesh, and Nigeria will also have greater populations than Russia by 2010. Indeed, Brazil already has a larger population and is becoming a focal point for business, as I will show in the next chapter.

Recall that we noted in Chapter 1 that Russia has slipped to a "third tier" status amongst world economies. We also discussed declining birth rates in Russia in Chapter 3. Both trends speak to the chaos and uncertainty, as well as the drop in living standards, in Russia following the collapse of the Soviet Union. However, some analysts believe that Russia has begun to turn around its economy, and that given its impressive population base and vast natural resources, it might once again become a powerful national economy. The *Financial Times,* noting the Russian stock market surge, observed that, "There is now renewed faith that Russia will develop into a 'normal' market economy, in which giant corporations, boasting prodigious assets, will generate exceptional returns for their shareholders."[15] However, the same article then detailed some of the problems Russia still faces, stating that "ministers predict the economy may contract again in 1997, its eighth consecutive year of decline, and expect it to grow only modestly next year." I also continue to hear firsthand reports of chaos, corruption, and violence in Russia (and some other parts of the former Soviet Union to its south). Thus, it is difficult to forecast Russia's future. Certainly it has the resources and scale to become a massive national economy, but its path to economic development and any form of stability is a long and uncertain one.

Table 6–1 provides the technical detail underlying this chapter's forecast model. It shows the growth assumptions needed to generate all our GDP forecasts (for national economies in Figure 6–1, and for regional economies under pessimistic and optimistic assumptions, respectively, in Figures 6–2 and 6–3). Table 6–1 also details *when* we add nations into various regional economies as we "extend the triad." Note the *deceleration* of growth rates in the next century as diminishing returns increasingly set in. However, the main driver of the model is that despite decelerating from their past, very high growth rates, China, ASEAN (after its 1998 slowdown), and India should be able to achieve growth rates that will exceed those slow rates experienced and likely to continue in the already quite economically advanced nations of the traditional triad. Thus, we will move from the three regional focal points implicit in a triad model to six great regional economies, with three new ones coming from the big emerging nations, as we add a focus for the 21st century.

THE SIX GREAT REGIONAL ECONOMIES MODEL

Recall from our prior discussion, particularly in Chapter 2, that business is increasingly looking at *regional* economies, not just national ones. The wisdom of taking such a regional approach is demonstrated by the continuing economic integration of major regions of the world. Thus, it will profit us to extend our national economies model to forecast the development of great *regionally integrated* economies as we move into the 21st century. A model of (macro) regional economic integration and development is the highlight of this chapter, and is summarized graphically in Figures 6–2 and 6–3. Note that there will be several great regional economies developing in the 21st century; we claim that these regional economies will provide the focal points for most industries as business looks to expand more globally.

TRADITIONAL TRIAD ECONOMIES

Specifically, I conclude that there will probably be at least six great regional economies in the new century. This means that a focus only on the three regional economies of the traditional triad is outdated and would likely make it more difficult to prosper in an emerging global economy. The economies of the traditional triad should not be ignored, however, as indeed we can see that all three are still in our model. Europe will remain a major focal point of business, under either a pessimistic or an optimistic

Table 6–1   Real GDP Growth Assumptions in the "Six Great Economies Model"
Assumptions for the Optimistic Scenario (all growth rates are annual averages)

	Through 2000	Through 2010	Through 2020	Through 2030
Americas[1]:				
U.S. and Canada	2.6%	2.6%	2.6%	2.6%
Latin America (e.g., Brazil)	3.8%	4.2%	3.6%	3.4%
"Europe 17" (e.g., Germany)[2]	2.4%	2.4%	2.2%	2.2%
"Central Europe 3"	5%	5%	3.5%	3.5%
Japan	2.4%	2.4%	2.2%	2.2%
ASEAN (e.g., Indonesia)	6%	6%	4.5%	4%
China	8%	6%	4.5%	4%
Hong Kong[3]	4%	4%	4%	4%
India	6%	6%	4.5%	4%

Assumptions for the Pessimistic Scenario
(note no change for advanced nations in Triad)

	Through 2000	Through 2010	Through 2020	Through 2030
Americas[1]:				
U.S. and Canada	2.6%	2.6%	2.6%	2.6%
Latin America (e.g., Brazil)	3.0%	3.0%	3.0%	3.0%
"Europe 17" (e.g., Germany)[2]	2.4%	2.4%	2.2%	2.2%
"Central Europe 3"	3%	3%	3%	3%
Japan	2.4%	2.4%	2.2%	2.2%
ASEAN (e.g., Indonesia)	3%	4%	3.5%	3.5%
China	6%	4%	3%	3%
Hong Kong[3]	4%	4%	3%	3%
India	4%	4%	3%	3%

[1]The Americas economy starts with United States, Canada, and Mexico, adds Chile in 1999, Argentina in 2000, Brazil in 2002, and the rest of the Americas in 2005.
[2]The European economy starts with the 15 nations in the European Union, adds Switzerland and Norway (in a de facto economic sense only) in 1998 to become the "Europe 17," and adds the "Central Europe 3" (Poland, Hungary, Czech Republic) in 2000.
[3]The Chinese regional economy adds Hong Kong in 1998.

Figure 6–2 THE SIX GREAT REGIONAL ECONOMIES OF THE 21ST CENTURY

(Pessimistic Scenario)

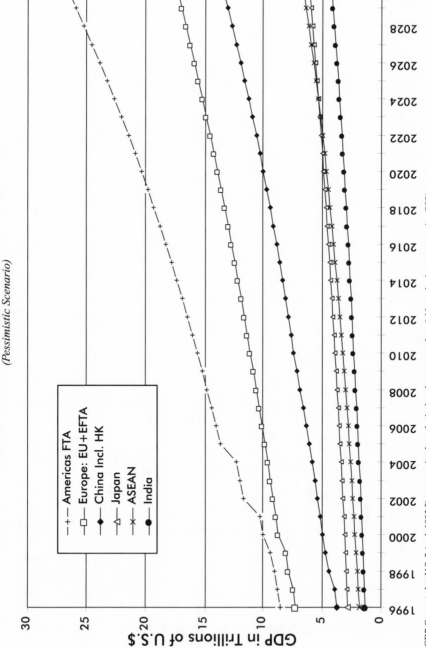

GDP Converted to U.S. $ (real, 1995 $) terms, using hypothetical exchange rates that yield purchasing power parity (PPP). Pessimistic implies slower growth in the developing nations if they do not fully open to capitalism and foreign investment.

Figure 6–3 THE SIX GREAT REGIONAL ECONOMIES OF THE 21ST CENTURY

(Optimistic Scenario)

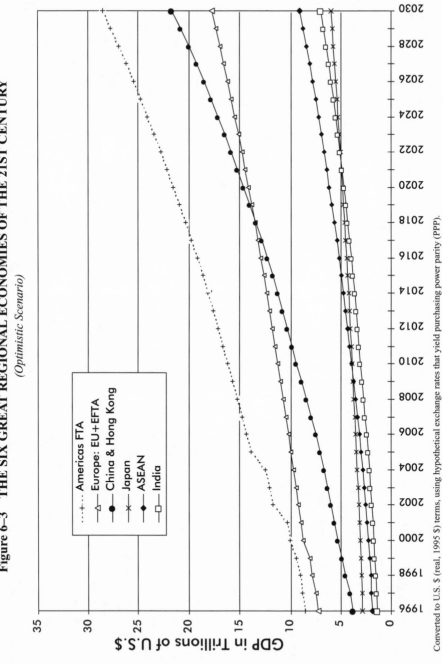

Converted to U.S. $ (real, 1995 $) terms, using hypothetical exchange rates that yield purchasing power parity (PPP).

scenario. I forecast that a European regional economy will grow for two reasons. First, there is much economic growth within each nation currently in the regionally integrated economy of the European Union. Second, there will be a continued expansion of the European regional economy to comprise more nations, particularly European nations to the east. Eventually adding nations such as Poland accounts for the "upward steps" in my forecast for the European economy shown in these figures. Likewise, Japan remains a major economy and a key regional economy in its own right, for any business that has global aspirations.

It is important to understand that the United States is now part of an emerging regional economy. Already we are part of NAFTA, a North American free trade area that is increasingly becoming an integrated economy. Furthermore, we discussed in Chapter 2 the plans to form a Free Trade Area of the Americas (FTAA). This further integration of the regional economy will likely happen in stages; therefore this reality is reflected in our forecasts. The Americas economy will grow as major nations such as Brazil become more integrated in an emerging Americas free trade area; these successive stages are reflected in the figures and summarized by the assumptions shown in Table 6–1. Before getting into more detail, let us understand how our main point was arrived at: how we move from the *three* major regional economies of the traditional triad to a model with *six* great regional economies.

CHINA AND INDIA: MAJOR REGIONAL ECONOMIES EVEN WITHOUT FURTHER INTEGRATION

We have seen that great economies for business are developing in populous emerging regions around the world. In particular, we have discussed the emergence of China as a growing economic force. Further, we noted that there is something of a "greater China" in a business sense, as investments from overseas Chinese, such as those in Taiwan, flow into mainland China. Even prior to the actual return of Hong Kong to the mainland People's Republic of China, the anticipation of this merger resulted in massive investment flows into the area.

For our purposes, I included the (still separately reported) projected GDP of what was Hong Kong in the China region, starting in the first full year of merger, that is, 1998. Although the very high productivity in Hong Kong leads to a little step up in China's GDP, it is important to realize that, at least in purchasing power terms, the Chinese economy in total dollar GDP already dwarfs that of Hong Kong. Even though the average Hong

Kong worker has a much higher level of productivity, the sheer mathematics of 1.2 billion people in China, compared to only 1/200th of that total in Hong Kong, means that the addition of Hong Kong provides only a small increase in China's total GDP.

Since we have discussed China in depth before, we will not analyze it at length here. The insight of the present model is that "greater China" is an economic force already. In addition, this area is on a growth path to become one of the great economies, perhaps *the* great regional economy, of the 21st century.

Reaping the insight of the initial six great national economies model, we realize that India also has such a huge population, and an impressive enough record of recent economic growth, that it can be counted among the great potential economies of the 21st century. You may wonder why I count India, China, and Japan as separate great economies, in contrast to the truly region-wide economies of Europe or the Americas included in this model. This is an important point, and it is based on my belief that China, Japan, and India are so distinct in terms of their economic structure, cultures, languages, and political structures, as well as strong historical antipathies, that it is unlikely that they will integrate deeply enough to be called one regional economy. Francis Fukuyama, in his influential book, *Trust: The Social Virtues and the Creation of Prosperity,*[16] analyzes the very different business cultures in major nations. He writes that China, a "low-trust society," favors extended family businesses, whereas Japan, a "high-trust society," is similar to the United States and Germany in favoring corporate forms of organization.

Each of these large Asian national economies (China, India, and Japan) has such a huge economic and/or population base that they do not *need* to integrate more fully in order to create regional economies of sufficient magnitude to generate the "economies of scale" needed for business efficiency. One can see why Ireland, Austria, Denmark, or Belgium, each with a small population and geographic base, would be eager to integrate into a pan-European regional economy. These nations need regional integration in order to attract business investment and to reach a large enough open market to generate the needed economies of scale to recover fixed costs of, for instance, research and development. In contrast, China and India will each have well over 1.4 billion people by the year 2030, so there is really no motivation for either nation to overcome cultural and historical divides to form a regional economy. Japan's economy is already large enough to afford economies of scale, even if its rather insular culture stops it from integrating regionally. A crucial underlying theme of my model is that these three Asian nations can reach an economic scale that will make them major focal points of business, even if they do not integrate further within the Asian region. The ability of all three to become huge economies is clearly portrayed in this chapter's graphics.

SOUTHEAST ASIA: A POTENTIAL SIXTH GREAT REGIONAL ECONOMY

The Southeast is the one area in Asia where regional economic integration is proceeding rapidly. This area contains economies that have been very dynamic, but some nations are not large enough to generate sufficient economies of scale. Thus, integration is a key component of economic growth. Notable is the economic integration that is progressing in the Association of Southeast Asian Nations (ASEAN), as presented in Chapter 2. ASEAN represents an emerging, powerful trading and economic bloc in Southeast Asia.

Indonesia is the demographic focal point of ASEAN, just as Brazil is the demographic giant of South America. Indonesia is populous, rich in natural resources, and has had a rapidly advancing national economy. Other nations of ASEAN, particularly Thailand, the Philippines, and Vietnam, also represent populous areas ripe with potential to provide efficient yet cheap labor, or future customers. Meanwhile, Malaysia and Singapore have demonstrated enviable economic growth records, as portrayed in Chapter 5, that provided lessons for their ASEAN neighbors. Brunei may be small, but as Atlantans discovered during the 1996 Olympic Games, the Sultan of Brunei, who rivals Bill Gates for the title of "the world's richest person," has the economic clout to rent out entire neighborhoods and buy blocks of tickets to the most prestigious events without making any dent in his bank account. After adding Vietnam in 1995 and Laos and Myanmar in 1997, ASEAN now has nine nations that individually could become economic dynamos and collectively are forming a regional economy that should be a focal point for business in the new century.

The large and growing total population in the ASEAN nations augurs well as an attractive *future labor force* for businesses looking to outsource some production. In addition, as these workers increase their productivity (thanks to additions of physical capital and training), they will eventually improve their standard of living, thereby becoming huge *emerging markets* for firms around the world. Already, this region has been one of the fastest growing destinations for U.S. exports as well as for U.S. foreign investment.

Further, I remain bullish on ASEAN despite recent currency turmoil, precipitated when Thailand's financial problems forced it to devalue its *baht* currency in July 1997. Currency "crises" that lead to devaluation, in effect, make a nation's products relatively cheaper in global competition. I predict that ASEAN will follow the lead of Chile, the United States, and Mexico, each of whom saw their exports surge within a year or so of their respective currency devaluations in 1982, 1985, and the winter of 1994–1995.

I concur with the assessment of MIT Professor Rudi Dornbusch, widely regarded as one of the world's leading and most practical economists, in his column in *Business Week*[17]:

> It is safe to argue that emerging Asia still has and will continue to have extraordinary dynamism. Over the past two decades, the standard of living has more than doubled. And it will probably do so again in the next two. . . . The other complicating factor is the shift from a strongly statist and regimented economy to the free market. That is new in Asia and comes as something of a shock. . . . There is turmoil involved in shifting from centralized to market economies, and Joseph Schumpeter's creative destruction is well under way in Asia. Close up, things look messy, and financial markets can mistake the transition pains for major problems with stability and economic growth. Yet if you believe in markets, this transition is ultimately good news. Beyond strikes and bankruptcies, the free-enterprise economy is freeing up the productivity gains that will keep Asia growing.

Thus, ASEAN is still evolving into one of the regional economies that I believe should be most exciting to business. Interestingly, it was barely on the radar screen just a few short years ago. In fact, one of my first versions of a model that attempted to help business look beyond the traditional triad was termed the *five* great regional economies. It has only been in the last few years that ASEAN has proven its desire to truly integrate into a regional economy. Further, its recent crisis contains a silver lining— the opportunity to reform by freeing its markets.

IMPLICATIONS OF THE SIX
GREAT ECONOMIES MODELS

Up to the 1990s, strategists told business executives to take a fairly balanced view of the global economy. At least they claimed it was a balanced view, as they recommended looking equally at three major regions: North America, Western Europe, and Japan or Northeast Asia. We have seen that this view was not really balanced, because it basically ignored the billions of people living in the Southern Hemisphere or equatorial regions. Here we see that although the three regions of the traditional triad will remain important to any business strategy, one should also devote a good share of attention to the big emerging regional economies as we move into the 21st century.

Here an interesting fact emerges. Look at the continents that the various members of the six great economies inhabit. Again, a perceptive analyst may see something of a lack of balance in what first appears to be a balanced framework. We have a European champion, a champion from the Americas, and then what are we left with? Four of my projected six great economies are in Asia! Indeed, other than India, the Asian ones are all in East Asia! Thus, *fully one-half* of the predicted major focal points for global business strategy are in *East Asia.* Given the present pessimism regarding Asia, this point cannot be overemphasized: the implication of this analysis is that business must eventually have a strong component of its strategic focus on East Asia. Rather than seeing East Asia as just one of the three legs of the traditional triad, our expanded model shows us that the Asian leg of the emerging global economy has a number of potentially powerful sub-legs. Indeed, instead of perching global business on a shaky stool with only three legs, we may be able to have a very firm stool with six legs, but it is important to realize that two-thirds of what will be supporting global business expansion are Asian legs. Thus, we once again see that it just no longer makes good business sense to focus exclusively on Europe or on transatlantic trade and investment.

The above arguments are not meant to diminish the continuing importance of Europe and the Americas as focal points for business in the new century. These two constituents of the original triad can remain a massive and powerful *two* of the *six* great economies I predict for the 21st century, if they proceed (as I and most economists advise) toward a broader integration of the economies in their regions.

Consider the example of the Americas. Recall that most forecasts show China eventually surpassing the United States as the largest national economy. But this point is being overstated by many analysts because they look at the United States as a national economy. I believe the United States as a national economy will grow to a massive $17 trillion by 2030. But in fact, the United States is already part of the North American regional economy, NAFTA. Further, we have seen that the plan is to extend this regional economy into a Free Trade Area of the Americas. Our model here anticipates such an expansion, in a step-by-step fashion, adding first Chile, then Argentina, then Brazil, and then other nations of this hemisphere. The upshot of this analysis is that the United States can remain *part* of the world's greatest economy, if it continues on the path of being the largest part and main engine of a growing and evolving regionally integrated economy of the Americas. Such an Americas regional economy, forecast to grow to nearly $29 trillion by 2030, will continue to far exceed the economic magnitude of China's economy (incorporating Hong Kong's separately reported data).

This chapter has added strategic focus by identifying the "hot spots" for global business expansion. We identified the continuing development of six great regional economies. The potentially biggest of these, that of the Americas, is anchored by the United States, which has recently performed well economically. However, Latin America will constitute an ever-growing portion of the Americas economy, while economic power is shifting inexorably toward Asia. Investing in these emerging hot spots holds great promise; therefore the next chapter provides a rationale for, and routes to, a more global strategy for both firms and individuals.

LEADER SPOTLIGHT

Ray Anderson Challenges Interface to Achieve Sustainable Development

At a recent CEO conference, after I had the opportunity to present my Six Great Economies model, one leading CEO came up to tell me I was absolutely crazy. After all, he pointed out, under my optimistic scenario, the sum of the GDP of all the nations eventually comprising the six great regional economies, even in real terms (i.e., constant 1995 dollars), nearly triples to roughly $90 trillion by 2030, from $30.6 trillion in 1998. He told me the Earth could not possibly sustain such a high volume of production; indeed, we are inexorably destroying our natural environment even at today's lower levels of production.

I answered, rather shallowly, that I was predicting that services would continue to rise as a share of GDP, whereas the more resource-depleting or environmentally threatening manufacturing, mining, and agricultural industries would continue to diminish as a share of the growing GDP pie. I also made the point that business leaders would have to follow the lead of European firms such as Swissair, changing business processes to become more sustainable and avoiding unnecessary environmental damage or resource depletion.

Little did I know that I was speaking with a CEO who is doing just that! Indeed, he has won major accolades, such as the inaugural Millennium Award from Global Green, presented by Mikhail Gorbachev. In addition, as a result of his leading efforts in fostering sustainable development, in April 1997 he was appointed co-chair of President Clinton's Council on Sustainable Development.

This CEO, Ray Anderson, in 1973 founded what is now over a billion-dollar multinational corporation. His company, Interface, Inc., is the world's largest producer of commercial floor coverings. One might expect that such an industry, based on modular carpet tiles, could easily damage the environment, depleting resources and filling landfills. However, Ray has challenged his people to achieve 100% sustainability. Interface is attempting to reach this "no harm to the environment" sustainable position through many initiatives: recycling, reducing resource use and waste by improving the efficiency of business processes, and influencing other firms to follow similar environmentally sound practices.

Ray Anderson sees Interface's efforts to foster more environmentally sustainable business practices as integral to its own sustainable competitive advantage. A recent article entitled "Business Achieves Greatest Efficiencies When at Its Greenest," in the the *Wall Street Journal*,[18] describes Anderson's strategy of achieving business success with a sustainable impact on the environment. The article shows how striving for resource efficiency is a key part of Interface's competitive strategy. Business processes can be improved to reduce environmentally harmful wastes, simultaneously improving productivity.

> "Looking at waste really forces you to look at how your systems are designed," says James Hartzfeld, a top Interface official. The crackdown has saved Interface a stunning $25 million since 1995, with another $50 million expected the next two years.
>
> The marketing benefits are even bigger. Everybody wants to do business with a green vendor, especially a low-cost green vendor. . . .
>
> Reaching $1 billion in revenue last year, Interface has regained world-wide leadership. . . .
>
> Only business can create a renewable future, and only by following nature's own example.

A more recent article in *Business Week*[19] amplifies Interface's successful strategy:

> Perhaps no CEO has embraced eco-efficiency as much as Ray Anderson . . . His goal is to create zero waste and consume zero oil

while making a healthy profit. . . . So far Anderson's "drive to zero" has resulted in cost savings of $25 million. Even better, it's attracting customers—architects like doing business with an environmentally friendly supplier. Interface's profits rose 30% last year and revenues 25%, to a record $1 billion.

Ray Anderson is a CEO who "practices what he preaches" with sincerity and intelligent business sense. Thus, fellow CEOs are taking notice of his creative initiatives, his commitment, and his consequent enhanced business success. A leader by example, Anderson deserves the final word: "There is a limit to what the Earth can supply and endure. When the Earth runs out of resources and the ecosystem collapses, future generations will be left to hold it up. . . . The answer is resource efficiency."[20]

PART III

A GLOBAL STRATEGY FOR PEOPLE AND PROFITS IN THE 21ST CENTURY

CHAPTER 7

PREPARING FOR THE GLOBAL CENTURY:

The Rationale, Route, and Tools for Diversifying Beyond the U.S. Market

A MODEL THAT MOTIVATES A MORE GLOBAL INVESTING STRATEGY

Why would anyone look beyond the large U.S. market and adopt a more global strategy? After all, the United States has by far the world's largest national economy. Furthermore, as we saw in the preceding chapter, claims that China will soon surpass the United States economy are overly extrapolative. Indeed, it will be at least a few decades before the United States is supplanted as the world's largest national economy. Clearly then, the United States continues to be the single richest national market for firms to pursue. The country also possesses large stock markets listing many firms for investors to add to their portfolios. By contrast, many of the world's emerging economies pose significant potential risks, forcing us to consider, in the preceding chapter, a possible pessimistic scenario for economic growth.

At this point, readers may be questioning the wisdom of a global strategic plan; speculating instead that a business or investment focus on the U.S. economy alone might be the best strategy. Such readers may feel that this country is the safest place on Earth to keep all their business or wealth. They might also point to the U.S. stock market's brilliant performance since the October 1987 crash, and for that matter, during the whole period since 1982. "Surely," they will say, "the U.S. dollar must be an admirable store of value?!"

This chapter will show that the United States is *not* a safe basket for "all of your eggs." As we move into the 21st century, the riskiest course will be to remain with a domestic concentration, *whereas the preferred strategy will be a much more global one.* I will support this claim by presenting an original model of the U.S. economy and its linkages with the increasingly global economy. The model suggests that the U.S. economy, despite many strengths (as reflected in the current low rates of inflation and unemployment), is nonetheless risky, due to the recent massive accumulation of debt. Furthermore, this debt problem exists in both the U.S. government and international (trade and payments) accounts. Once we understand this dynamic, rather depressing, model of U.S. debt accumulation and its implications, we will be able to highlight the key aspects of the appropriate response: the implementation of a more global strategy.

Thus, this chapter aims to do three things. First, I will present an original economic and financial model that should provide motivation for diversifying well beyond a reliance just on the U.S. market. Second, we will apply the insights and implications of this model to *firms,* urging them to consider a time-phased global strategy for expansion. Third, we will see that *individuals* wishing to prosper in the emerging global economy should diversify their personal or family investments by including a strong "global investing" component.

We will examine a less technical version of a dynamic model I have developed over the years to illustrate the interlinked system of deficits and debt that characterizes a significant aspect of the U.S. economy. I title this model, "The U.S. as Global Debtor: The Dual Vicious Circles of Deficits, the Dollar, and Debt." My goal is to help readers understand how international economic and financial concepts, such as deficits and debt, the dollar foreign exchange value, and the balance of payments (BOP) accounts, are related within an economic system. The model will also help readers understand the linkages between currency fluctuations, trade, economic performance, interest rates, and the reality of U.S. deficits and debt accumulation. Once readers understand these linkages, the need to explore global investment opportunities will become paramount.

Despite the risk that it may seem ethnocentric, we focus here on the U.S. position in the world economy. Many firms and investors focus exclusively (or almost exclusively) upon the United States because it is still such a large market. What are the *economic* reasons to focus our discussion on the United States here? This country is still, by far, the largest economic unit in the world. It is currently more than twice the size of any other national economy, as we demonstrated in the last chapter.[1] As such, the U.S. economy is much larger than any other economic entity, be it nation or global corporation. But this distinction should not lull readers into a false sense of security, so that they miss the lessons of diversification highlighted in this chapter. Indeed, a significant key feature of U.S. interaction with the rest of the world—trade deficits—will point out the major weakness of the U.S. economy.

THE CURRENT ACCOUNT PERFORMANCE HIGHLIGHTS THE WEAKNESS IN THE U.S. ECONOMY

Let us look at the international economist's favorite set of accounts—the balance of payments (BOP). The BOP is a summary of all of a nation's international business transactions over a period of time. The BOP accounts include two major subcategories: *a current account,* which essentially summarizes a nation's current business operations with the rest of the world, and *a capital account.* The external current account is the broadest trade balance measure, comprising trade in goods, trade in services, net income on foreign investments, and unilateral transfers (net foreign aid received or given).[2]

The key trend of the U.S. balance of payments accounts over the past few decades is the continual massive external or international current account deficits the country has been running since the early 1980s. Indeed, the deficits are the largest in world history! Prior to the continual record-setting deficits, the economic recessions the United States suffered in 1980 and again in 1981–82 temporarily improved the current account balance. This improvement was the result of curtailed individual and business income, which limited spending, and particularly important for our concerns, shrunk spending on imports. After 1982, economic recovery and a rising value of the U.S. dollar (until 1985) in foreign exchange markets led to a surge in imports, ballooning merchandise trade deficits and a corresponding overall current account deficit.

International deficits in the current account (broad trade balance) have significant implications. A current account deficit needs to be financed by *net foreign borrowing.* In other words, such a deficit implies a need to attract foreigners' savings or investment into the economy to fund the excess expenditures. The continued large U.S. current account deficits since 1982 have resulted in massive foreign borrowing. We have needed *net capital inflows,* via the incursion of debt or the sale of assets to foreigners, to finance our broad trade deficit.

Indeed, massive foreign investment did flow in during the 1980s, as foreigners purchased assets in the United States or extended loans to U.S. institutions. A number of books have been written on this subject; some bemoaning that the United States is "for sale" or implying that foreigners are cheating or dominating us. The truth is that the foreigners have done us a favor! Americans, by their own choice, are spending more internationally than they are earning, and thereby incurring deficits. Thus, we *need* someone more willing to save than we are to step up and provide the requisite financing. Furthermore, the good side of this equation is that the inward flow of foreign investment helped the U.S. economy grow, creating tens of millions of jobs since the early 1980s. These benefits should indeed be appreciated, but bear in mind that our model shows such benefits do come at a cost: a rapidly accumulating "net debt to foreigners position."

Figure 7–1 shows the international current account performance of the United States from 1982 onwards. The bars reveal the shift to numerous massive annual deficits. The rapidly falling line in the figure displays the result of these deficits: the declining net worth (rise in net debt) of the United States vis-à-vis the rest of the world. This trend of rising assets sold or liabilities incurred to foreigners fueled the United States' historic transition from the world's largest net international creditor nation (highest net foreign worth) to its present dubious honor—the world's biggest net foreign debtor. In fact, the combined total debt of the previous largest debtors, Brazil and Mexico, pales in comparison to the U.S. net debt to foreigners. Indeed, Figure 7–1 shows preliminary estimates that U.S. net foreign debt exceeded $1 trillion by the end of 1997!

The important question for us is: Why did the United States make the shift to continual massive international current account deficits and what are the ultimate implications of all these deficits? Figure 7–2 reveals that the U.S. federal government deficits appear to be an important influence. U.S. government deficits started ballooning after 1980,[3] and we see in the figure that the external current account shifted to similarly large deficits after a time delay. By the mid-1980s, the United States had huge deficits of over $150 billion on both accounts, prompting a new theory of "twin deficits."[4]

The twin deficits theory captures the insight readers can derive from examining Figure 7–2: after the U.S. government deficits started growing dramatically, the U.S. dollar rose sharply in value against the other major currencies in the world. The rise in the foreign exchange value of the dollar made U.S. products relatively expensive, which most analysts believe was a major channel by which the United States moved into massive merchandise trade and, more broadly, current account deficits. This linkage between government deficits and trade (or the broader current account) deficits, operating through a rising currency foreign exchange value, is the essence of the "twin deficits" theory.

Figure 7–1 THE LEGACY OF TRADE DEFICITS

U.S. shifts into a vicious circle of foreign debt

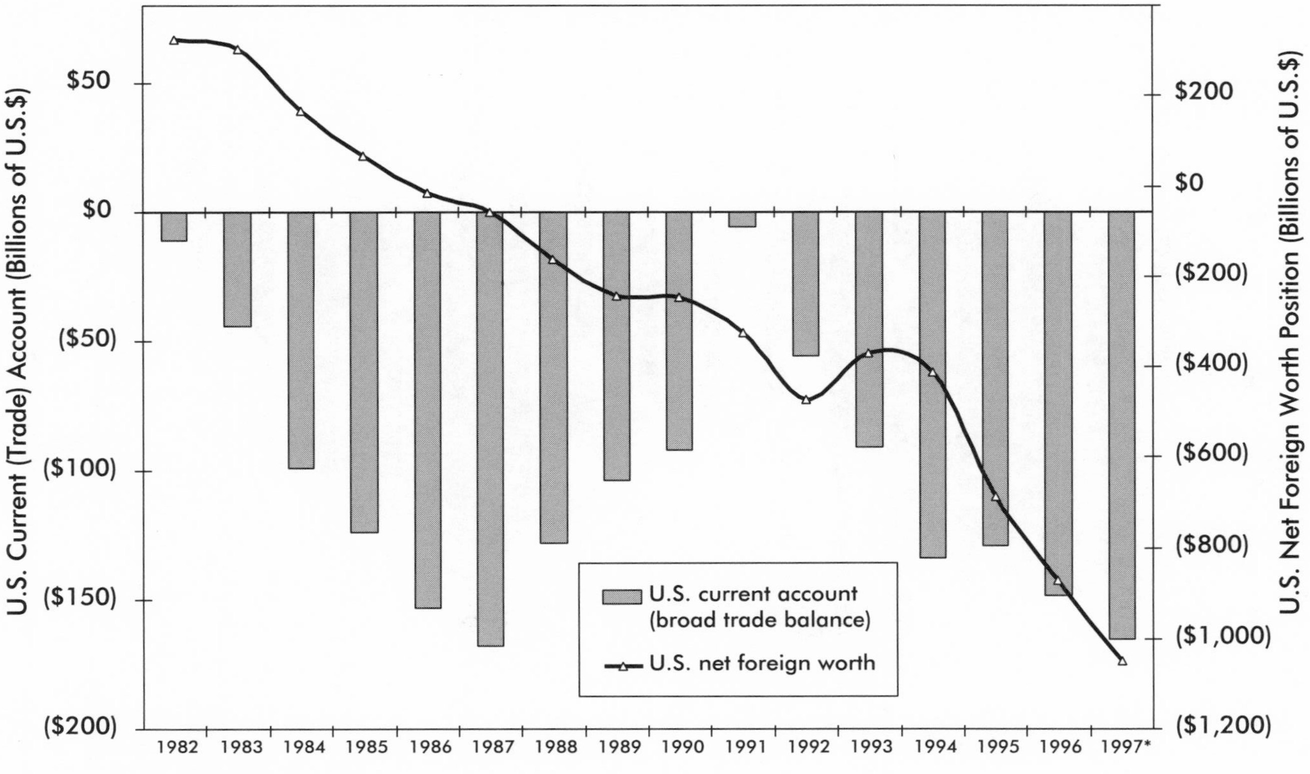

Data Source: U.S. Department of Commerce.
*preliminary

175

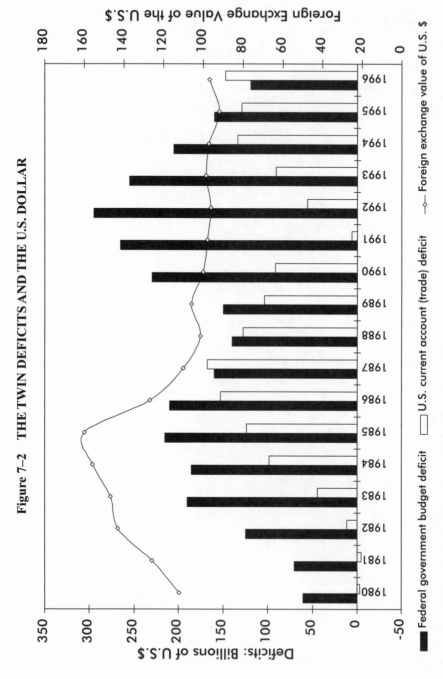

Figure 7–2 THE TWIN DEFICITS AND THE U.S. DOLLAR

Foreign Exchange Value of the U.S.$

Deficits: Billions of U.S.$

■ Federal government budget deficit   ☐ U.S. current account (trade) deficit   ◇— Foreign exchange value of U.S. $

Data Sources: U.S. Department of Commerce, *Survey of Current Business*, July 1997.
IMF real trade-weighted average of U.S. $ foreign exchange value: Index 1990=100.

Further evidence of the twin deficits linkage is provided in Figure 7–2. In the mid-1980s, the government deficit declined for a few years and the U.S. dollar's foreign exchange value declined with it. We see that the current account deficit again seemed to follow the government deficit, as it also started declining after a delay. Unfortunately, the more negative pattern repeated in the early 1990s: first, the substantial rise in the government deficit, then a worsening in the U.S. international current account balance.

We will now build a model to help us understand all these developments and economic relationships. Figure 7–3, a summary of the "Dual Vicious Circles of Deficits, the Dollar, and Debt," illustrates my latest attempt to capture all these dynamic linkages in one explanation.[5] This model traces the *future* implications of continued deficit spending, by extending the rather static twin deficits story ("these two deficits appear to be similar or related") into a more dynamic framework that is much more useful, because it allows us to see where trends are developing and where they may lead the U.S. economy within the global economy. This, in turn, can help us plot a strategy to prosper in the future.

THE DUAL VICIOUS CIRCLES OF DEFICITS, THE DOLLAR, AND DEBT

In the top part of Figure 7–3, we see that the twin deficit chain initiates the model; that is, the system was begun with the increased federal government budget deficits of the 1980s. In 1979 President Jimmy Carter had appointed Paul Volcker as chairman of the nation's central bank, the U.S. Federal Reserve System. Volcker's plan was to fight high inflation by means of a tightened supply of money or credit. This policy, combined with the federal government budget deficits, led to the very high interest rates seen in the United States in the early 1980s. Many readers will remember the pain of paying interest rates of 18% or even higher, especially on consumer loans and credit cards. The government deficits were then further exacerbated by extra federal spending, which existed in an unholy alliance with President Ronald Reagan's tax cuts.

Foreign investors were attracted by the high returns (interest rates) and low taxes[6] that became available here, so they increased their loans to and investments in the United States. In order to invest here, however, foreigners first had to buy U.S. dollars on the foreign exchange market. The increased market demand lifted the foreign exchange value of the U.S. dollar. We see in Figure 7–3 that the rising foreign value of the dollar (until 1985) pushed the United States toward a trade deficit in services and a massive trade

Figure 7–3   THE DUAL VICIOUS CIRCLES OF U.S. DEFICITS, THE DOLLAR, AND DEBT

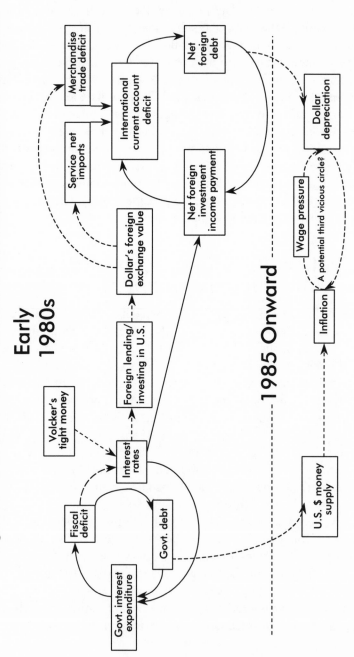

Key: After large U.S. federal fiscal deficit increases, all items in the boxes increase.

⟶ Means that by accounting definition an increase occurs.

- - -▸ Means hypothesized increase: a standard economic relationship is assumed.

178

deficit in merchandise, by harming the global price competitiveness of U.S. firms. The result was the historic shift to huge U. S. current account deficits that we saw in this chapter's earlier figures.

This model goes beyond the twin deficit story by tracing the implications of the continual deficits experienced by the United States in both the government and the international current accounts. First, on the left side of Figure 7–3, we see that the federal budget is turning into a vicious circle—one of deepening feedback between government deficits and debt. Each year a large federal deficit fosters the need for further government borrowing; that is, the deficit flows into an increased stock of government debt. This growing level of debt needs to be serviced; people will only buy or hold the debt, which is in the form of U.S. Treasury securities, if they earn a return in the form of interest payments. If the government deficits lead to high interest rates and/or if the accumulation of deficits leads to a high level of debt, the interest payments on this debt become mammoth. Since interest payments are a necessary expenditure in future federal budgets, huge interest payments will push future government budgets toward larger deficits.

The process of deficits leading to increased debt, the servicing of which helps cause future deficits, which in turn results in more debt, feeds on itself and becomes a "vicious circle." Such a vicious circle system is not confined to governments. It has bankrupted many firms, such as Eastern Airlines, which was choked to death by the high interest payments it had to make on its "junk bonds." In addition, it has bankrupted many individuals who held too much high interest rate debt (e.g., credit card debt).

The vicious circle that has developed in the U.S. federal government account is a major unfortunate legacy of the 1980s and 1990s to future generations. Total U.S. federal debt was barely less than $1 trillion at the end of 1980, when President Jimmy Carter left office, but it grew dramatically as the government budget deficits surged. Strikingly, it took 205 years of U.S. history to accumulate the first $1 trillion of federal debt, but only about *six* years to add another trillion dollars! After this, interest payments on the swelling level of debt massively boosted the vicious circle of government deficits and debt, and the next few trillion dollars of debt accumulated even more quickly. The gross federal debt total has swelled to more than $5.5 trillion in 1998, indicating that the United States is locked into massive interest payments that will push all future federal budgets toward large deficits. Despite recent political rhetoric and promised plans, it will be very difficult to balance the budget once baby boomers start to retire.[7] Consider the ramifications of a debt that could soon hit $6 trillion. Even if average interest rates on U.S. Treasury securities were slightly below 6%, the government would have to pay a gross interest bill of roughly *$350 billion* annually!

A method to determine if the level of debt is problematic is to compare it to the level of income. Fortunately for the United States, this crucial ratio of total federal government debt to national income (GDP) is not as high as it is for some debtor nations. For example, Italy and Belgium have worse ratios of debt to income. Nonetheless, one should not draw very much comfort from the fact that our fiscal problems appear more benign when compared to those of Italy! The important point is that U.S. federal government debt has risen sharply as a share of U.S. GDP since 1980, and is now near record levels,[8] as a result of the United States piling on new debt to service (pay interest on) old debt.[9]

This is explained by the misleading nature of the current reporting system for the government deficit; the reported deficit is reduced by the inclusion of the current surplus cash flow on Social Security and similar accounts that are building trust funds to prepare for baby boomers' retirements. Most of us economists think this inclusion is improper, because the current Social Security surplus cash flows are forced to be invested in U.S. government bonds that are not truly independent assets of the government—they are already earmarked for our retirement.

Unfortunately, there is a second dangerous "vicious circle" developing, this time in the U.S. international accounts. The international *current account* balance is the global operations "budget balance," or international income statement bottom line. The continual recording of massive deficits in this broad trade account since the early 1980s has led to a large and rapidly accumulating *net debt* in the United States' international position, as seen in Figure 7–1. This net debt position could eventually lead to large net servicing payments overseas on foreign loans to, or investments in, the United States. Indeed, we can see the rising trend in these payments abroad by examining the U.S. balance of payments accounts.

The BOP accounts reveal that the servicing payments that the United States must make on its growing foreign liabilities are rapidly rising. Income payments to foreigners on their investments in the United States nearly *sextupled* in the period from 1980 to 1997, whereas our receipts for U.S. investments made abroad barely tripled in the same period. Such income payments on foreign investments can be interest, profits, rents, or dividends. By 1997, U.S. income payments on foreign assets in the United States (or foreign debt incurred by the United States) exceeded $250 billion, compared to only $79 billion in 1986, $14.2 billion in 1977, and a minuscule $1.3 billion in 1962.

Data for 1997 disclose that the United States has sunk to an unprecedented position: its *net* income on foreign investments became negative.[10] In other words, payments on liabilities to foreigners now exceed U.S.

earnings on investments abroad. As a result, we see a deficit of $14.3 billion in the "net investment income" balance, a component of the international current account. These net income deficits will exacerbate the overall U.S. current account deficits. At the same time, broad trade deficits imply a need for further foreign borrowing, foreshadowing a continuing buildup of U.S. net debt to foreigners. This increased net foreign debt will generate even higher investment income payments in the future; pushing future U.S. current accounts further into deficit. Thus, if the United States does not tame its current account deficit soon, a *second vicious circle will develop,* in the international accounts (recall that the first vicious circle involved the federal government accounts).

In the bottom part of Figure 7–3, we see that from 1986 onward, the basic twin deficit story was somewhat altered. The United States, perhaps recognizing the negative long-run implications of the burgeoning twin deficits, shifted its policy mix toward tighter budgetary or fiscal policy (reducing deficits in accordance with the Gramm-Rudman Law) and looser monetary policy. The U.S. government policy was designed to make U.S. firms (or for that matter, any production facilities located in the United States) more competitive by depreciating (lowering) the U.S. dollar's foreign exchange value. This move aimed to eventually spur U.S. exports (making them cheaper to foreigners) and retard U.S. imports (making them more expensive in the United States), thereby reducing the massive trade deficit.

Our model predicts that there is a natural tendency for a nation trapped in dual vicious circles of deficits and debts to eventually print money and incur a depreciating (losing value) currency. How might this occur? First, surging international deficits and debt could lead foreign exchange traders to sell a nation's currency, thereby causing it to depreciate. Second, the need to finance massive government deficits, magnified by the interest payments required to service a swelling debt level, could eventually lead the government to print money.

In the case of the United States, during the mid-1980s we resorted to large increases in the money supply, as well as in U.S. Treasury securities, in order to finance the deficit. This printing of money could engender inflationary implications, as we saw in the United States after 1986.[11] Hoping to forestall accelerating inflation, the U.S. monetary authorities tightened money and credit, boosting interest rates from mid-1987 well into 1989. Recession ensued in 1990–91, leading to a new round of expansionary monetary policy and declining interest rates. This easing of monetary policy again began to engender inflationary expectations; in any event, it helped lead to new lows in the U.S. dollar's average foreign exchange value by 1992–94 (particularly against Europe's "hard currencies" such as the German mark and Swiss franc). Once again, hoping to forestall inflation, the U.S. Federal Reserve boosted interest rates in 1994 and early 1995. Large capital losses were incurred on long-term U.S. Treasury securities, as increased interest rates implied falling bond prices. Even the increased U.S. interest rates could not stop the dollar from hitting new lows versus Japan's yen in spring and summer 1995, as the U.S. merchandise trade deficit with Japan stayed stubbornly, and to many observers and foreign exchange traders, rather surprisingly, near $60 billion. Fortunately, the U.S. trade deficit with Japan did decline (improve) after that, as U.S. exports were boosted by the super-cheap dollar. Also, the dollar stabilized, rising significantly against the yen during the second half of 1995 through early 1997, before flattening out.

What will the future bring, from the perspective of the dual vicious circles model? Obviously, it all depends on the future course of U.S. government fiscal (and, perhaps to a lesser extent, monetary) policy. Perhaps because he perceived the increasingly "vicious circle" momentum building in the U.S. federal budget accounts, Ross Perot made fiscal policy a major issue in the 1992 presidential campaign. President Clinton had little choice but to make the U.S. federal deficit a central preoccupation of his first administration. By 1995, Republicans were a majority in Congress and pushed for a "balanced budget amendment." Sadly, the 1996 Presidential campaign seemed to generate more rhetoric (and potentially dangerous tax cut promises) than action to deal with the reality of our burgeoning debt. Robert Dole tried to resuscitate his unsuccessful candidacy in 1996 by proposing a 15% income tax cut, while not specifying spending cuts. This did not raise his low standing in opinion polls: a healthy sign, perhaps, that the American people are finally cognizant of the long-term damage of policies that would exacerbate the federal government deficit. However, the bipartisan plan to eventually eliminate the federal deficit passed in 1997 seems rather "front-end loaded" with tax cuts. Politically expedient no doubt, but this plan may repeat some mistakes made in the early 1980s—mistakes that helped ignite our current vicious circle debt trap, a negatively reinforcing system.

IMPLICATIONS OF THE U.S. "DUAL VICIOUS CIRCLES" MODEL

The major ramification of this "dual vicious circles, model" is that if a process of debt accumulation is allowed to continue long (or pile high!) enough, the process can take on a life of its own. Huge servicing payments on the massive debt practically guarantee future deficits, as the interest payments swamp the budget, furthering the debt accumulation process. This original model may suggest to readers that, eventually, a vicious circle of *international* deficits and debt could push the dollar's foreign exchange value down further, while federal government debt accumulation could lead to inflationary increases in the U.S. money supply. Figure 7–3 hints that a potential third vicious circle, exhibited previously in many poor debtor nations, may assert itself: a feedback between domestic price inflation and declines in the foreign exchange value (purchasing power abroad) of the nation's currency.

The main implication of this and my conclusion: Americans may want to diversify some of their wealth into investments in foreign assets and currencies. Having recommended this, I will offer some hints as to the "how" and "why" of personal global investing in the concluding section of this chapter. Meanwhile, the next section portrays how firms should likewise diversify themselves away from a strict reliance on the U.S. market, by adopting a time-phased global strategy for expansion. The upshot of the above model is that both firms and individuals should see the wisdom of investing in less debt-trapped foreign markets.

What of policy implications? The only hope for the United States is to stop talking about balanced budget amendments (or front-end loading tax cuts in "plans to balance the budget by 2002") and actually take some actions *now* to reduce the growth in federal government gross debt. Given the massive and rapidly increasing interest-payments-to-service-government-debt component of federal expenditures, serious action is needed. To break the dynamics of dual vicious circles of debt in the U.S. case will probably eventually require both tax increases (sorry, I do not like them either) and cuts in more areas of government expenditure (such as entitlement spending). Given that massive U.S. trade deficits are partly caused by low savings rates in the United States relative to other major trading nations, increased consumption taxes that would twist the tax structure to favor efforts to grow income and to save and invest would help. This could be accomplished through a value-added tax (VAT), as is relied upon by European nations, or a national sales tax, partly offset by decreased taxation of income or savings.[12]

Of course, it is much easier for politicians to talk about balanced budget amendments, or what the *next* Congress and administration will do, than it is to cut spending on entitlements or to raise consumption taxes. This is why I encourage the prudent firm or person to begin learning about a globally diversified investment strategy. We now turn to such strategies.

A. TIME-PHASED GLOBAL STRATEGY FOR BUSINESS EXPANSION

The first section of this chapter showed that a market reliance solely on the U.S. economy, despite its many strengths, is risky because of cumulating foreign and federal debt burdens. In addition, Chapter 3 showed us that a market reliance on the United States ignores more than 95% of the world's people. Fortunately for business expansion strategy, many of these non-U.S. residents are gaining purchasing power and viability as future customers, as discussed in Chapters 5 and 6. Thus, for many U.S. firms, a global expansion strategy seems the clear route to sustainable and significant growth in the 21st century.

My advocacy of a global expansion strategy does not imply, however, that predominantly domestically oriented firms should try to "go global" all at once. Most firms do not command the financial or human resources needed to succeed in hundreds of new markets spread over distant continents at this time. A lack of focus would dilute resources and return only disaster. I do advocate gradually developing a more global business structure, with regard to both new customer markets and new production sites, by sequentially implementing a time-phased global strategy for business expansion.

Essentially, a firm embracing a time-phased strategy will take discreet steps toward global expansion; sequencing the steps every few years as potential-market regions develop sufficiently. In so doing, the firm does not waste money investing in an emerging region prematurely. In addition, the firm will have time to absorb the expansion and to develop its resource base sufficiently before taking on other regions.

Clearly, the time-sequencing pattern may differ depending on the industry. However, after examining a variety of U.S. firms that are implementing global expansion strategies, I find that a common time-phasing pattern seems useful for many industries.

1. TO THE TRIAD AND BEYOND

First, any domestically oriented firm hoping to grow should not ignore the basic lesson of Chapter 1: most of the world's wealth is concentrated in a triad of wealthy nations. Indeed, the 20th century will end with the vast majority of purchasing power still concentrated in North America, Europe, Japan, and the four Asian "Tigers" (NICs). Thus, the first step beyond the United States should be to develop markets in similarly affluent nations such as Canada, Japan, Hong Kong, Taiwan, and those of Western Europe.

Residents of the non-U.S. parts of the triad have sufficient purchasing power to be of interest to many industries that sell relatively expensive items, including information and computing products, high-end transportation equipment, graduate and executive education, financial services, medical diagnostic equipment, and health care products. An excellent example of a "take the triad now" strategy is the massive expansion of leading U.S. investment banks into Europe and East Asia. Another example is the historical focus of the "Big Three" U.S. auto manufacturers on Canada and Western Europe, combined with a recent push into East Asia. Moreover, we saw in Chapter 2 that the triad itself is in the process of market growth, as all three legs regionally expand further. The current fascination of the auto industry with some of the key areas for triad extension, such as Brazil, Eastern Europe, China, and Thailand, clearly illustrates this point.

Conclusively, then, the first step toward global extension is to consider the wealthy and historically largest markets for U.S. goods and services: North America, the European Union, and Japan. Canada, in particular, remains a huge market for U.S. firms. Meanwhile, Hong Kong and its fellow NICs, Taiwan and Singapore, also represent markets boasting living standards comparable to our own.

2. LATIN AMERICA EMERGES AS A BUSINESS PRIORITY

Beyond the triad, the next step for many U.S. firms will be Latin America. Indeed, many firms are already in Mexico. As a result of its NAFTA membership, large population, and close proximity, Mexico has surged ahead of all nations, save Canada and Japan, as a U.S. export market. Mexico has made serious progress toward free-market economic reform, and important initial movements toward political and electoral reform. Thus, firms not already in Mexico should consider it a priority possibility for near-term expansion.

Second, at least three nations in South America have sufficient scale and/or speed, with regard to economic development, to warrant serious strategic consideration. Many U.S. businesses are already focusing their expansion on the "ABC" countries of South America: Argentina, Brazil, and Chile (or Colombia, depending on the industry). Chile is the most economically advanced; so despite a relatively small population, it has been able to attract many firms. For example, The Home Depot made Chile its first step outside of North America. Argentina combines a good-sized population with quite promising economic progress, under the market-opening and stabilizing reforms initiated by President Carlos Menem. Brazil is the demographic giant of Latin America, and as economic reforms begin to open up its potential market of over 160 million people, a range of U.S. firms have moved it to the front burner. For example, firms in financial or credit-related industries, such as Equifax and Total Systems Services, as well as firms in basic manufacturing, such as Southwire, have visionary leadership (Tom Chapman, Jim Blanchard, and Roy Richards, Jr., respectively) that recognizes Brazil's middle-class customer market could grow explosively during the next decade.

Data that can support Latin America as the likely next step for many U.S. firms' expansion strategy is provided by the World Bank in *World Development Indicators 1997*. In its own summary of big emerging markets, the World Bank lists (p. 129) the ten largest economies in the developing world, three of which are in Latin America. Crucial for our strategy, these nations appear to have the purchasing power *now* (converting to U.S. dollars using actual market exchange rates) to become major markets and sources of profits for firms' consolidated income statements. Indeed, converting to dollars using market exchange rates, Brazil has the second largest economy in the developing world, Mexico the fifth, and Argentina the sixth.[13] Furthermore, a key strategic element is that many industries require at least lower-middle-class consumers, and Latin America is in the process of adding millions of these potential customers. Its lead in purchasing power is demonstrated by *per capita* GDP statistics, where Argentina leads all ten of the largest developing nations, and Mexico and Brazil rank in the top four.

Critically, Latin American leaders appear to have learned from past mistakes, and are now stabilizing their economies with widespread economic reforms. Research conducted at the Inter-American Development Bank, led by chief economist Ricardo Hausmann and lead research economist Michael Gavin, was highlighted in an article entitled "In Latin American Economy, Fiesta-or-Famine Cycle May Be a Thing of the Past."[14] The article noted that:

> Analysts are talking up the notion that Latin economies have undergone a "secular change" that will smooth out volatility and raise long-term growth rates. Heeding the call, investors are pouring money into what has already been a booming market.

3. AFTER LOOKING SOUTH, LOOK WEST NEXT: TO EAST, THEN SOUTH ASIA

We saw in Chapter 6 that Asia will be hard to miss as a key to global expansion strategy. Indeed, four of our projected Six Great Regional Economies will be Asian, and three of those will be East Asian. Clearly then, most industries should turn their focus to East Asia, perhaps right

FIRM SPOTLIGHT
BellSouth Expands Further South

BellSouth, the largest of the original "baby Bells," perceived more than a decade ago that global expansion was a wise route to growth, given its regulated domestic market. To achieve global expansion, BellSouth recruited Mylle Bell Mangum, a leading global businesswoman featured in our next chapter, to be the founding president of its BellSouth International (BSI) division. Rather than expand globally all at once, BSI has always focused on selected markets—choosing those with consumers likely to have enough purchasing power to become telephone customers. Markets chosen for expansion included Australia, Mexico, Western Europe, Israel, and increasingly, South America.

Recently, BellSouth, under the leadership of CEO Duane Ackerman and current BSI President Charles "Buddy" Miller, has honed its time-phased global strategy. While doing business in the above-mentioned places, and positioning itself for eventual large-scale expansion in Asia, BellSouth is a prime example of a U.S. firm succeeding with a southward focus, anticipating the extension of NAFTA into Latin America. BellSouth's strategy seems particularly sensible for two key reasons. First, telephone firms need markets with many potential customers who are at least reaching lower-middle-class incomes. Clearly, Latin America fits this bill, particularly given its encouraging economic growth prospects portrayed in Chapters 5 and 6.

Second, in the current intense competition for Latin America's telephone markets, employees that both understand the business *and* speak Spanish are a clear asset. This explains the growing success of Spain's phone company, Telefonica de España, in Latin America. Given that Florida is its largest market domestically, BellSouth also can draw upon a deep reserve of Spanish-speaking employees, many of whom are also bicultural. Thus, BellSouth's Hispanic employee base is a great asset to its expansion focus on Latin America.

BSI has been investing serious money in Latin America, and is already receiving positive net income flows from the region. A recent article summarizes this important stage in BellSouth's time-phased expansion strategy: "BellSouth Corp. continued its march across Latin America on Friday, winning its second Brazilian wireless license in two months with a $512 million bid. The Atlanta-based company, the most aggressive U.S. phone company in making Latin American investments . . . now has interests in nine of the region's countries, where demand for phones outstrips supply."[15]

after Latin American subsidiaries are established enough to generate cash flow.

One of the three East Asian forecast focal points, Japan, already has the purchasing power to support almost any product. A core member of the wealthy triad, Japan is a booming market for U.S.-made products. The decline of the U.S. dollar from its 1985 peak, combined with gradual but steady deregulation and market opening in Japan, has enabled U.S. exports of goods and services to flourish. U.S. total exports to Japan surpassed $100 billion in 1996, increasing more than three times from 1985. U.S. firms who exhibit patience and a willingness to understand the Japanese culture and market are growing profits. Japan's strategic importance to one industry was highlighted in the Spotlight in Chapter 5, which showed that firms in the U.S. travel and tourism industry would be wise to add Japan's huge and open market to their growth strategies.

Beyond Japan, the focal point of all global business may soon shift to the three potentially massive regional economies of Asia: Greater China, ASEAN, and India. We saw the evolution of these regional economies in Chapter 2, learned of their demographic potential in Chapter 3, analyzed their past world-leading economic growth in Chapter 5, and forecasted their economic potential in Chapter 6. Nearly 60% of the world's people currently *do,* and in the future *will,* live in Asia. Asian nations have the fastest economic growth rates on Earth, led by China, with its dramatic speed of economic development and top-ranked demographic scale. I once asked Robert Oxnam, a renowned expert on China who for many years was president of the Asia Society, if we now stand at the "dawn of the Asian century." He offered a critical insight for the next big stages of a time-phased global strategy:

> Never before has a region combined such great scale with such tremendous speed. This unique combination of scale (population) and speed (rapid economic growth) is most compelling in China. China, along with ASEAN and India, *must* be part of a global expansion strategy. Asia is so important in business strategies being formed even now that it is *not* "the dawn of the Asian century," it *is already* "mid-morning in the Asian century."[16]

4. LOOK TO THE HUMAN AND NATURAL RESOURCES OF AFRICA AND SOUTH AND CENTRAL ASIA

A glance back at Figure 5–4 reveals that Africa and the southern, central, and western regions of Asia contain very few truly middle-class consumers at this time. This huge area has tremendous population, but precious little purchasing power. Thus, only firms that have both great foresight and products that people with only a bit of disposable income can afford, are currently finding markets in the vast stretches of the Populous South. Coca-Cola is a prime example of such a company, as highlighted in Chapter 4's Spotlight. Nestlé would be another.

Sadly, the vast majority of people in this area are unable to purchase phones, let alone personal computers or Porsches. However, we saw earlier that economic reforms and a spread of capitalism are yielding some examples of success and hope for the future. Furthermore, our term "Modern-Day Fertile Crescent" was coined to remind us that this region will command a large and ever-growing share of the world's burgeoning population. The human resource potential of these presently poor regions is huge, which is why I advocate that firms at least put the Populous South onto their radar screens.

It is clear that in a time-phased strategy, the big investments *now* should be in the extended triad, that is, Latin America or East Asia (cheap now!), but firms can gain a first-mover advantage by scanning other parts of Asia and Africa for profitable investment opportunities. The strategic plan is to seek out future opportunities and future potential leaders in these emerging regions now, and to begin forming relationships that can grow dramatically in coming decades. Growth can emerge, as long as enduring and deep economic reforms stabilize the economies of Africa and non-East Asia. Engaging these nations now can catalyze a win-win strategy, in which the provision of needed capital, technology, and managerial capability can help these nations stabilize and grow. By solidifying market-opening economic reforms, this more stable economic growth can, in turn, lead to profits for the pioneering firms.

Two key features lead me to stress that firms ought to eventually find a place for Africa, the Middle East, and Central Asia in a time-phased global expansion strategy. First, the region has vast untapped human resources, people who want an opportunity to learn and obtain a better life. Second, the region has immense natural resources. The world's expected significant economic growth will require the mineral resources of Africa. In addition, the already intense dependence on this region for worldwide energy needs will deepen. While the oil of the Middle East is now a key fuel for global business, I predict that the vast oil and gas reserves of Central Asia (e.g., Kazakhstan) will become a major focal point. Indeed, these vast oil fields are already being coveted by the leading oil companies of the United States, Europe, Russia, and China. Thus, joint ventures and investments in the billions of dollars are taking place, even while geopolitical intrigue and possible struggles seem likely.

Concluding the strategic tour, I would like to stress that, despite Asia's current problems, most business expansion roads must eventually lead there. Chapter 6 made it clear that Asia is likely to resume its position as the "hot spot" for economic growth in the 21st century. This claim is validated by that continent's immense demographic scale, combined with its speed of economic progress. Paul Krugman, the prescient debunker of the notion of an "Asian miracle," concluded his recent article in *Fortune:*

> Asia's growth will probably resume, driven, as before, by education, savings, and growing labor force participation. It probably won't be as fast as it was. . . . But there are still a lot of peasants in China waiting to be pulled into the modern world, and there are even more in other places where the process of joining the modern world has barely begun. No doubt Asia will eventually account for most of gross world product—but only because most human beings are, after all, Asian.[17]

Readers wishing to learn more about how to implement a globalization strategy are referred to George S. Yip's book, *Total Global Strategy: Managing for Worldwide Competitive Advantage.*[18] This book analyzes an industry's particular globalization drivers, and links this analysis to the appropriate global strategy implementation.

THE CHANGING FACE OF THE U.S. COULD FUEL GLOBAL EXPANSION

A time-phased global strategy can work for U.S. firms and fuel their growth, but only if the United States can continue to compete and lead in the 21st century. To do so, we must learn to manage our firms and our lives in a way that truly respects and promotes the diversity of our own population. My own analysis reveals that the "face of the world" is changing dramatically, as portrayed in Chapter 3. The U.S. population, arguably more so than any other national population, will reflect future global diversity. Firms that can make this diversity an asset will prosper, while those that do not are likely to lose out, by missing potential leaders, workers, and customers.

Figure 7A-1 shows the base scenario projection for the U.S. population mix in the middle of the upcoming century.[19] Note its diverse nature: while non-Hispanic whites will still comprise a majority of U.S. population, 52% is a thin majority in dramatic contrast to this group's current 73% share. Most of this diminished share is attributable to the rapid growth of the U.S. Hispanic population, from 11% now to nearly one-quarter of our total population in 2050. Likewise, Asian-Americans gain significant share, rising from 4% today to nearly 9% in 2050. And the share of African-Americans is projected to rise from 12% currently to 15%.

The crucial point is that the "face of the United States" will mirror the "changing face of the world." Recall from Chapter 3 that world population shares are shifting inexorably toward Africa and parts of Asia; and that the population growth of the Americas is shifting steadily southward to Latin America. These major trends match the projected transition in the United States, where population shares are shifting toward Hispanic-Americans, African-Americans, and Asian-Americans, as non-Hispanic whites comprise a steadily shrinking share.

If we truly extend educational and employment opportunities to all, and work together productively through the appreciation of people from diverse backgrounds, we will gain a tremendous competitive advantage. Our firms can be uniquely situated to go out to world markets and credibly say "We understand and value your culture," because so many of us will have deep roots in African, Asian, or Latin American cultures. Contrast this with Japanese firms that are likely to continue having managerial teams and boards of directors dominated by Japanese men. The fit between global and U.S. demographic trends should make our diversity a source of strength— indeed, of sustainable competitive advantage. If we fail to learn to work together equitably, to manage diversity wisely, to respect and appreciate each

Figure 7A–1 MANAGING FOR DIVERSITY: A GLOBAL FIT
(U.S. Demographic Projection for Year 2050)

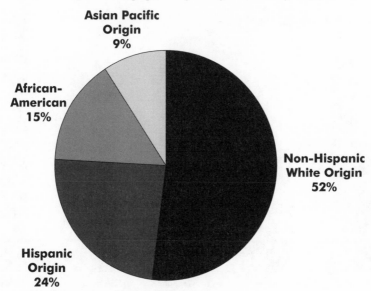

Data Source: U.S. Bureau of Census, *Current Population Reports*, 1997.

other, then we will lose the opportunity for global leadership. Our people can and should be our greatest asset in the implementation of a time-phased global strategy leading to successful business growth.

B: PERSONAL GLOBAL INVESTING STRATEGIES

This section highlights the rationale for and the route to a more global *personal* investment strategy. Earlier in Chapter 7, the dual vicious circles model implied that the U.S. financial system and the U.S. dollar are perhaps not such safe stores of value. Finance courses preach the value of diversification; that it never pays to hold all your eggs (assets) in one basket. A lack of diversification makes even less sense if you have a "leaky" basket: one backed, as the U.S. economy is now, by over $5.5 trillion of government debt and over $1 trillion of net foreign debt. Indeed, despite its partial recovery upward during 1996–97, the U.S. dollar has not been a good store of value over the last dozen years, or for that matter, the

Figure 7B–1   IS THE U.S. DOLLAR A SAFE STORE OF VALUE?
U.S. $ value in units of major foreign currencies, in 1997 compared to 1960 and 1985)

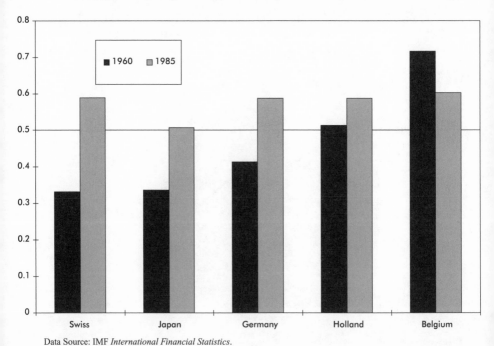

Data Source: IMF *International Financial Statistics.*

last two generations. Figure 7B–1 graphically illustrates how the dollar has lost tremendous value relative to the safer stores of value—specifically, the hard currencies of western continental Europe and Japan.

The first bar in Figure 7B–1 shows the average value of the U.S. dollar in 1997 (in terms of how many units of various foreign currencies the U.S. dollar could buy), compared to its exchange value in 1960. For instance, the first bar reaches to only 0.33, which means that in 1997 the dollar could only buy one-third as much of the Swiss franc as it could buy during 1960.[20] The second bar compares the amount of foreign currency units a U.S. dollar could buy in 1997 to the amount it could buy when the dollar hit its recent peak in 1985. Note that once again the dollar has lost close to half its value against other major currencies after its peak in 1985. Thus, the U.S. dollar has not been a good store of value either in the last dozen years or over the last few generations. What, then, is a U.S. investor to do?

Figure 7B–2 highlights the obvious strategy for U.S. investors or money managers. This figure, which I titled the "Power Curve of Global Investing," shows the expected return-versus-risk profile of portfolios that can be invested in various mixes of U.S. and foreign assets. Recall that many people call economics the "dismal science" because, in general, everything is a trade-off; "there is no such thing as a free lunch." The basic message is: if you want more of something good, you often lose on another dimension. Specifically, when considering finances and investments, people usually assume there is a trade-off of risk versus return. The higher the expected return we wish to achieve, the more risk we must assume, by investing in potentially faster-growing, but therefore riskier, assets. For example, growth stocks or junk bonds have a higher expected return than money sitting in an insured bank account, but the higher expected return assets are more risky. With a bank account the risk is minimized; you know exactly how much money you'll have at the end of the year.

The curve in Figure 7B–2 defies this usual trade-off and points to the value of a globally diversified investment strategy. We see that for much of the curve, there is the usual trade-off; that is, the usual upward-to-the-right or positive slope where a higher expected return implies more risk. However, note that a significant part of the curve slopes upward to the left, that is, it has a negative slope. This means that if you start at the bottom at point A, with a portfolio invested 100% in U.S. assets, you can actually improve on both dimensions by adding some global diversification to your investment strategy. "Improving on both dimensions" means that, by moving from point A to point B, you can have a higher expected return, while at the same time, lowering the risk or variance of your portfolio. For once, we break the cruel law of economics; here *is* a way to have a free lunch, to gain on both dimensions rather than trade off one versus the other.

Figure 7B–2   THE POWER CURVE OF GLOBAL INVESTING
(Improve both risk and return by diversifying globally)

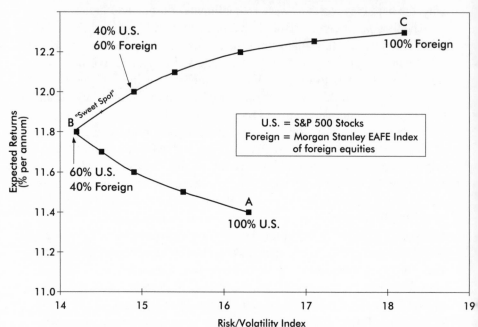

How can this magical outcome be possible? The insight is that point A, a purely domestic portfolio, is a very inefficient strategy. It is dominated by a more globally diversified strategy, such as those represented by portfolio mixes anywhere along the curve from point B to point C. Putting all your eggs in one basket, particularly in the U.S. economy (as in point A), is not a sensible strategy because it does not provide any of the basic gains available from diversification. Diversification generally yields the benefit of risk reduction, by protecting you if one economy or one industry or one stock in your portfolio happens to perform poorly. The insight from the earlier part of this chapter is that the U.S. basket may be leakier than many people think: the U.S. economy and the *dollar* are threatened by the massive debt accumulation in the government and the international accounts. Thus, in order to reduce the risk of our wealth portfolios, we should invest in some assets outside of the United States and/or the U.S. currency.

Furthermore, we saw in Chapter 5 that while the U.S. economy is growing faster than a few other advanced or mature economies, we are essentially confined to long-term real GDP growth rates of between 2% and 3%. Most forecasters see this rather stagnant U.S. growth trend continuing. By contrast, there are some very dynamic economies where growth rates between 7% and 9% have been achieved, and where, as we saw in Chapters 5 and 6, healthy, albeit decelerating, growth is likely. Thus, an investor may achieve a higher expected return on assets outside of the United States. Of course, the U.S. stock market achieved a record performance during 1995–1997. However, one reasonable conclusion is that the *future* bargains may be found in emerging markets.

The insight in this section is that American investors or money managers can break the dismal story line of much of economics. Rather than face a trade-off, investors can improve their likely future living standards by adopting an investment strategy that both increases their expected return and minimizes their risk. Obviously, the message is to begin to *globally diversify your wealth*—not all at once, and not to the risky point C, where all your investments are in foreign assets, but eventually to at least what I call the "sweet spot" of the global investing power curve—the range of portfolio mixes from point B up toward point C. Your position along that segment of the curve is determined by your own tolerance for risk. If you are young and do not mind a little risk in the hopes of ultimately achieving a higher average return, you can move further toward point C, perhaps even to a point of 60% foreign exposure, 40% U.S. exposure. On the other hand, if you are older or risk-intolerant, you should begin to move your portfolio toward point B, or 40% foreign involvement.

Any stock market could have good long-run characteristics, yet be subject to sharp downturns in the short run. Therefore, it is probably best to move toward a more globally diversified mix over time. I suggest buying into foreign assets as you learn more about them and find some you are comfortable with, as opposed to rushing into some foreign market without a good feel for whether it is one with imminent risk of a large downturn. Still, the basic logic of finance is that any stock or bond market can have an unexpected large downturn, including the U.S. market; thus it is unwise to leave all your assets in any one nation's market.

TOOLS TO DIVERSIFY YOUR INVESTMENTS BEYOND THE UNITED STATES[21]

Many Americans who do not have the time to analyze (or are suspicious of) foreign stock markets or foreign companies still try to gain some benefit of global diversification and some of the high expected returns of emerging markets by purchasing shares in U.S.-headquartered firms that are truly global in scope and sales patterns. Such investors often favor firms that seem very likely to participate in global growth, such as Intel, Microsoft, Hewlett-Packard, Motorola, Coca-Cola, McDonald's, Boeing, Citicorp, and

General Electric (perhaps even Chrysler as the Jeep becomes a status symbol for the emerging group of yuppies worldwide). Of course, many of these equities already trade at very high stock market valuations (i.e., price/earnings ratios) because the whole investing community recognizes these firms' excellent global strategies for growth.

Therefore, if you broaden your investments to companies headquartered around the world, rather than in the United States only, you will have a more truly diversified equity (stock) portfolio and higher potential gains. Adding firms that can grow fast in various rich or emerging international markets will enhance your portfolio return as well as lower your overall portfolio risk by providing more avenues for diversification. *How do we purchase shares in such promising foreign-based firms?* A number of approaches or tools are now readily available, even to the so-called "average investor." Let us examine the various instruments by which readers can invest more globally.

Direct Purchases

Anyone can directly invest in foreign stocks, provided that one's broker can execute the transaction. Most of the larger brokerage firms have overseas offices and are able to invest in many different stock markets around the world. However, transaction costs can be high and it may be difficult to obtain enough information to follow the investment. Also, because direct investments are made in the local currency, the return depends on exchange rate fluctuations in addition to the performance of the investment itself. These limitations apply to direct purchases of foreign bonds as well. Average citizens often have neither the money nor the time to acquire foreign currencies or to go poking around in foreign countries deciding exactly what stocks to buy. Thus, generally speaking, direct purchases are not an efficient way for the individual investor to invest internationally. Fortunately, we now have easier and more affordable methods to begin globally diversifying our own portfolios.

American Depository Receipts (ADRs)

ADRs are certificates issued by a U.S. depository, usually a bank, that represent ownership of foreign securities held by the depository. ADRs are traded on U.S. exchanges, and investments are made in U.S. dollars. Even though ADRs are quoted in dollars, exchange rate risk is not eliminated entirely, because exchange rate fluctuations will be reflected in the ADR's price. Another potential shortcoming is that many of the companies whose stocks are traded as ADRs are large multinationals, which are already past their growth stage. Small capitalization foreign stocks, which may offer some of the greatest growth potential, are generally not traded as ADRs.

In spite of these potential drawbacks, the number of ADRs listed on the New York, American, and NASDAQ stock exchanges has grown steadily. In 1997 alone, 245 firms launched ADR programs, with Citicorp estimating that 65% of the total $17 billion raised through ADRs during that period was for issues based in emerging economies.[22] Trading volume has also grown rapidly. Not all ADRs are listed, however, because listing requires adherence to U.S. Generally Accepted Accounting Principles (GAAP) standards and SEC disclosure requirements. Examples of ADRs that are popular investments for Americans include Sony, British Petroleum, Nokia, SmithKline Beecham, Honda, Telmex, and YPF (the Argentine oil company).

Closed-End Country Funds

Closed-end country funds invest in a portfolio of stocks of one particular country or region. They can be a convenient way for individual investors to buy foreign stocks. Closed-end funds are traded on the stock exchange in the same way that regular equities are traded. They are called "closed-end" because a fixed number of shares are issued. The fund's price is market-determined by the relative supply of and demand for shares of the fund, but it is ultimately dependent on the value of the fund's underlying assets (the net asset value or NAV). Also, exchange rate fluctuations will be reflected in the price. Significantly, closed-end funds often trade at a discount to their NAV, meaning that the shares can be purchased at a price below their underlying value.

I have found it personally advantageous to invest in closed-end country funds. My own rule is only to invest in funds under two conditions: (1) the fund's market price reflects at least a 15% discount to its underlying NAV, and (2) the fund invests in a country or region that has good growth prospects and stock markets that are not overvalued. For example, in the past I have prospered by investing in a single country fund for Mexico and one for Ireland. Of course, the usual disclaimer holds that we cannot use the past to predict future investment performance. You can find information on funds' discounts and the like in tables in *Barron's* weekly and in Monday's editions of the *Wall Street Journal* or the *New York Times*.

Open-End Mutual Funds

Open-end mutual funds provide the most convenient opportunity for the individual investor to invest abroad. There are global funds (but they may still contain many U.S. stocks), widely diversified international (non-U.S.) funds, funds specializing in specific regions, and funds specializing in specific countries. The price of an open-end fund is based on the net asset value per share, sometimes with an added sales charge called a "load." "No-load" mutual funds carry no sales charge and can be purchased directly from the fund distributor. My favorite funds are low fee, no-load, international index funds.

PERSONAL GLOBAL INVESTING SUMMARY

The aim of this section was to show you that diversifying your investment portfolio beyond U.S.-based securities should help you prosper well into the next century. Some readers may still fear investing in firms not based in this country, choosing instead to invest exclusively in the United States, but in assets that appear less risky than stocks, such as bonds, or in cash equivalents, such as money market funds. This, however, is not a wise strategy, as a total reliance on the U.S. dollar, even in so-called "safe" money market securities, was shown earlier in this chapter to involve substantial exchange rate risk. Even for Americans, who typically purchase items using U.S. currency, a total concentration of wealth in U.S. dollars leaves them subject to reduced purchasing power for the many imported goods and services they are likely to consume in the 21st century, if our burgeoning debt eventually leads to a further devaluation of the U.S. dollar. Figure 7B–1 showed us that the dollar has substantial exchange rate risk, as it has lost significant value versus other major currencies since 1960.

Most importantly, studies have always, and rather uniformly, shown that in the long run, investment in equities (stocks) yields a higher average return than investment in bonds or in money market securities. Again, a reliance on stocks may seem risky, but the insight we gain from Figure 7B–2, the "power curve of global investing," is that the risk can be reduced by global diversification of the portfolio. Many empirical studies have suggested the following rules of thumb are reasonable estimates of the long-run average annual return available to different investment strategies: 12% average return on globally diversified equities; 8% average return on U.S. bonds; 4% average return on U.S. money market or cash equivalents.

We will now look at the potential power of global equity investing. Many readers of this book are likely to be about 39 years old, as the U.S. baby boom peaked about that many years ago. Let us see how much money these readers may have at age 75 if they invest $10,000 now in three alternative investment. Recall from Chapter 5 the very useful "Rule of 72": divide the growth rate of any magnitude into 72 to see how many years it takes to double. Global equities, because they grow on average 12% per year, will double roughly every six years on average. This means that after 36 years, a normal scenario would imply that your retirement fund could double six separate times by the time you attain age 75. Doubling six times is an impressive geometric growth that means a magnitude ends up 64 *times* its starting amount. In other words, the $10,000 investment in global equities may grow to nearly two-thirds of a million dollars!

Meanwhile, investing exclusively in bonds will earn an investor 8% on average annually, or two-thirds the growth rate of global stocks. Over a lengthy time horizon, even small differences in growth rates compound to huge differences in final outcomes. Bonds that yield an 8% return double every nine years; in 36 years the bond investment has the opportunity to double four separate times under a normal scenario. This means the initial amount increases 16 times, for a tidy retirement sum of $160,000 by age 75. This is a nice growth over the original $10,000 investment, but note that it is only *one-fourth* of the money available under the global-equity-investing scenario.

Finally, the person relying only on money market accounts or other interest-bearing cash equivalents may have felt safe, but I fear he will feel relatively poor upon retirement. Growing 4% a year, these so-called safe investments will take a full 18 years to double. Consequently, the initial amount will only double twice before retirement, increasing by four times to a mere $40,000.

This chapter has shown that a true global diversification of your port-folio can help you reduce some risk and increase return. The person who starts saving early and invests in a globally diversified equity portfolio may likely, if the above scenario holds true, retire to a house on the beach. The only sure thing about leaving all your money in short-term U.S. dollar financial instruments is that your retirement fund will not buy you a house on the beach—it probably won't even buy you a small condo on a bus route to the beach 10 miles inland!

The major insight in this chapter is that, just as you would not put all your wealth in any one foreign currency or foreign stock market, there is no logic to putting all your eggs in the leaky basket of the debt-ridden U.S. dollar. The risk-reducing benefit of diversification is a fundamental prin-ciple of modern finance, and geographic or global diversification has become the new frontier of efficient investment strategies. Speaking of new frontiers, the next chapter will discuss strategies to enhance your *human capital* by preparing you for career success in the emerging global economy.

CHAPTER 8

TWENTY-FIRST CENTURY CAREER STRATEGY:

Becoming a Global Manager

The preceding chapter highlighted the need for firms to grow through a time-phased global strategy. The U.S. economy, although by far the world's largest national economy, is neither dominant enough nor likely to grow fast enough to justify a solely domestic focus. This chapter outlines and discusses the skills that will be needed by 21st century leaders—skills the reader must master to build a successful career as a global manager.

In spite of the fact that the economies of the United States and triad nations are expected to grow 3% or less annually, shareholders of most firms are demanding double-digit growth in earnings. Obviously, established firms with a large market share will have a difficult time achieving this growth rate in slow-growing domestic economies. For example, consider the telephone industry in the triad. With population in the triad nations growing slowly at best and actually declining in some places, and virtually every individual in these nations already possessing a telephone line, firms in this industry are unlikely to achieve double-digit growth if a domestic strategy alone is followed. Preceding chapters should have made it clear that such firms can achieve a higher growth rate only if they increasingly work overseas and focus their growth strategy toward more global diversification. This need to focus more globally hints at the type of young executives these major firms, even ones in the United States, are *now* hiring.

The irony, or perhaps the important lesson, of recent years is that even as headlines bemoan the fact that major firms are laying off tens of thousands of employees, MBA students from globally oriented business schools are being recruited and hired by these very same firms. A reasonable conclusion is that the new MBA hires must be bringing skill sets critically needed by these otherwise downsizing firms. This is indeed the case; firms are hiring executives who offer skills or experience that will help the companies grow in the more global, technologically linked market. Obviously, the "first draft choices" are executives who are comfortable doing business internationally; that is, they are both multilingual and multicultural (a distinction we will pursue later), as well as technically savvy.

Harvard Business School's authority on leadership, John P. Kotter, in his influential book *The New Rules,* observes that "a shift in what is required to succeed is being driven by many factors, none of which is more important than the globalization of markets and competition."[1] Thus, on page 57, Kotter states his New Rule #2: "to succeed, one must capitalize on the opportunities available in the faster-moving and more competitive business environment while avoiding the many hazards inherent in such an environment."

The main goal here is to study, analyze, and portray the skill sets and range of experiences needed by executives who are surviving, who will continue to survive, and who will ultimately prosper as future leaders of firms that are becoming more global. Today's leaders are comfortable operating in what we earlier portrayed as an emerging global economy. By examining the traits portrayed by these current leaders, the reader will essentially gain a road map for career success and personal leadership development.

This chapter relies heavily on personal observations and informal interviews I have conducted with many outstanding global leaders, primarily from business but also from politics, over the past nine years. I have had the opportunity to interact with and observe an unusually diverse set of leaders during my years at Emory University in Atlanta. As an Olympic city and a hub for travel, Atlanta has enabled Emory to attract great leaders to speak here through three main avenues: (1) our Business School dean has a speakers series that attracts roughly a half dozen top CEOs each year; (2) Emory had a Center for Leadership and Career Studies, founded and directed by former Professor Jeffrey Sonnenfeld, that garnered a reputation as the world's foremost "CEO college," attracting literally hundreds of CEOs to Emory each year; and (3) my "Global Perspectives" course, required for all Emory MBAs, based on a unique design that has integrated ultimately dozens of top global leaders in business and politics as distinguished lecturers. Knowing it could help my students and readers, but realizing that they may not have the same opportunity to interact with these visiting global leaders, I always ask our distin-

guished lecturers this question: "What are the skills and attributes or capabilities *you* look for in an individual when you have the opportunity to
promote or hire an executive?"

This chapter reflects a commonly held view that the best way to learn
about leadership is from role models—from observing current global
leaders. What do they look for when hiring managers? Not only what do
they publicly profess to believe in, but what distinguishing skills or talents
do these leaders themselves embody? Warren Buffett, in a recent Dean's
Lecture Series presentation at Emory, added a useful perspective on this
general theme: he has derived significant benefit in his life from having
role models, or what he more clearly described as "heroes." Some of
Buffett's heroes are his father, former Coca-Cola Company president
Donald Keough, and investment analyst guru Benjamin Graham. The
people described below have earned the title of hero or role model from
many cohorts of MBA students as well as young executives globally.

SmithKline Beecham's vice president and director of worldwide
recruitment and leadership planning, Lou Manzi, points out that there are
critical competencies—critical for a firm's success—that must be embodied in the people they hire and promote. Skills, or what we often term
competencies or capabilities, are what successful businesses are looking
to hire. No longer is it sufficient to have gone to the "right school" or to be
"our type of guy" or to "have a network" or to "be loyal and follow orders"
or whatever. SmithKline Beecham is not just replacing people but is
recruiting with the corporation's future needs, as driven by their strategic
intent, in mind. SmithKline Beecham is practicing "competency recruitment"—seeking out people with the specific competencies needed to
contribute to flexible teams that will be formed to achieve a firm's strategic vision. Manzi points out that the goal is to find people who will have a
positive impact, following the "i model" of competencies: intelligence,
interpersonal skill, innovation, initiative, and integrity.

More generally, what are the competencies of a future global manager
that top leaders currently personify or look for in their hires and promo-
tions? The eight competencies highlighted in Figure 8-1 are among the
most valuable I have seen during nine years of classroom visits by the
distinguished leaders who embody the various competencies.

First, and fortunately for us educators, global leaders still place great
emphasis on an education that is both broad and deep. The keys here are
the ability to think both *globally* and *strategically,* combined with a *multi-
functional* business education. Consider a situation in which a global business sends an executive to Bulgaria to open a new office. At first, there
may not be sufficient business opportunity to justify sending a whole
team, so the lone executive must be competent in a range of business func-

Figure 8–1   Learning from Global Leaders
Competencies of a Global Manager

---

1. **Broadly educated: trained to think strategically and globally**

   • Edwin Artzt, Former Chairman and CEO, Procter & Gamble
   • P. J. Patterson, Prime Minister of Jamaica

---

2. **Multicultural competence and sensitivity**

   • Daniel Amos, CEO, AFLAC
   • Ambassador Andrew Young

---

3. **Integrity, character, ethical values**

   • Former President Jimmy Carter
   • Bernie Marcus and Art Blank, Co-founders, The Home Depot

---

4. **Flexible, responsive, and able to move quickly**

   • Tom Johnson, CEO, Cable News Network (CNN)
   • M. Douglas Ivester, Chairman and CEO, Coca-Cola

---

5. **Personal attributes: energy, worldly appearance and manners**

   • Jan Leschly, CEO, SmithKline Beecham
   • The late Michael Manley, Prime Minister, Jamaica
   • Thomas Chapman, CEO, Equifax

---

6. **Communications and interpersonal skills**

   • Donald Keough, Chairman, Allen & Company, Inc.
   • Bernie Marcus, Co-founder and Chairman, The Home Depot
   • Jan Leschly, CEO, SmithKline Beecham

---

7. **Command of information systems and technology**

   • Jackie Ward, CEO, Computer Generation, Inc.
   • Mylle Bell Mangum, EVP, Carlson Wagonlit Travel
   • Nicholas Shreiber, President & CEO, TetraPak Americas
   • Derek Smith, CEO, ChoicePoint

---

8. **Fluency in several key languages**

   • Kazuo Chiba, Mitsui, former Japanese Ambassador to the U.K.
   • The late Roberto C. Goizueta, Chairman & CEO, Coca-Cola
   • Erik Vonk, CEO, Randstad Staffing Services

---

tions: finance, accounting, marketing, human resource management, and organizational strategy. Political leaders such as Jamaica's Prime Minister P. J. Patterson, as well as business leaders such as Edwin Artzt, former chairman and CEO of Procter & Gamble, display the depth of education that leads to a powerful ability to think both strategically and globally.

John Kotter emphasizes the growing importance of a quality education for anyone aspiring to future leadership: "Globalization has added significant new levels of complexity to decisions, and those able to handle that complexity increasingly seem to be individuals with a good education, often from excellent schools."[2]

The emerging, more global economy adds a powerful force that should inspire people to pursue both a deep and a broad education. The minimum investment for all individuals ought to be a full college education. Not surprisingly, the relative incomes of low-skilled laborers are falling compared to college-educated workers (see below), and this trend will continue. Emerging nations in the global economy have an almost infinite supply of low-skilled labor willing to work for very modest wages, and this force will be able to compete very effectively against low-skilled workers in the United States. The picture is not completely bleak, however, because as emerging global economies grow, there will be a corresponding rise in huge markets for the products and especially the services yielded by workers with an excellent college education. It is universally acknowledged that the United States still has the world's best university system.

Studies clearly show that there has always been an earnings disparity in the United States, with college graduates earning much higher incomes than those with less formal education. The Research Department of the Federal Reserve Bank of Cleveland summarizes the evidence on the high returns given by college education: "In the early 1960s, the median earnings of a person who continued past college were about 1.6 times more than those of an individual with less than 4 years of high school. By 1993, that gap had more than doubled."[3]

Indeed, those Americans with more than four years of college now earn three times the income of their compatriots who did not finish high school. Further, they earn almost twice as much as Americans who completed between one and three years of college, but did not finish their college degrees. The Federal Reserve Bank of Cleveland's report goes on to state: "For females, the difference is larger yet. Note also that the disparity is still increasing for both of these groups. For blacks and women, the wage premium due to education is greater than it is for white males." Thus, education at the college level is a minimum competency a future global leader must pursue. An advanced degree from a highly regarded globally oriented business school will greatly enhance the career and professional reputation of any executive.

The second competency is multiculturalism. As discussed before, the area of rapid growth for many firms will be among the over 95% of the world's people not living in the United States, and thus, a premium will be placed on adding new executives who are multiculturally competent. This competency entails an understanding and appreciation of cultures beyond one's own, with a sensitivity to cultural and political nuances. Two leaders who both stress this and personify it are Ambassador Andrew Young and Daniel Amos, CEO of AFLAC.

Former mayor and U.N. ambassador Andrew Young played a critical role in Atlanta's successful bid to win and host the Centennial Olympic Games. He then chaired the committee that the city formed to oversee the Games. The respect held for Ambassador Young by leaders throughout the developing world, particularly but not exclusively in Africa, was a key element of his success. Andrew Young always demonstrates his multicultural competence and sensitivity, in venues ranging from his central role in the memorial service held after the tragic bombing in Centennial Olympic Park, to my Emory classroom where he held students enthralled and answered questions informally well after the class officially ended.

Daniel Amos, CEO of AFLAC, an insurance company based in Columbus, Georgia, also demonstrates multicultural competency. AFLAC has been described by the *New York Times* as one of the most successful U.S. companies at doing business in Japan. Roughly 80% of its profits and asset base typically come from AFLAC's Japanese subsidiary. The global record of outstanding market penetration and growth that AFLAC has achieved in Japan is well recognized. This record derives from the understanding of and sensitivity to the unique cultural and political traditions of Japan that have been carefully demonstrated by CEO Daniel Amos and his predecessor, John Amos. Profits flowed only after years of patience during which trusting relationships and mutual understanding were given time to develop.

It is hard to overstate the importance of multicultural capability for future success in increasingly global business. Readers wisely desiring to deepen their knowledge of the cultural dimension of international business should read the book with that title by Gary P. Ferraro.[4] Particularly, his chapter 8, "Developing Global Managers," contributes a useful look at themes and competencies similar to those portrayed here, as well as a focus on the importance of cross-cultural training. For example, Ferraro details the importance of flexibility, which we approach in our own way as our fourth competency (discussed below).

Third, a global manager must demonstrate strong integrity. Leaders are necessarily people who operate from a solid base of ethical values. The importance of this competency has been demonstrated repeatedly by former President Jimmy Carter. President Carter's work on behalf of human rights, democracy, and development throughout the world speaks for itself. The success of The Home Depot owes a great deal to the ethical values infused and embodied by its co-founders, chairman Bernie Marcus and CEO Arthur Blank. The Home Depot's rapid and principled response to the suffering caused by Hurricane Andrew or by the tragic bombing in Oklahoma City are two such examples. All three of these leaders speak eloquently to business executives and students of the need for ethics in business. Their actions in the community also testify to the depth of their concern for diverse stakeholders. Warren Buffett is another great leader who both stresses and personifies the importance of an ethical character for business success.

Fourth, people hoping to succeed in business as it increasingly globalizes will find a correspondingly increasing emphasis placed on a trait best termed *flexibility.* Firms hire and promote individuals who are responsive to the rapidly changing nature of our business world, and who are willing and able to move quickly. Lack of flexibility due to geographic or other self-imposed restrictions will increasingly limit professional growth opportunities.

Both Coca-Cola and CNN are examples of organizations demonstrating extraordinary flexibility in building and maintaining a global presence. Coca-Cola chairman and CEO M. Douglas Ivester, along with his precedessor, the late Roberto Goizueta, helped pioneer a new strategic vision within the global corporation. To succeed globally, organizations must be capable of fast reaction to external forces. The Coca-Cola annual report of 1990, particularly Goizueta's message to shareholders, is a must read for its discussion of how flexibility may be replacing the ability to manage complexity as the key organizational competency. CNN has used this competency to gain global competitive advantage over its less flexible traditional broadcast network television competitors. Tom Johnson, a journalist and businessman who is the CEO of CNN, stresses that network's flexibility and fast response time as one of the keys to its global success.

Fifth, a global manager must display personal attributes such as high energy level and professional appearance and manners. These attributes will facilitate doing business in any culture. SmithKline Beecham CEO and former tennis champion Jan Leschly personifies, as well as emphasizes, the importance of physical fitness, which provides an executive with the capability and energy to enthusiastically pursue opportunities on a global scale (see Leader Spotlight box).

Thomas F. (Tom) Chapman, CEO of Equifax, is another leader who embodies great energy and charisma. He is an impressive public speaker, a visionary leader who exudes the presence and stamina of a star athlete. Indeed, Tom Chapman was a professional baseball player! Yet another great leader who personified worldly appearance, manners, and energy is the late Michael Manley, the former prime minister of Jamaica. He was widely seen as perhaps the most eloquent voice of the Third World during the 1970s and 1980s. Manley's intelligence, concern for the welfare of all people, and charisma made him a compelling leader over many decades.

LEADER SPOTLIGHT
CEO Jan Leschly of SmithKline Beecham

Jan Leschly, the CEO of SmithKline Beecham, is credited with building SmithKline into one of the world's leading health care companies. He is truly a global executive—jetting each month between dual headquarters offices in London and Philadelphia. One reason for the merger of SmithKline Beckman of Philadelphia and Beecham of London was to achieve global scale, so necessary in the pharmaceutical industry which is characterized by huge fixed costs for research and development. Jan Leschly has enhanced the global status of his firm by maintaining headquarters on each of the two major continents for his industry. Mr. Leschly believes passionately in the need for a global strategy and in the benefits from building global scale; he has actually been involved with two of the pharmaceutical industry's megamergers, as earlier he had served as president of Squibb and helped lead its merger with Bristol-Myers.

In addition to a very successful business career, Jan Leschly achieved greatness as an athlete as well. As one of the world's top ten tennis players in the late 1960s he led Denmark's Davis Cup team and played in sixteen straight Wimbledon tournaments. Leschly achieved a feat rare in today's society—the combination of a world-class education with degrees in pharmacology and business administration, and top professional athlete status.

I choose Leschly as a role model here, but I cannot claim any originality on that score. Leading publications also identify him as a notable global leader. A major profile of Leschly was published in *The Financial Times of London*,[5] and *Business Week* identified Leschly as one of the best managers in a feature article on top global leaders.[6]

Leschly can not only attest to the qualities needed by a global leader

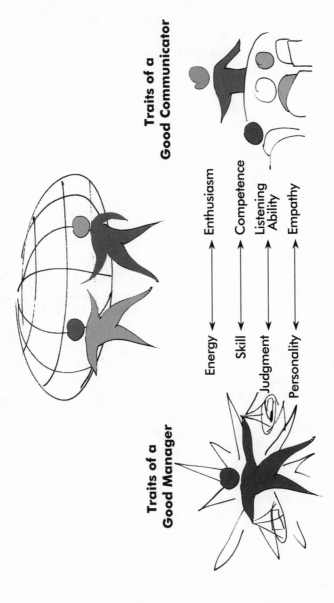

Figure 8–2   GLOBAL LEADERS EMBODY TRAITS COMMON TO GOOD MANAGERS AND GOOD COMMUNICATORS

Traits of a Good Communicator

Traits of a Good Manager

Energy ———→ Enthusiasm

Skill ———→ Competence

Judgment ←——→ Listening Ability

Personality ←——→ Empathy

Sources: Jan Leschly, CEO, SmithKline Beecham; Professor Jag Sheth, Goizueta Business School; Bernie Marcus, Chairman, Home Depot.

based on his own experiences, but also, he has had to think deeply about the capabilities needed by successful executives in the future, as he has promoted at least 16 executives to senior management (they report directly to him) since assuming the helm at SmithKline Beecham. Leschly maintains consistently that he looks for four things when interviewing management candidates: energy, intellectual skill, good judgment, and interpersonal skill. These four traits are summarized on the left side of Figure 8–2. These crucial indicators of management potential cannot be found merely on a résumé, they must be personally embodied and demonstrated in interviews and in performance.

The first trait is energy. Managers in a global enterprise need a high energy level, as they may often need to fly all night and then work effectively all day. One way to demonstrate this is with energetic enthusiasm. Leschly highlights what I've heard repeatedly from CEOs: a positive attitude as shown by genuine enthusiasm is a necessary trait for any individual reporting to them.

Leschly also looks for intellectual skill. This presupposes an education of sufficient depth and breadth, but goes beyond a knowledge base. A leader must constantly demonstrate the ability to understand, analyze, and resolve complex issues or problems. Increasingly, in this information age, a leader must have the intellectual skill not only to find and analyze data, but also to sift rapidly through the overwhelming amounts of information available.

The third trait is hard to measure, yet critical for business success. Leschly looks for individuals capable of exercising good judgment. A résumé can list degrees and awards, but a business ultimately needs leaders able to consistently make sound judgments and to exercise an uncommonly high level of common sense. In order to assess this trait, Leschly might probe in an interview to see if a candidate has enough judgment to respect and listen to various people: customers and secretaries as well as top executives.

Finally, an effective manager needs good interpersonal skills. A personality type that can motivate others and earn their respect is essential, because the best managers are those that others want to follow.

Jan Leschly is one of the most popular and respected business leaders regularly visiting university campuses. What the students always admire is his personal balance, including his commitment to his family and to his employees, customers, and shareholders. In essence, students find Leschly an ideal role model because he can talk about a global vision and the attributes needed to prosper in the emerging global economy, and obviously, he also "walks" this great talk.

Sixth, it is hard to overstate the importance of competency in communication as well as interpersonal skills. The ability to communicate well with people, through listening, speaking, and writing capability, is absolutely necessary for success as a manager, particularly in global business. Communication skills are even more crucial for leaders: global executives such as Bernie Marcus or Jan Leschly can articulate strategic visions for their firms that motivate top individuals to join their teams and work creatively together to achieve the vision they communicate so clearly. In the past one might hear someone say "He's a good manager, he just doesn't enjoy speaking up or communicating." But in our current globally linked business environment, one must be able to communicate easily and clearly, both orally and verbally, if one is to obtain leadership opportunities.

What makes a good communicator? The Home Depot is nearly unique in having two great communicators, chairman Bernie Marcus and CEO Arthur Blank, at the top. These two have instilled a corporate culture of skilled listening whereby top executives listen to their employees and customers, and in turn, all employees (called associates) listen carefully to their customers' needs before empowering them with "do it yourself" solutions. Bernie Marcus and Arthur Blank have shown that the ability to truly listen is the necessary trait of a good communicator. This message is clearly communicated throughout The Home Depot, to the roaring approval of shareholders as well as the retail home improvement market. We can see a two-way link between the critical communication trait identified by Bernie Marcus—listening ability—and that identified by Jan Leschly in being an effective manager—judgment (see Figure 8–2). It is a demonstration of good judgment to listen well to diverse people, while listening and learning is one sure way to develop judgment, including common sense.

What are the other traits of a good communicator? My colleague, Professor Jagdish Sheth, who has won awards as the world's leading marketing professor, has researched this important issue and unearthed three additional traits: enthusiasm, competence, and empathy. Figure 8–2 illustrates how these three traits can also be mapped to the corresponding traits of a good manager. Jan Leschly looks for enthusiasm as a necessary sign of a high energy level. Competence corresponds closely to intellectual skill, an able intelligence combined with knowledge. Finally, empathy is often the result of an open and accepting personality, including a pleasing sense of humor and the ability to laugh at oneself.

The importance of empathy (including the ability to listen carefully and attentively) not only in great communication, but also in leadership success, is receiving wider notice. For instance, in 1996, *Fortune* magazine focused one issue on "A Complete Guide to Your Career."[7] A feature on the importance of executives' "emotional intelligence" highlighted the significance of empathy, defining it as the ability to see life as somebody else sees it. One expert even called empathy "a fundamental skill of management."[8]

Interpersonal skills are an important component of good communication. Often, a good indicator of the type of attractive and resilient personality needed in global business is a sense of humor. The ability to laugh with others, make others laugh, and laugh at yourself clearly aids in surviving and even enjoying the rigors of international business. Consider a leader evaluating a potential hire who will be accompanying her on trips to South Africa someday. The individual with an attractive personality and a good sense of humor clearly will gain an edge as the leader contemplates the long flights required as part of a truly global business strategy. A current top executive at Coca-Cola once shared with me a keen insight regarding personality. When Coke's legendary former leader the late Robert Woodruff said that a young executive "seems to be a solid person, but he has no sense of humor," it could be taken essentially as a "kiss of death." That individual could expect to rise no further in the Coca-Cola ranks, and indeed was often eventually let go. Robert Woodruff was clearly ahead of his time; his sentiments are now echoed by many who have followed the trail he blazed in focusing his firm on the global market.

Donald Keough is the chairman of Allen & Company, Incorporated, and was a long-term president of Coca-Cola during its heyday of global growth. Allen & Company was portrayed in a *Forbes* cover story as a creative, powerful, and unique investment bank.[9] Keough's ability to be a great leader in such diverse businesses derives from his wonderful communication skills and his capacity to form and maintain meaningful personal relationships. One striking testament to Keough's personal character and depth is the tribute paid him by Warren Buffett, who described Keough as one of his heroes.

Thus, global managers, particularly future leaders, must be good communicators. Fortunately, communication skills are not just a gift of birth; we can all work to improve our skills. Particularly, we can constantly strive to *listen* more attentively, and we can gain empathy by working to understand others' cultures and putting ourselves into the shoes of diverse people.

Seventh, a ready command of technology, particularly information systems technology, is a competency highly valued in global managers. Nicholas Shreiber is the president and CEO of TetraPak Americas. The firm has a decentralized structure where leaders such as Shreiber run multibillion dollar businesses in large regional areas (e.g., the Americas).

Shreiber is a global business leader and strategist, yet he is also an expert in information and communication technologies. He keeps informed of recent developments and potential applications of such technologies. Shreiber makes a forceful case that managers of the future must be personally competent in these productivity-enhancing technologies. Peter Sealey, former director of global marketing for Coca-Cola, once stated that managers will be at a competitive disadvantage if they rely on a "technology chauffeur."

Mylle Bell Mangum is another top global manager who both stresses and personifies a competency for the emerging information technologies. She is the executive vice president of Carlson Wagonlit Travel, and a former president of the Committee of 200, a group of leading business-women worldwide. She was the founding president of BellSouth International. While a leader at Holiday Inn Worldwide, she brought her knowledge of communication technologies to the hotel chain. The firm had always seen itself as having a competitive advantage in the business of providing hotel rooms. Mangum's role was to secure a competitive advantage in a global reservations and information system, comprising the latest useful technologies and applications. Her strategy and skill helped transform Holiday Inn from what was essentially a real estate firm into essentially an information firm.

Jackie Ward has leveraged her deep knowledge of information systems and technologies into a highly successful career as the CEO of Computer Generation. This firm is growing strongly thanks to its global orientation. Indeed, Jackie Ward's combination of technical skill and experience with a truly global vision proved the right mix for Computer Generation, but is also valued beyond her firm. After a very successful stint as vice chair—international for the Metro Atlanta Chamber of Commerce, she became the first woman ever to chair this national-award-winning chamber in 1997.

Derek Smith rose to become the president and CEO of ChoicePoint by age 42, thanks largely to his successful blend of technical abilities and superb interpersonal skills. He has a degree in computer science as well as an MBA, and is pursuing a doctorate researching the impact of technological innovation. And like Jan Leschly, Derek Smith focused on a useful education while excelling in sports—he played football for Joe Paterno at Penn State.

Developing at least some command of information systems and technology is needed by any future executive. Of course, becoming a true expert in technology—for instance, becoming a software developer or systems designer—can lead to a secure and lucrative career path in our current more information-technology linked global economy. An interesting article in the

Wall Street Journal pointed to the premium placed on potential employees who can master new technologies[10]: "Demand for high-tech workers, already strong, has intensified . . . touching off recruiting wars for techies that resemble the scramble for big-time basketball prospects." The article points out that those with the skills in demand can prosper even in a generally gloomy job market for middle managers and other professionals: "In an era of downsizing, the hiring craze in technology provides a counterpoint to the often bleak assessments of the current economic recovery's power to produce jobs, particularly high-paying ones."

Finally, no list of competencies for globally oriented executives is complete without stressing fluency in several key languages. Obviously, English is the primary language of global business and many managers are able to "get by" with only English. Further, referring back to earlier key attributes such as communication ability and the ability to think strategically and globally, it is more important to have something meaningful to say in one language than to speak fluently but mindlessly in many. Nevertheless, an ability to speak an important language or two besides English is a clear asset. Becoming fluent in Spanish or Chinese will maximize the reader's attractiveness to increasingly global businesses, as Chapter 6, Six Great Economies of the 21st Century, clearly revealed.

Recall that the Americas, if the region integrates as we suggest in Chapters 2 and 6, could become the world's leading regional economy. Spanish, therefore, would be a very useful second language for readers who now speak only English. And Spanish fluency will pay tremendous dividends within the United States, as early in the 21st century this nation will contain over 30 million primarily Spanish-speaking residents. Clearly, a business person who speaks Spanish as well as English will have a definite advantage in this hemisphere.

The six great economies model also highlighted the central importance of East Asia for any future business strategy. China will become the largest of these Asian economies, particularly when one looks at a "greater China economic area." Thus, the model offers compelling reasons to start studying Mandarin Chinese. Chinese is a difficult language for native English speakers, for whom Spanish will come much quicker. However, for people willing to spend the time, an ability to be even somewhat fluent in Mandarin Chinese will be a key differentiating asset in the job search process.

Many schools in the United States geared up during the last decade or so to teach French and Russian. French used to be considered a global language, at least for diplomacy, and Russia was seen as the other superpower in the world. Our earlier analysis suggested that Russia is no longer a superpower from a political standpoint, and from a business standpoint, it may not even be a viable economy. Thus, my own economic models have clear implications for school systems throughout the United States: give students the opportunity to learn Spanish or Chinese, preferably starting in kindergarten. French, Russian, and even German or Japanese are useful as well, but not as primary options.

Two truly multilingual leaders are Erik Vonk and Kazuo Chiba. Erik Vonk, the CEO of Randstad Staffing Services, is as comfortable working in the United States as he is in his native Holland. Indeed, Erik Vonk is the type of young leader who helps us understand why The Netherlands plays such a disproportionately large role in our Figure 1–1, "The World According to Trade," as he embodies his compatriots' multilingual capability. Vonk's ability to conduct business globally is enhanced by his knowledge of English, German, French, Dutch, and some Arabic. Ambassador Chiba, now a senior consultant with Mitsui and Company, was formerly Japan's Ambassador to Britain. He demonstrated remarkable eloquence in English and French, in addition to his native Japanese, on his last visit to Emory. Both leaders offer truly global perspectives, coupled with unique abilities to communicate globally.

Further, the late Roberto C. Goizueta was a role model for aspiring global managers. It is fitting that Coca-Cola, seen by stock market and other analysts as *the* most truly global U.S.-based company, was led for 16 years by a chairman/CEO who could articulate a clear vision in the two most crucial languages for business, Spanish and English.

The competencies described above lead us to an ideal role model for aspiring global leaders: an executive who combines technical strength with multilingual and multicultural finesse. Two executives that seem to embody all the competencies previously mentioned are the late Roberto Goizueta and Dr. Mario Corti, chief financial officer at Nestlé. Roberto Goizueta, the multilingual chemical engineer from Yale who increased his firm's stock market valuation more than any other CEO in history, showed this balanced strength. Mr. Goizueta and his protégé, Coke's current CEO Douglas Ivester, appeared on the cover of *Fortune* for a probably unprecedented three times within ten months. First, Mr. Goizueta was cited as the champion CEO in terms of creating the most market value added (MVA) for his firm's shareholders.[11] Second, Mr. Goizueta was on *Fortune*'s March 4, 1996 cover as the CEO of America's most admired company. Third, Coke's then president Douglas Ivester appeared on the cover of *Fortune* October 28, 1996. The accompanying story, "How Coke is Kicking Pepsi's Can," pointed out that "Goizueta has created more wealth for shareholders than any other CEO in history." The article cited both Mr. Goizueta's technical expertise and his multicultural background as key elements in Coca-Cola's trouncing of Pepsi Cola in global markets.

Another leader who embodies both technical and multilingual skill is Dr. Mario Corti, Nestlé's chief financial officer. Nestlé is the world's leading food company and Switzerland's largest industrial company. A truly global corporation, Nestlé has the smallest percentage of its total employees in its home country (6,000 out of 220,000!) of any company in the world. Dr. Corti, a Swiss-Italian, combines his technical mastery of finance and economics with a command of numerous languages useful in business. He has stated that multicultural sensitivity is the most important ingredient at Nestlé.

THE GLOBAL LEADER: A ROADMAP FOR PROSPERING IN THE 21ST CENTURY

Figure 8–3 represents my latest attempt to construct a visual image of the ideal 21st century executive. This composite future leader is drawn from both the talk that great global leaders now talk and the walk that I observe them walking. Few of us will ever reach anywhere close to perfection on the many attributes shown in this figure. Indeed the excitement of life is the striving toward an ideal; it is the nature of humans to reach toward perfection even if it is never achieved. However, I offer this figure in the hope that it will be a useful roadmap to guide readers in pursuing further studies and experiences. It would be sad to work hard to improve, only to end up wasting those efforts because of a lack of a strategic target.

The eight key competencies of global leaders enumerated above and in Figure 8–1 are expanded into a dozen capabilities in Figure 8–3, as if each hour on the clock represents time to improve on one of these crucial twelve dimensions. I have expanded the list of eight key competencies to twelve to include such important items as environmental consciousness and the willingness to strive for continuous improvement.

Environmental consciousness is already a necessity for business in Europe, where a political "green movement" and consumer awareness are both strong. Many European consumers have a sincere interest in purchasing products that show environmental sensitivity in their design. This trait of environmental concern is also becoming increasingly useful for those trying to do business in the United States or Japan. Indeed, Chapters 4 and 6 show the need for all business leaders to be extremely sensitive to the environmental impact of their work, because with the forecast continued population and economic growth, the fate of the planet will hinge on such environmental consciousness.

In interesting articles in the *Journal of Economic Perspectives*[13] and in the *Harvard Business Review,*[14] Michael Porter and Claas van der Linde

Figure 8–3 THE 21ST CENTURY LEADER:
A Global Businessperson

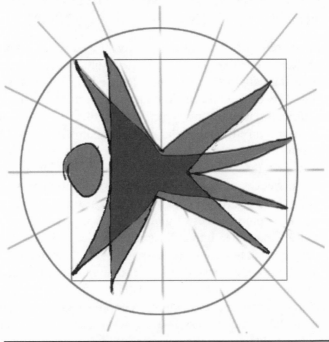

Business education to:
"Think globally, act
multi-functionally"

Command of
information
systems and
technology

Written & oral
(speak & listen)
communication
skills

Charisma:
worldly
appearance and
manners

Environmentally
conscious

Interpersonal skill: works
well on diverse teams and
maintains relationships

Fluency in several
key languages

Multicultural
competence

Backbone:
integrity,
character, ethical
values

Flexible and
responsive:
can and will
move quickly

Avoids complacency:
continuously
improves

Energy to glob-trot: can
fly all night, work all day

focus on the current state of environmental regulation, but conclude that what is most needed is global managers who can innovate to preserve the environment and use natural resources efficiently. Porter and Van der Linde make a strong case that business will need managers with enough vision and environmental consciousness to change even the most basic business processes. Managers must offer a dynamic (as opposed to the traditional static) strategy to help corporations ameliorate their impact on the global natural environment. Essentially, a firm can improve its competitiveness *and* benefit the environment by innovating to increase its *resource productivity.*

Another added feature in Figure 8–3 is the need to strive for continuous improvement. Leaders are people who avoid complacency and never rest on their laurels. A feature of Emory University's Goizueta Business School is our Dean's Speaker Series. Top leaders who have been dean's speakers, such as Bernie Marcus of The Home Depot or Sir Alex Trotman of Ford, do not want to waste their time listening to flattery and praise, but rather seek out constructive criticisms. More impressively, they act on that criticism in an effort to ward off complacency and to improve themselves and the firms they lead.

The reader who only faintly resembles the future leader pictured in Figure 8–3 should not despair; it is an idealized composite of the best traits of outstanding managers. It represents a goal to work toward, not someone you may actually meet in competition. Be reassured that many successful leaders prevail despite a few relatively weak links in this competency chain. The important point is to identify where you excel, and continue to build that into such a strength that it will differentiate you from others attempting to get to the executive suite. Further, assess which of the twelve listed attributes is a weakness so potentially damaging to you that it could become an Achilles' heel. Enhance your greatest potential strength in order to have a clear selling point, and minimize your greatest weakness in order to protect yourself from a fatal attack on your career. The appendix to this chapter presents a simple worksheet to help you categorize your strengths and weaknesses on these twelve crucial attributes of future success. Use the worksheet as a driver to strive for continual improvement in order to prepare yourself to prosper in the emerging global economy.

My hope is that this final picture provides a useful roadmap. Many of us want to continue with both our personal and professional development, yet our efforts will not be efficient unless we have a strategy to reach a targeted goal. Select work experiences (including overseas assignments) and college courses (degree or non-degree) that help you build real competencies. Many young executives reading this will be offered an overseas assignment as their firm attempts to adopt a more global strategy. This will be a major life-changing decision for you as it may mean uprooting a family, renting your home for a few years, and so on. However, accepting such an assignment could not only represent a chance for exciting personal growth and family experiences, it may also provide a boost to your career. Moreover, refusing such an offered assignment may show a lack of flexibility that, given our above discussion, could start to knock one off the fast track. A major headline at the top of a section of the *Wall Street Journal* in 1996 pointed to a new reality, one echoed by many leading CEOs: "An overseas stint can be a ticket to the top."[15] The accompanying article points out that these days even the executive suite is going global. "With nearly every industry targeting fast-growing foreign markets, more companies are requiring foreign experience for top management positions. Major corporations required candidates with international experience in 28% of senior-level searches last year, up from 4% in 1990. But finding qualified global executives can be tough."

If firms are increasingly searching for global executives, yet having difficulty finding qualified candidates, then there will be a demand/supply imbalance. The lack of supply implies that the value placed on qualified global executives will continue to rise. Developing enough competencies to at least start resembling the 21st century leader portrayed in this chapter should ultimately lead to a very rewarding career. Meanwhile, you will become a more interesting person and a better citizen, outcomes which in themselves are rewards for a lifelong pursuit of learning, of competency, and of a truly informed global perspective.

APPENDIX:

PREPARING FOR GLOBAL LEADERSHIP

The following worksheet (pages 220–221) lists the twelve attributes discussed in this chapter. It is an aid for self-assessment, and should be used as a personal development guide. Space is provided to list your current status on each global leadership trait, which you should evaluate on a 1 to 10 scale. Fill out the greatest strength and most costly weakness section next, bearing in mind that no one is expected to be perfect on all dimensions, but these are the two most critical, as discussed above. Next, consider and list your short-term (one-year) as well as intermediate-term (three- to five-year) goals. Finally, there is space for you to list specific actions to take to meet these goals.

The worksheet guide is meant to be a dynamic model, so that you might refer back to it over the course of your professional development and reassess where you stand. Use it to structure your goal setting and career strategy. Becoming a global leader is truly a lifelong pursuit, and this worksheet can help you plot your course.

BECOMING A GLOBAL LEADER
Personal evaluation and goal setting
(Use a 1-to-10 Scale)

	A	B	C	D	E
Capability (skills)	Where I am now Self-assessment Rating Date: ____	Where I hope to be 1 year from now	1 year from now: Evaluate, compare to B Date: ____	Where I hope to be 3 (or 5) years from now	3 (or 5) years from now: Evaluate, compare to D Date: ____
Communication skill: Listening, speaking, writing					
Multifunctional business education					
Trained to think globally and strategically					
Interpersonal skill: Builds relationships, team player					
Fluency in several key languages: English, Spanish, Chinese					
Multicultural competence and sensitivity					
Character, integrity, and ethical values					
Flexible, responsive, able to move quickly					

Energy to globe-trot: Health and stamina			
Charisma: Wordly appearance and manners, humor			
Command of information systems and technology			
Environmentally and socially responsible			

What is my greatest strength? Make a strategy to enhance and "play to" that personal comparative advantage.

What is my most glaring/costly weakness? Make a strategy to build competence here, before it becomes an Achilles' heel.

What specific actions will I take to help me meet my goals?

CHAPTER 9

PEOPLE AND PROFITS:

A Win-Win Global Strategy for the 21st Century

The main objective of this book has been to illustrate how businesses can grow and prosper well into the 21st century by adopting, over time, a more truly global strategy. We have seen that "more truly global" means extending beyond the traditional triad of wealthy nations into populous emerging markets. In doing so businesses would be wise to approach new markets sequentially as the potential consumers within those markets reach the stage of economic development needed to become customers—that is, businesses should adopt a time-phased global strategy.

A secondary aim of this book has been to show that the best hope for the majority of the world's people who are not currently wealthy is to embrace the global spread of capitalism. Regions or nations that set their policies to educate all their people and to encourage profit-seeking investment can follow the model of nations such as Chile and Singapore and achieve rapid economic development. Our optimistic vision of the next century requires sensible and forward-looking policies and actions on the part of developing nations, advanced nations and their multilateral institutions, and most importantly, business leaders.

This book has often identified trends that support my basic optimism. However, we have also seen that there is much suffering and dislocation at the end of the 20th century. Fundamentally, the world seems perched on a knife-edge as the 21st century approaches. Depending on the actions of business and political leaders throughout the world, we can envision either optimistic or pessimistic scenarios prevailing. In Chapter 4, for example, we showed that large and populous parts of the world are now trapped in vicious circles of poverty, population explosion, and environmental degradation. If these vicious circles are allowed to spiral ever larger, they will spin out of control in the next century, with dire consequences for everyone on this Earth. Fortunately, many nations or regions have achieved both a demographic transition and substantial economic development, and have lifted themselves out of vicious circles to more optimistic scenarios. Examples such as Singapore embolden us to believe that many nations can break out of the vicious circle trap, and move toward a more virtuous circle of enhanced education, productivity, incomes, and engagement with the growing capitalist world.

Ultimately, I claim that there is a great challenge facing the world as we enter the new millennium: *the challenge of a more truly global development.* The 20th century, particularly the last quarter, witnessed unprecedented progress in global economic development. East Asia has achieved economic development on a scale and at a speed never before accomplished. Fortunately, this successful model of capitalist economic development, particularly the welcoming of foreign investment, now seems firmly entrenched in Latin America and is increasingly prevalent in Central and Eastern Europe. There are even signs of progress in Africa and South Asia. Nonetheless, many nations are barely touched by such progress or such free-market capitalist policies, and the world still contains over a billion people living in dire poverty. Whether these nations can find catalysts to make the transition to more virtuous circles of economic development is perhaps the most significant issue facing the world in the imminent new century.

A MODEL OF CATALYSTS NEEDED TO MEET THE CHALLENGE OF GLOBAL DEVELOPMENT

Figure 9–1 summarizes my view of the world as we approach the new millennium. On the left-hand side, we see a model of the vicious circle that is currently spiraling out of control in many poor nations. We must all worry about the consequences of such vicious circles, as they put great strain on the Earth's resources; both from degradation of its environment and the explosion of people living in dismally poor circumstances. This figure incorporates much of the insight shared in Chapter 4, including the key driver of such tragic vicious circles—the lack of empowerment of women in many poor nations of the Populous South.

Fortunately, our vision of the world as we enter the 21st century also embodies very optimistic target scenarios. This positive outcome is summarized on the right-hand side of Figure 9–1, which portrays a virtuous circle. In this circle, rapid economic and social development are achieved. A crucial ingredient for such development is the opportunity for *all* people to become skilled, through investments in education and training. A key to this circle

Figure 9-1   THE CHALLENGE OF GLOBAL DEVELOPMENT
Catalysts Needed to Lever World off the Knife-Edge and into the 21st Century

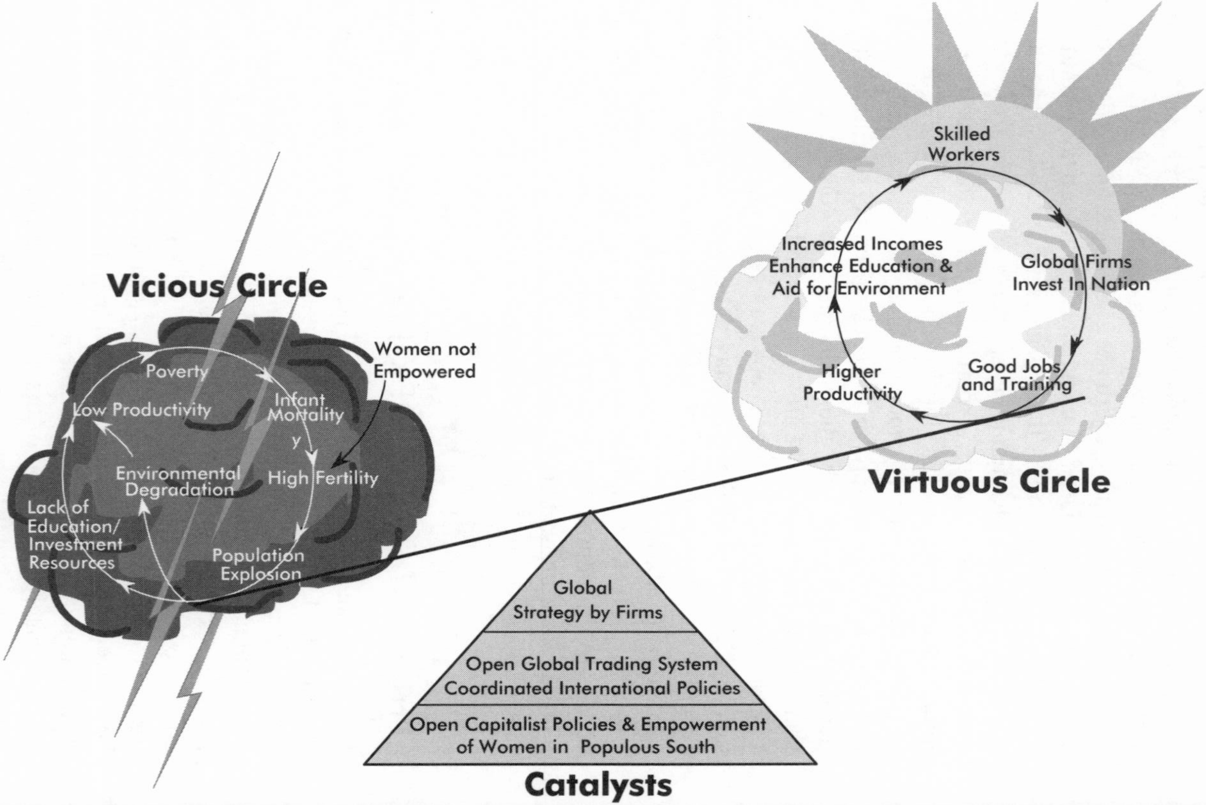

Vicious Circle

Women not Empowered

Infant Mortality

High Fertility

Poverty

Population Explosion

Low Productivity

Environmental Degradation

Lack of Education/ Investment Resources

Virtuous Circle

Global Firms Invest In Nation

Skilled Workers

Good Jobs and Training

Increased Incomes Enhance Education & Aid for Environment

Higher Productivity

Catalysts

Global Strategy by Firms

Open Global Trading System Coordinated International Policies

Open Capitalist Policies & Empowerment of Women in Populous South was described by former U.S. Labor Secretary Robert Reich in a famous article in the *Harvard Business Review*.[1] Well-trained workers attract global corporations, which invest in the developing nation and provide good jobs, and this in turn generates additional training. My own model also addresses the importance of enhanced action to protect the natural environment. This added emphasis is critical, given the role of environmental degradation in the vicious circle on the left-hand side of our model.

Thus, we stand on the threshold of a new millennium with two possible, starkly disparate, scenarios looming ahead of us. In our optimistic scenario, we envision nations embracing capitalism, welcoming foreign investment, and thereby attracting capital, technology, and training, which can boost workers' productivity. This enhanced productivity, in turn, will raise incomes in these formerly poor nations, leading to further educational and environmental investment. This may sound like a very optimistic, or even an idealistic, portrayal, but we have seen numerous examples of just such success. Again, Singapore is the obvious example. The important point for our purposes is *the ever-wider range* of successful examples. Consider that each of these nations has attracted foreign investment and moved to a more virtuous pattern of economic development: Argentina, Botswana, Brazil, Chile, China, Ghana, Hungary, Indonesia, Malaysia, Poland, and Uganda.

What are the catalysts needed to ensure that more of the world ends up on the optimistic side of our knife-edge? That is, what policies can ensure that the world achieves some leverage in the massive task ahead of it, that of lifting whole populous regions out of vicious circles to a higher economic realm? Figure 9–1 shows a hierarchy of policies needed to catalyze this world transition. It incorporates the catalysts into a fulcrum upon which we can exert leverage to shift much of the world from the poverty of a vicious circle to the enhanced incomes and education of a more virtuous circle. Note also that I portray the catalysts in a three-part hierarchy.

First, progress will only occur if the nations constituting the presently poor Populous South themselves adopt the policies which, as shown throughout this book, have led to development in other parts of the world. Crucial among such policies are those encouraging economic reform toward more open, capitalist, free markets. Only through such open policies and deregulation can developing nations hope to attract the foreign investment needed to achieve economic development. Because the firms able to make such investments of massive capital, technology, and training have many potential hosts around the world, they will only seek out those nations adopting open capitalist policies.

One example should suffice: China is eager to attract billions of dollars of investment in its electricity generation and distribution infrastructure, which is a critical prerequisite to its continued industrialization.

However, in the past Chinese authorities have stated their intent to put a cap on the rate of return potentially earned by such investments. Rightly so, firms in the industrial triad have looked elsewhere to make investments as part of their global expansion strategies. China's policy implies that such firms should bear substantial risk, but be barred from earning a compensating high profit return. Such governmental policies, which overly regulate the workings of the market, clearly deter the massive investment needed to continue rapid economic progress.

Along with open capitalist policies, the first tier of our catalyst hierarchy also lists policies that will lead to the empowerment of women in the Populous South. Nations that waste half of their human resource potential are not preparing themselves for progress and leadership in the new century, nor are they likely to attract foreign investment. Moreover, we saw in Chapter 4, as well as in the vicious circle portrayed in Figure 9–1, that the lack of empowerment of women is a crucial driver of the present vicious circle of poverty, population explosion, and environmental degradation that traps much of the developing world. A further transition of nations into more optimistic scenarios must begin with the adoption of policies that extend freedom and the opportunity for education and economic empowerment to all citizens.

In the second tier of our triangular hierarchy of catalysts needed to lever the whole world toward optimistic scenarios are policies related to the global economic system. These policies logically lay between the first tier, which comprises policies embraced by nations, and the final tier, which comprises the policies adopted by firms. In the middle tier, we focus on the supranational policies that enable firms to compete more globally. The most important driver here is the continued movement toward a free and open global trading system, a prerequisite for a more global spread of economic progress. Policies in this tier were discussed in Chapter 2's review of the hopeful signs of movement to a more open trading system. Once again, the formation of the World Trade Organization (WTO) deserves special note.

In spite of enormous steps forward, we enter the 21st century with the continued progress toward an open global trading system very much in doubt. Recent political developments in European nations, particularly France, and the lack of progress in the United States toward expanding NAFTA readily illustrate the setbacks and concern. I remain optimistic that progress toward free trade will continue, both on a regional and a global basis. Yet a massive educational effort will be required, as many self-serving politicians attempt to exploit voters' feelings of job insecurity by attacking our free trading system. To be sure, the insecurity regarding jobs is real in many nations, such as France and Spain. Job insecurity, however, is more often due to inflexible regulations, particularly regarding employment practices, than to the movement toward an open global trading system. Indeed, the movement toward free trade has been a prime driver of the unprecedented economic progress witnessed in the second half of the 20th century.

Pop Internationalism,[2] by Paul Krugman of MIT, is an excellent source for those readers desiring to distinguish solid economic analysis from the shaky yet seductive arguments of political rhetoric. The importance of preserving and extending an open global trading system, a prime feature of our fulcrum needed to tilt the world to a more virtuous circle in the upcoming century, is eloquently portrayed by Krugman (pp. 67–68):

> If the West throws up barriers to imports out of a misguided belief that they will protect Western living standards, the effect could be to destroy the most promising aspect of today's world economy: the beginning of widespread economic development, of hopes for a decent living standard for hundreds of millions, even billions, of human beings. Economic growth in the Third World is an opportunity, not a threat; it is our fear of Third World success, not that success itself, that is the real danger to the world economy.

The second tier of our fulcrum also requires coordinated international policies to protect the important elements of the global trade and investment infrastructure, such as confidence in the international financial system. Intervention by governments and supranational official institutions should occur only in instances where the stability of the system may be threatened. As an illustration, the U.S.-led coordinated financial aid to Mexico in 1995 was clearly a useful strategy, stabilizing the system. Incidentally, the loans extended by the United States were paid back both early and with a profitable rate of return for U.S. taxpayers. In the same light, the coordinated financial assistance provided to Thailand beginning in summer 1997 (and later to Indonesia and Korea), led by the IMF and Japan, was clearly part of a "win-win strategy," intending to further extend global economic progress.

The third tier of our triangular hierarchy needed to lever the world firmly onto the optimistic side of its present knife-edge consists of the policies of firms. These business strategy policies are listed last, because they require the successful implementation of the first two stages of our hierarchy; that is, freedom-preserving and stable policies on the part of governments are necessary before firms can adopt global strategies in the best interest of their shareholders. As such, the apex of the catalytic pyramid in Figure 9–1 is the adoption by firms of more truly global strategies. Given the right preconditions, the ability of the world to meet the great challenge of the 21st century—the challenge of a more global economic development—will be largely in the hands of business leaders.

Populous emerging nations need capital, technology, good management, and training to develop economically. The best sources of this needed fuel of economic progress are the successful firms currently termed transnational or multinational corporations. These firms, by becoming truly global, will provide the leadership needed to catalyze the transition of the world into more virtuous circles in the 21st century. We discussed the nature of "time-phased global expansion strategies" in Chapter 7. Our claim here is that the world's progress will rely, to a large extent, on the foresight of business leaders to adopt such global expansion strategies and implement time-phased strategies. I hope that this book has inspired current and aspiring business leaders to fill this crucial catalytic role. The ability of business to fulfill the final tier of the three-part pyramid of needed policies will largely determine two crucial items: (1) whether firms will continue to grow and prosper well into the 21st century, and (2) whether the world as a whole will continue to grow, prosper, and eradicate the present massive poverty and environmental degradation.

Ultimately, business will only fulfill this crucial role if a more truly global expansion strategy is seen as in the best interests of shareholders. This book has shown that this is indeed likely to be the case, and "tomorrow's customers" are likely to reside outside of firms' traditional markets. Below I present an example of an industry that can find its own continued growth and prosperity through a *truly* global expansion strategy. An important consequence of such a strategy is the ability to move millions of people into a more optimistic or virtuous circle of enhanced health and productivity.

A VISION OF GLOBAL STRATEGY LINKING PEOPLE AND PROFITS: THE HEALTH CARE INDUSTRY

Figure 9–2 suggests how a more truly global strategy on the part of industry could link, and simultaneously advance, people and profits. The example is drawn from the health care industry, specifically the pharmaceutical industry, which quite clearly has a great effect on the well-being of people. Note, however, that I do not see this as the only possible example of a strategy linking people and profits. Telecoms, information distribution, university education, and adult education and training are other industries that could be used to illustrate global strategy as linking potential profit growth and enhanced living standards.

Figure 9–2 displays the linkage of two rather virtuous circles. Thus, this figure represents something of a "dual virtuous circles" model—a

**Figure 9-2   EXAMPLE OF HOW A GLOBAL STRATEGY COULD
ADVANCE PEOPLE AND PROFITS:
HEALTH CARE VIRTUOUS CIRCLES**

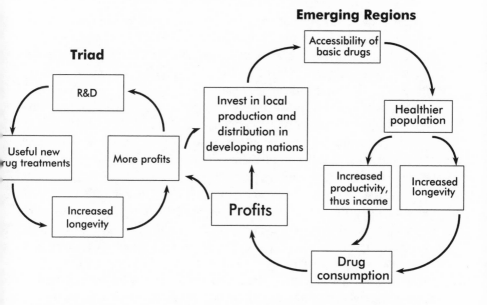

useful antidote perhaps to the less optimistic "dual vicious circles" model presented in Chapter 7. I am indebted to a number of fine alumni of Emory's Executive MBA program, particularly Dr. Ira Isaacson of Egon Zehnder International, for helping develop this example.

Successful firms in the pharmaceutical industry conduct business primarily in the traditional triad, as illustrated in the left-hand side of the virtuous circle. The innovative feature in this figure is the potential *second* virtuous circle, which can be generated by extending key aspects of a pharmaceutical business to the world's lesser-developed or emerging regions. A critical driver of this second circle is that to expand profits, a firm must find new markets by undertaking the risky strategy of investing in local production and distribution in many developing nations. This is due to the key feature of the pharmaceutical industry: the massive investment in research and development (R&D) needed to discover, test, and develop useful new drug treatments.

The use of the word "massive" in this case is almost an understatement, as useful new drugs generally cost hundreds of millions of dollars in R&D and testing before ever being brought to market. Thus, the pharmaceutical industry is characterized by huge fixed costs of development, and then much lower marginal costs of actual production. Clearly, then, the key to efficiency in this industry is the achievement of *economies of scale,* as mammoth investments in R&D required to pioneer useful new drug treatments can only be recovered in huge markets.

Increasingly, leaders in this industry are realizing that global expansion can provide the gargantuan scale needed to achieve adequate rates of return on the ever-increasing investments in R&D. This means of recouping R&D investments is preferable to the alternative: charging painfully high prices. Furthermore, only by looking beyond the obvious big emerging markets to even less-developed nations can firms achieve both optimal economies of scale and positive impact on people's health and lives worldwide. Particularly, expansion strategies of these firms must consider investments in the poor yet populous nations of Africa, the Middle East, and South Asia, in order to catalyze future business growth and partially leverage the world away from vicious circles.

As such, the model portrayed in Figure 9–2 starts with continued investments in R&D by the leading pharmaceutical firms in the wealthy triad. This investment will lead to useful new drug treatments that can increase longevity, as well as improve lives. Of course, efficacious new treatments can be priced at profitable margins within the wealthy triad. Many people have the willingness and ability to pay prices sufficiently above marginal costs, thus providing pharmaceutical firms with high rates of return and further motivation to innovate. In the wealthy triad, we (or our insurance companies) are willing to pay prices that justify further R&D investments by private firms, because such investments can lead to enhanced health and longevity.

On the "Emerging Regions" side of the figure, the crucial ingredient is the investment in local production and distribution in developing nations. Such an investment can be seeded now by the growing profits of innovative and successful triad pharmaceutical firms, such as SmithKline Beecham, Merck, Pfizer, Novartis, Roche, and Glaxo Wellcome. While these investments are beginning to occur, the distribution must be greatly extended throughout Africa and the poor regions of non-East Asia. Only through investments in production and distribution can there be a nearly universal accessibility of basic and desperately needed pharmaceutical products. Quite obviously, access to essential drugs, such as antibiotics, and vaccines, can lead to healthier populations and increased longevity. Thus, these profit-seeking firms have a key role to play in breaking the tragic vicious circle in which some nations have life expectancies of less than 40 years (see Chapter 4). Healthier populations, through enhanced abilities to learn and work, will increase productivity and thus incomes. In our optimistic scenario, the combination of eventual increased incomes and enhanced longevity will allow residents of presently very poor nations to one day have the purchasing power to provide profitable effective demand for pharmaceutical products. Thus, by providing access to needed basic drugs now, firms will be ensuring future growth through emerging markets; markets that will one day increase the use of needed medicinal drugs and the ability to pay *profitable* prices for them.

Once emerging markets are able to pay sufficiently high prices for necessary pills, these markets will provide both a further source of needed economies of scale and added profits to truly global pharmaceutical firms. The profits that will eventually flow from now poor yet populous regions will be added to the profit flow coming from the wealthy nations of the triad. Figure 9–2 illustrates that this combined flow of profits can both fund and justify future massive investments in R&D. Thus, the linkages in the figure show that emerging regions can partially generate the economies of scale necessary for R&D expenditures to find cures for the dreaded diseases now prevalent. The figure also shows that a virtuous circle can emerge in the developing regions, whereby healthier populations will eventually reach the productivity and thus income standards to be a source of new profits for health care firms—profits which can both fuel further R&D and be reinvested in these emerging markets themselves. Such reinvestment will ultimately fund R&D in laboratories in the developing nations, as well as further production and distribution of life-enhancing medicines throughout the Populous South.

One of the most important linkages in this hypothetical model is that between the availability of needed medicines and healthier, more productive people. The *World Bank Research Observer*, in a recent issue, focused upon service, quality, and cost impacts on education and health. Issues of access to health services were studied in an article entitled "Household Responses to Public Health Services: Costs and Quality Trade-offs," by Harold Alderman and Victor Lavy.[3] These authors point out that in Ghana and Côte d'Ivoire, poor nutritional status, denial of access to antibiotics and drugs (through high prices), and mortality were all linked (pp. 14–15). In their conclusion, Alderman and Lavy state (p. 18) that: "Unlike facilities, equipment, and human resources, drugs and vaccines can be readily provided by governments and can generate a rapid improvement in public health." One reason for my own optimism is that this rapid improvement in public health is being facilitated not only by governments, but by farsighted firms such as SmithKline Beecham and Merck. Both of these firms have greatly extended the provision of vaccines and drugs to the poorest of people, often working with nongovernmental organizations.

Merck has been working with President Jimmy Carter's Center in Atlanta to fight river blindness disease (onchocerciasis). Likewise, early in 1998 SmithKline Beecham CEO Jan Leschly (see Chapter 8 Spotlight) announced a collaboration with the World Health Organization to eliminate lymphatic filariasis (elephantiasis), one of the world's most disfiguring and disabling tropical diseases. This huge effort will entail SmithKline Beecham's donating several billion doses of its drug albendazole.

Finally, the link to increased productivity also derives from the finding that the availability of drugs and vaccines not only improves children's health, but also enhances learning standards. In a separate article in the same issue of the *World Bank Research Observer*,[4] Jere Behrman summarizes a number of studies regarding the effects of health on productivity in the developing world. Behrman points out that (p. 33):

> The evidence suggests that better health and nutrition may pay off in terms of economic growth as well as equity concerns by improving the educational performance of poor people in the developing world. That productivity and equity concerns probably are in harmony is an important plus. Policymakers, therefore, should seriously consider how various policies affect child health and nutrition and identify those policies that would improve it. . . . Improving the health and nutrition of children can be an efficient way to improve school attendance and enhance economic growth.

The "dual virtuous circle" model portrayed in this hypothetical example is admittedly optimistic. Indeed, I hope for something of a "self-fulfilling prophecy," that the eventual increased demand and enhanced profitability will inspire investments in currently poor nations and young people *now*. Such investments could provide the path to profitable growth well into the 21st century.

FREEDOM, GROWTH, AND A CALLING FOR BUSINESS

Ultimately, this book is about a vision for the imminent new century: a win-win strategy in which poor nations extend freedom and open their markets, while firms' investment in poor nations grows profits but also raises living standards. This is an optimistic vision, but one based on the empirical trends portrayed throughout this book. Nations that have opened their markets to capitalism and to foreign investment, such as Singapore, Chile, and Poland, have begun to spread prosperity among their citizens. Meanwhile, the firms that pioneered investment in such nations derive an increasing share of their growing profits from their new global partners.

Importantly, both empowering *all* people and enhancing freedom are being seen as the path to prosperity by many developing nations. Freedom can come in many forms. For example, in Chapter 4, we saw that a key element of the vicious circle of population explosion and poverty is that women are not empowered, or even free to choose aspects of their own fertility. Societies cannot truly enhance local living standards if many of their citizens suffer from coercion. Dasgupta, in his excellent survey article cited in Chapter 4, offers an important conclusion:

Political and civil liberties are positively and significantly corre-lated with *improvements* in income per head, life expectancy at birth, and the infant survival rate. Correlation is not causation, but there are now reasons for thinking that such liberties are not only desirable in themselves, but also have instrumental virtues in empowering people to flourish in the economic sphere.[5]

Significantly, a number of recent studies show that freedom can be a contributing element along the path to prosperity. A major article in *The Economist,* entitled "Economic Freedom: Of Liberty and Prosperity,"[6] examines the age-old debate on whether government intervention helps or hinders economic progress and concludes that the important research in a major book, *Economic Freedom of the World: 1975–1995,* mostly resolves the debate.[7] Indeed, the conclusion of this research from 102 countries over 20 years could scarcely be more emphatic (*The Economist,* p. 21):

[T]he more economic freedom a country had in that period, the more economic growth it achieved and the richer its citizens became. . . . the ratings reveal a strong correlation between economic freedom and wealth especially for countries that main-tained a high level of freedom for many years. Before individuals and companies will respond to new-won freedom, they must believe that it is likely to last. It is no coincidence that the six countries that have persistently high ratings throughout the 1975–1995 period (Hong Kong, Switzerland, Singapore, the United States, Canada and Germany) were also all in the top ten in terms of GDP per head in 1993–95. . . .

Most noteworthy, perhaps, are the ratings given to the fast-growing economies of East Asia, and to Japan, for many people assume that in these countries economic freedom is heavily curtailed. Yet Singapore comes in second place, Malaysia is sixth, Japan is ninth, and South Korea is twelfth.[8]

At the beginning of this chapter I presented a model, summarized in Figure 9–1, that portrayed a hierarchy of policies needed to catalyze a transition of more nations in the developing world, from vicious circles to the more virtuous circles of our optimistic scenario. Countries need to adopt policies that will empower people and provide freedom for individual energies and imagination to flourish; firms must then look to such developing nations as a key part of their expansion strategy. I believe that it is through a more truly global expansion strategy that firms will be able to sustain healthy growth, by linking people and profits.

CONCLUSION

This book has shown that the burgeoning populations of developing nations, although often poor today, represent "Tomorrow's Customers" for firms looking to grow well into the 21st century. Firms who adopt a "time-phased global strategy" can indeed grow and prosper. Moreover, extending investments to previously poor nations who embrace the global spread of capitalism can constitute a "win-win strategy" for both the firm and host nation.

Business leaders hold the key to the 21st century, as their actions will largely determine on which side of its present knife-edge perch the world will settle. Michael Novak, in his book, *Business as a Calling*,[9] offers us an eloquent conclusion:

> In particular, business has a special role to play in bringing hope—and not only hope, but actual economic progress—to the billion or so truly indigent people on this planet. Business is, bar none, the best real hope of the poor. And that is one of the noblest callings inherent in business activities: to raise up the poor.

The world *can* move off its present knife-edge into a widespread virtuous circle, the optimistic scenario. Freedom for people, particularly women, is critical. If more free-market, growth-oriented policies are adopted by governments worldwide, business will likely fulfill its end of the bargain. It will be in firms' best interests to expand globally, for this will be the path of future business growth and prosperity. In turn, a truly global strategy can help everyone "win the global game," by linking profits and all the world's people.

LIST OF ACRONYMS

ACRONYM	PROPER NAME
ABB	Asea Brown Boveri
ADR	American Depository Receipt
AFTA	ASEAN Free Trade Area (proposed)
APEC	Asia-Pacific Economic Cooperation forum
ASEAN	Association of Southeast Asian Nations
BEM	Big Emerging Markets
BEN	Big Emerging Nations
BOP	Balance of Payments
CIS	Commonwealth of Independent States
EFTA	European Free Trade Association
EMU	European Economic and Monetary Union
EU	European Union
FDI	Foreign Direct Investment
FTAA	Free Trade Area of the Americas (proposed)
G-7	Group of Seven (largest advanced industrialized nations)
GATT	General Agreement on Tariffs and Trade
GDP	Gross Domestic product
GNP	Gross National Product
HDR	Human Development Report (a UNDP annual)
HPAE	High-performing Asian Economies
IMF	International Monetary Fund
ITN	Industrialized Trading Nations (secondarily, an Information Technology Network)

ITU	International Telecommunication Union
MNC	Multinational Company
NAFTA	North American Free Trade Agreement
NIC	Newly Industrialized Country
PPE	Poverty, Population Explosion, and Environmental Degradation
PPP	Purchasing Power Parity (hypothetical exchange rates)
PRC	People's Republic of China
PWPP	People with Purchasing Power
RIC	Recently Industrializing Country
SSS	Surviving-Son Syndrome
TFR	Total Fertility Rate
UNCTAD	United Nations Conference on Trade and Development
UNDP	United Nations Development Program
WDR	World Development Report (a World Bank annual)
WIR	World Investment Report (an UNCTAD annual)
WTO	World Trade Organization

NOTES

INTRODUCTION: GLOBALIZATION OR "GLOBALONEY"?

1. The late Clare Boothe Luce deserves credit for popularizing the term "globaloney."
2. John Whalley and Colleen Hamilton, "The Trading System After the Uruguay Round," *Institute for International Economics* (Washington, DC), July 1996, Table 2.2, p. 14.
3. *Wall Street Journal,* 21 October 1996, p. A1.
4. I often call this recession the "recession that CNN brought to us," because so many people were watching the excellent coverage of the Gulf War on CNN that they forgot to go out and grow their businesses; or if they didn't forget, they were afraid of terrorism and were unwilling to make business trips.
5. This globalization trend is even more dramatic if we look at the whole second half of the 20th century. The *Economist,* in an article entitled "World Trade: All Free Traders Now?" (7 December 1996, pp. 21–23), used WTO data to show that the volume of world trade increased more than fifteenfold from 1950 to 1995, whereas world GDP increased less than sixfold. Trade volumes in 1995, fifteen times larger than in 1950, clearly show that booming international trade gives some meat to the term "globalization."
6. William Gates III, *The Road Ahead,* rev. ed. (Penguin Books, New York, 1996).
7. John Maynard Keynes, *The Economic Consequences of the Peace* (New York: Harcourt, Brace and Howe, 1920), pp. 10–12. My colleague, Terry Clark, kindly brought this passage to my attention.
8. *The Economist,* 27 April 1996, p. 113.
9. *Global Economic Prospects and the Developing Countries* (Washington, DC: World Bank, 1996), p. 21.
10. Bank for International Settlements, May 1996 Report, Basle, Switzerland.
11. *The Economist,* 1 June 1996, p. 102. Recall that FDI is foreign *direct* investment, where "direct" implies some managerial control. Direct investment stands in contrast to mere "portfolio" investments, which imply no direct influence on management.
12. See, for example, *Survey of Current Business,* U.S. Dept. of Commerce, July 1997, pp. 24–33.
13. *World Investment Report 1997* (New York and Geneva: U.N. Conference on Trade and Development), p. 313.
14. *Survey of Current Business,* June 1997, p. 61.
15. Twenty-percent shares of many key magnitudes seem common for the developing world; an "80/20 split" that we will explore in Chapters 1 and 5.
16. *World Investment Report 1997* (New York and Geneva: UN Conference on Trade and Development), p.5.
17. ibid, pp 3–8.
18. The World Bank confirms the FDI trend in its publication, *Global Development Finance.* For example, it reports that FDI inflows to China rose to over $42 billion in 1996.

19. Nicholas R. Lardy, *China in the World Economy* (Washington, DC: Institute for International Economics, 1994).

PART I. REGIONAL ASPECTS OF A GLOBALIZING ECONOMY
Chapter 1. The Limited World of Business at the End of the 20th Century

1. United Nations Development Program, *Human Development Report 1996,* p. 1.
2. *Global Economic Prospects and the Developing Countries,* World Bank, 1996, p. 20.
3. United Nations Development Program, *Human Development Report 1996,* p. 2.
4. Ibid.
5. This attitude is reflected in numerous jokes, one example being "someone who speaks three languages is trilingual; two languages is bilingual; and someone who speaks only one language is termed American."
6. Kenichi Ohmae, *The Borderless World: Power and Strategy in the Interlinked Economy* (New York: Harper Business, 1990).
7. Paul Kennedy, *Preparing for the Twenty-first Century* (New York: Random House, 1993), pp. 53–63.
8. The exception is the substitution of Chile for South Korea. I promoted South Korea into our first-tier ITN, as it is no longer considered a developing country by the World Bank or OECD, despite the Commerce Department's including it as an "emerging market" and its recent economic troubles.
9. Of the remaining four ASEAN nations, three have small economies and the fourth, Singapore, is in our ITN group.
10. The Commerce Department effort was led by Jeffrey Garten, who has since moved on to become Dean of Yale's School of Management. In his influential book, *The Big Ten,* he returned to a focus on the original ten big countries. At times in his book, rather than just discussing Indonesia, he speaks of ASEAN as a whole. In my own analysis, I find it compelling to add to our Second World BENs the other large economies in ASEAN: Thailand, Malaysia, Vietnam, and the Philippines.
11. *Wall Street Journal,* 6 January 1998, p. A2.
12. H. Kennedy, *Preparing for the Twenty-first Century,* p. 24.
13. 13 April 1996, p. 102.
14. *Wall Street Journal,* 26 September 1996, p. B6.
15. "*Fortune*'s Global 500: The World's Largest Companies," *Fortune,* 4 August 1997, pp. 102–109, F1–F42.
16. Interestingly, *three* out of these four "top 200" firms outside the ITN are dominated by oil or gas revenues, not manufacturing. Further, the 1996 *World Investment Report* points out (p. xiv) that: "The world's largest 100 TNCs (excluding banking and financial institutions), ranked by foreign assets, are all based in developed countries."
17. *Trends in Private Investing in Developing Countries,* International Finance Corporation, Discussion Paper No. 28, December 1995, p. 1.
18. World Bank, *1996 Global Economic Prospects and the Developing Countries,* p. 22.
19. Edward M. Graham, *Global Corporations and National Governments* (Washington, DC: Institute for International Economics, 1996).
20. Ibid., p. 1.
21. Ibid., p. 2.
22. United Nations Conference on Trade and Development, *World Investment Report 1996* (New York and Geneva, 1996), p. xiv.
23. Ibid., p. xvi.
24. Data from U.S. Commerce Dept., *Survey of Current Business,* June 1997, p. 61.
25. *WIR 1996,* p. xvii.
26. Data from U.S. Commerce Dept., *Survey of Current Business.,* July 1996, pp. 52–54.
27. *WIR 1996* (p. 48) also details the tragic absence of Africa from significant FDI inflows from Japan.

Chapter 2. Business Strategy into the 21st Century: Extending the Triad

1. John Whalley and Colleen Hamilton, *The Trading System after the Uruguay Round* (Washington, DC: Institute for International Economics, July 1996).
2. For a useful discussion, see Charles R. Carlisle, "Is the World Ready for Free Trade?" *Foreign Affairs,* Vol. 75, No. 6 (November/December 1996), pp. 113–126.
3. E.g., Kenichi Ohmae, "Putting Global Logic First," *The Harvard Business Review,* January-February 1995.
4. Kenichi Ohmae, *The End of the Nation State: The Rise of Regional Economies* (New York: The Free Press, 1995).
5. Ibid., e.g., pp. 5, 80.
6. Ibid., pp. 80–81.
7. Peter F. Drucker, "The Global Economy and the Nation-State," *Foreign Affairs* (September/October 1997), pp. 159–171. Another interesting article that argues that a nation (the nation-state), although not what it used to be, will still have an important role for quite a while, appeared in *The Economist,* 5 January 1996. The article, "The nation-state is dead. Long live the nation-state," concludes that nation-states will live longer than most people may think.
8. Kenichi Ohmae, "The Rise of the Region State," *Foreign Affairs,* Spring 1993, pp. 78–87, at p. 80.
9. Fast-track authority is given by Congress and empowers the U.S. president to negotiate trade treaties with foreign countries, and then present them to Congress for a yes-or-no vote without amendment.
10. The *Wall Street Journal,* in an article titled "Clinton to Begin Campaign for 'Fast-Track' Authority" on 24 July 1997 (page A4), clarifies this issue: "The administration wants fast-track authority to gain entry for Chile to the North American Free Trade Agreement as the first step to expanding a free-trade zone throughout the hemisphere. That effort has been stalled for several years." However, when Clinton finally asked Congress for fast-track authority in September 1997, it was a half-hearted attempt, as the *Financial Times* reported in an article (12 September 1997, p. 14) titled "Fast Track Bogged Down." This attempt failed, at least temporarily.
11. *The Economist,* 1 March 1997, p. 43.
12. Mercosur is also called "Merco*sul,*" which is the Portuguese spelling of it.
13. Yoichi Funabashi, *Asia Pacific Fusion: Japan's Role in APEC* (Washington, DC: Institute for International Economics, October 1995), p. 166.
14. Reduced from four independent 'little tigers' or 'dragon nations' when Hong Kong reverted to China in July 1997.
15. Ashoka Mody, and Fang-Yi Wang, "Explaining Industrial Growth in Coastal China: Economic Reforms . . . and What Else?" *World Bank Economic Review,* Vol. 11, No. 2, May 1997, p. 294.
16. See for example, Ohmae's pp. 82–83.
17. *Wall Street Journal,* 16 July 1997, p. A1.
18. Lester Thurow, *Head to Head: The Coming Economic Battle Among Japan, Europe and America* (New York: William Morrow and Company, 1992).
19. *Financial Times,* 22 October 1997, p. 20.

Chapter 3. The Populous South: Will Markets for Growth or a Tragic Human Trap Emerge?

1. For the definitive study of the significance to all business of the overseas Chinese linkages, see Murray Weidenbaum and Samuel Hughes, *The Bamboo Network: How Expatriate Chinese Entrepreneurs are Creating a New Economic Superpower in Asia* (New York: The Free Press, 1996).
2. Kennedy, *Preparing for the 21st Century,* pp. 23–25, 32.
3. Ibid., pp. 41–46, 274–76.

4. See Lester Brown, *Who Will Feed China?* (Worldwatch Institute, W.W. Norton & Company, New York, 1995).
5. *World Population Projections,* 1994–1995 ed., the World Bank (Baltimore: Johns Hopkins University Press, 1994). Current World Bank projections still build off of the model shown in this book—this is the latest edition.
6. *The Economist,* 9 November 1996, p. 64.
7. Report compiled by Richard Holman, *Wall Street Journal,* 31 October 1996, p. A18.
8. See the article by Nicholas D. Kristof, "Not for Love or Money: Japan's Women Say No to More Kids," *International Herald Tribune,* 7 October 1996.
9. *The Economist,* 16 December 1995, p. 98.
10. Jim Rogers, *Investment Biker* (New York: Random House, 1994).
11. Ireland's attributes include an educated and literate (and fairly young and growing by European standards) population. It is attracting FDI and has achieved the highest economic growth rate in western Europe since 1993 (over 7% per year). For these reasons an investment I made in the Irish Investment Fund in 1994 turned out to be highly profitable. However, Ireland's total population of less than 4 million is less than three months of population growth in India.

Chapter 4. The Challenge of Development:
Ending the South's Vicious Spiral

1. Peter M. Senge, *The Fifth Discipline: The Art and Practice of the Learning Organization* (New York: Currency Doubleday, 1990).
2. United Nations Development Programme, *Human Development Report 1997* (New York: Oxford University Press, 1997), p. 3.
3. For a useful and more detailed and nuanced treatment of the issues and linkages embodied in this crucial dynamic model, see the survey article by Partha Dasgupta: "The Population Problem; Theory and Evidence," *Journal of Economic Literature,* Vol. 33 (December 1995), pp. 1879–1902.
4. Thankfully, many East Asian nations display diminished gender bias.
5. As an aside, note the hopeful sign that India is a bit of an exception.
6. World Bank, *World Development Indicators 1997,* p. 32.
7. Dasgupta, "The Population Problem."
8. The World Bank, *Population and Development* (Washington, D.C., August 1994).
9. The U.N.'s *Human Development Report 1997* shows both economic motives for high fertility (p. 71): "The need for children to support parents in old age and the security that comes from having many children when many die in childhood are well known. Less well understood is the need for more children in households that face demands on time just for survival. Children in the poorest families are often out of school and working from a very young age, as young as five. They do the work that their mothers lack the time to perform. In rural areas where environmental degradation adds to the time needed to fetch water and fuel, a solution for already overworked women is to have more children. . . . Thus it is a rational coping strategy in the face of acute time shortage."
10. *World Development Indicators 1997,* p. 94–96.
11. The U.N.'s *Human Development Report 1997* points out (p. 28) that: "Around 17 million people in developing countries die each year from such curable infectious and parasitic diseases as diarrhea, measles, malaria and tuberculosis."
12. *Human Development Report 1997* reports (p. 28): "The developing countries have one doctor for every 6,000 people, the industrial countries one for every 350. Among developing regions the ratio ranges from one doctor per 18,000 people in sub-Saharan Africa to one per 1,000 in Latin America."
13. Anne Platt, "Water-Borne Killers," *World Watch,* Vol. 9, No. 2 (March/April 1996), pp. 28–35.
14. Interestingly, men in Japan can expect to live only 77 years. Although this is much

longer then the life expectancies for certain nations of the Populous South, it is clear that men in Japan expire on average well before their wives. Stress on the job is probably part of the explanation. But I think the lion's share of the difference is accounted for by the bourbon drinking, smoking, and beef-eating habits that symbolize success to a Japanese businessman. I wonder how much of this behavior is done emulating a notion of what successful American businessmen consume. Ironically, most American businessmen I know have not only cut down or stopped drinking and smoking, they are even beginning to emulate Japanese women by eating fish (including sushi) without heavy sauces and plentiful servings of fresh fruits and vegetables, and rice.

15. Startling success stories, comparing 1970 to 1995 infant mortality per 1,000 live births, include: Algeria 139 to 34, Brunei 57 to 9, Chile 77 to 12, Costa Rica 62 to 13, Hong Kong 19 to 5, Italy 30 to 7, Malaysia 45 to 12, Oman 119 to 18, Saudi Arabia 119 to 21, Singapore 20 to 4, Spain 28 to 7. Examples are based on data in the *World Development Indicators 1997,* pp. 6–9.

16. See, e.g., Lawrence H. Summers, "Investing in All the People: Educating Women in Developing Countries," World, Bank *EDI Seminar Paper 45,* May 1994. This article provides "sound reasons why targeting funds to educate girls and women can yield the best investment returns in the developing world and provide enormous economic benefits. The discussion explains how such funding can reduce environmental pollution, fertility rates, and female mortality and help prevent the spread of AIDS."

17. Ibid, pp. 23–24.

18. All data cited here are from The World Bank's *World Development Indicators 1997,* pp. 6–9.

19. Dasgupta (p. 1898) summarizes the evidence: "The analysis presented here suggests that the way to reduce fertility would be to break the destructive spiral where such a spiral is in operation. Because parental demand for children, rather than an unmet need for contraceptives, in great measure explains reproductive behavior in poor countries, we should try to identify policies that would so change the options men and women face that their reasoned choice would be to lower their fertility."

20. Obed Galor and David N. Weil, "The Gender Gap, Fertility, and Growth," *American Economic Review,* Vol. 86, #3 (June 1996), pp. 374–387.

21. Minority populations who are underserved by healthcare (such as prenatal care) suffer even higher infant mortality rates in the rural U.S. South. Fortunately, progress is now being achieved on this front by a valiant coalition of doctors working with leaders from government and business.

PART II. THE POTENTIAL OF MORE GLOBAL ECONOMIC PROGRESS
Chapter 5. Tomorrow's Customers: The Middle Class Goes Global

1. Kenichi Ohmae's book *The Borderless World* (New York: HarperBusiness, 1990) presents a good example of this point. His borderless world is in reality just a borderless traditional triad of Japan, North America, and western Europe. He barely mentions the Southern Hemisphere throughout this otherwise interesting book.

2. The World Bank, *The East Asian Miracle: Economic Growth and Public Policy* (New York: Oxford University Press, 1993), pp. 1 and 2.

3. Stiglitz, Joseph E., "Some Lessons from the East Asian Miracle," *The World Bank Research Observer,* Vol. 11, No. 2 (August 1996), pp. 151–177.

4. Note that Chile has since adopted a democratic form of government. *The Financial Times of London* reports (30 July 1997, p. 7) that this return to democracy, plus "Chile's growing integration in the Latin American region" (which we detailed in Chapter 2), is spurring continuing record levels of foreign direct investment into Chile. Indeed, the estimate of FDI flows into Chile in 1997 exceeds $6 billion, a remarkable attraction of capital by a nation of only 14 million people.

5. "If Europe's dead, why is GE investing billions there?", *Fortune,* 9 September 1996, pp. 114–118.
6. I created this mapping by adapting some data from "The Emerging Middle Class," *Business Week,* 18 November 1994, pp. 178–185. The article contained a sensible data analysis, unlike the euphoric claims in many other popular reports, on the emerging global middle class.
7. This makes us at Emory University, with our $2.5 billion-plus endowment of Coca-Cola stock, very happy.
8. One frequently hears or reads of "India's 300 million middle-class consumers." India contains many fewer than 30 million telephones, so it surely does not have nearly 300 million PWPP. My best guess is that someone, noting that India's population exceeds 900 million, stated that "300 million people must be in the middle third." Next, someone improperly inferred that this meant "300 million middle-class Indians." My point is business must realize there are tens of millions of what we would consider "middle class" people in India, but not *yet* hundreds of millions.
9. This first phone will probably be a mobile one, as newly emerging economies have the benefit of jumping to the latest technology rather than building up an already obsolete infrastructure of copper wires.
10. One negative result of the new middle class is that Korea is currently experiencing tremendous pollution and traffic congestion problems due to an increased usage of the automobile and a decreased utilization of the more environmentally friendly modes of transportation, the bus and the bicycle.
11. *Global Economic Prospects and the Developing Countries,* 1997 ed., (Washington, DC: The World Bank), p. 92.
12. Lionel Demery and Lyn Squire, "Macroeconomic Adjustment and Poverty in Africa: An Emerging Picture," *World Bank Research Observer,* Vol. 11, No. 1 (February 1996), pp. 39–59.
13. Italics are as in original.
14. East Asian economic development helps fuel this surge in middle-class residents of developing nations. Indeed, Yoichi Funabashi in *Asia Pacific Fusion* (Institute for International Economics, October 1995), cites "the emergence of a solid middle class in all of the societies in the region. By the year 2000 there will be more than 230 million people in Asia living in households with incomes greater than $10,000 per year."

Chapter 6. Strategic Focus: The Six Great Economies of the 21st Century

1. We discussed this briefly in the beginning of the book, where I gave the example of buying a large bunch of bananas in India for the equivalent of only one-quarter of a U.S. dollar.
2. Paul Krugman, "The Myth of Asia's Miracle," *Foreign Affairs,* Vol. 73, No. 6 (November/December 1994), pp. 62–78.
3. This crucial notion is consistent with our emphasis in Chapter 4 on making *primary education* available to all children, particularly the currently underserved girls, throughout the "Populous South."
4. Unfortunately, they often catch and kill small fish inappropriately, thereby limiting the ability of later generations to sustain the increased productivity in terms of catching fish to eat. This is a classic example of Senge's type of "systems thinking" as detailed in our Chapter 4.
5. Darren McDermott, "Singapore Swing: Krugman Was Right," *Wall Street Journal,* 23 October 1996, p. A19. Total factor productivity is a measure of efficiency, as it shows output per units of input.
6. The classic work on scenario planning is by Peter Schwartz, *The Art of the Long View: Planning for the Future in an Uncertain World* (Currency Doubleday, 1996). Schwartz begins (pp. 3–6): "This book is about freedom. . . . To act with confidence,

one must be willing to look ahead and consider uncertainties. . . . Scenarios are a tool for helping us to take a long view in a world of great uncertainty. . . . Scenarios are *not* predictions. It is simply not possible to predict the future with certainty. . . . Scenarios allow a manager to say, "I am prepared for whatever happens." *It is this ability to act with a knowledgeable sense of risk and reward that separates both the business executive and the wise individual from a bureaucrat or a gambler."* (Italics as in original.)

7. *Harvard Business Review,* Vol. 75, No. 3 (May–June 1997), pp. 38–49.
8. Of course, we also should mention that the European leg of the triad comprises a number of important national economies besides Germany, notably France, Great Britain, and Italy. Furthermore, grouping the "Benelux" countries adds another very important economy, particularly given their longstanding orientation toward and success in international trade and investment. Finally, Spain is a rising economic force and has been ever since its restoration of democracy progressing into the 1980s.
9. Nicholas R. Lardy, *China in the World Economy* (Institute for International Economics, 1994), pp. 14–18.
10. See the article in *The Economist* entitled "How Poor Is China?" 12 October 1996, pp. 35–36.
11. Martin Wolf, "China as Next Superpower?" *Financial Times of London,* 7 November 1994, p. 22.
12. Yoichi Funabashi, *Asia Pacific Fusion: Japan's Role in APEC* (Washington, DC: Institute for International Economics, 1995), p. 154.
13. Discussed in Funabashi, p. 153.
14. Many Americans invested in Russia through "closed-end country funds," a vehicle for international investing which I will discuss in Chapter 7.
15. John Thornhill, "Funds Put Their Faith in Russia," *Financial Times of London,* 14 July 1997, p. 24.
16. The Free Press (New York, 1995).
17. "The Asian Juggernaut Isn't Really Slowing Down," *Business Week* (14 July 1997), p. 16.
18. Thomas Petzinger, Jr., "Business Achieves Greatest Efficiencies When at Its Greenest," *Wall Street Journal,* 11 July 1997, p. B1.
19. "When Green Begets Green," *Business Week,* 10 November, 1997, pp. 98–106.
20. Ray Anderson, Annual Keynote Lecture at the Emory University Center for Ethics in Public Policy and the Professions, on 25 February 1997.

PART III. A GLOBAL STRATEGY FOR PEOPLE AND PROFITS IN THE 21ST CENTURY
Chapter 7. Preparing for the Global Century: The Rationale, Route, and Tools for Diversifying Beyond the U.S. Market

1. Measured using purchasing power parity (PPP) exchange rates to compare each nation's GDP by converting to a common currency.
2. Recall that in accounting, a net or balance item is measured as receipts minus expenditures. In international accounts, this is usually export revenues minus import expenditures. A balance that is positive is termed a "surplus," versus a 'deficit' or net negative balance.
3. Most observers attribute the ballooning federal deficits to President Reagan's tax cuts and increased defense spending, combined with congressional Democrats' increased domestic spending.
4. For more information on the "twin deficits" theory and evidence, refer to my article with Ellis Tallman in the Federal Reserve Bank of Atlanta's *Economic Review,* May/June 1991, that deals with U.S. government and trade deficits. A more technical treatment appears in Jeff Rosensweig and Ellis Tallman, "Fiscal Policy and Trade Adjustment: Are the Deficits Really Twins?" *Economic Inquiry,* Vol. 31, No. 4 (October 1993), pp. 580–594.

5. My first published version of this model appeared in the Federal Reserve Bank of Atlanta *Economic Review* in October 1985. I have tried to refine and extend this model ever since. Sadly, new data keep adding support as U.S. federal government and U.S. net foreign debt have exploded in the direction predicted all along by the model.

6. These were especially attractive in light of the relatively low returns and high taxes then available in Japan and in continental Europe.

7. While a "plan" to balance the federal budget by early in the next century is in place, I probably do not need to remind readers that not all government promises become reality. The recent forecasts of an imminent move to budget surplus set off a race among politicians to see who could "spend the surplus," even before it materialized.

8. Except for the aberration caused by financing World War II.

9. Indeed, the *gross federal debt* continues to rise significantly, despite the very low recent values of the reported government deficit.

10. Interestingly, the United States had maintained a slight positive balance on net investment income until 1997, despite the large net foreign debt position the United States has dug itself into in the past decade. The reason our earnings on our foreign investments exceeded our servicing payments on our liabilities to foreigners, despite the greater magnitude of our foreign liabilities versus our foreign assets, is that our assets abroad earn very high financial rates of return. Indeed, until a recent data revision, the U.S. Commerce Department had reported that our net investment income balance sank to a negative position even earlier than 1997. The recent revision revealed that U.S. income returns from our past foreign investments actually are quite high, even higher than previously estimated. Of course, these data substantiate the main point of this chapter and much of this book—the wisdom of investing beyond the United States' borders.

11. Readers interested in learning more about the crucial policy choices facing the United States and our major trading partners, as a result of the *dollar*'s peak in 1985 and its subsequent sharp downturn, are referred to the landmark book by Stephen Marris, *Deficits and the Dollar: The World Economy at Risk* (Washington, DC: Institute for International Economics, rev. ed. August 1987).

12. I refer readers wishing to learn more about U.S. economic performance and its interplay with economic policy to Paul Krugman's clear and useful book, *The Age of Diminished Expectations: U.S. Economic Policy in the 1990s*, third edition (Cambridge, MA: MIT Press, 1997).

13. Even if comparisons are made using hypothetical PPP exchange rates (which boost the relative incomes of Asian nations with low or undervalued market exchange rates), Brazil trails only the hugely populous nations of China and India. Meanwhile, Mexico is sixth and Argentina falls to a tie for ninth of all developing nations' total economies when converting using PPP exchange rates.

14. Thomas T. Vogel, *Wall Street Journal*, 31 July 1997, p. A14.

15. Michael E. Kanell, *Atlanta Journal/Atlanta Constitution*, "BellSouth Wins $512 Million Brazilian Wireless Bid," 9 August 1997, p. C3.

16. Discussion with Robert Oxnam at Annual Conference of the Society of International Business Fellows, 26 September 1996, in Hot Springs, Virginia.

17. Paul Krugman, "What Ever Happened to the Asian Miracle," *Fortune*, 18 August 1997, p. 26.

18. George S. Yip, *Total Global Strategy: Managing for Worldwide Competitive Advantage* (Englewood Cliffs, NJ: Prentice-Hall, 1995).

19. The U.S. Bureau of the Census deserves credit for making these projections, as well as similar ones for every fifth year to 2050, available on its Web site.

20. I chose 1960 as representative of the fixed exchange rate era created after World War II.

21. I am indebted to Martha D. Volcker for helping me analyze and write this section of the book.

22. Financial Times, "Asian turmoil puts ADR listings on ice," 22 December 1997, p. 21.

Chapter 8. Twenty-First Century Career Strategy: Becoming a Global Manager

1. John P. Kotter, *"The New Rules: How to Succeed in Today's Post-Corporate World* (New York: The Free Press, 1995), p. 5.
2. Ibid, p. 55.
3. *Economic Trends,* Federal Reserve Bank of Cleveland, July 1996, pp. 12–13.
4. Gary P. Ferraro, *The Cultural Dimension of International Business,* 3d ed. (Upper Saddle River, NJ: Prentice-Hall, 1998).
5. Daniel Greene, "Team Player Leschly Likes to Prove a Point," *Financial Times of London,* 29 July 1996, p. 7.
6. *Business Week,* 8 January 1996, p. 56.
7. *Fortune,* 15 January 1996.
8. Daniel Goleman, "Looking Out for Number One," *Fortune,* 15 January 1996, pp. 33–37.
9. Dyan Machan, "Herbert Allen and His Merry Dealsters," *Forbes,* 1 July 1996, cover plus pp. 68–72.
10. Sewell Chan, "In Frenzy to Recruit, High-tech Concerns Try Gimmicks, Songs," *Wall Street Journal,* 9 August 1996, p. B1.
11. *Fortune,* 11 December 1995, p. 80. "What MVA really measures is how efficiently the chief executive has been able to use the capital entrusted to him—how well he has been able to keep his eye on the ball. By that standard, Goizueta and Welch are genuine champions. Goizueta created nearly all of Coca-Cola's MVA—$59 billion—during his own tenure.
12. "America's Most Admired Corporations," *Fortune,* 4 March 1996, p. 90. Coke was named "most admired corporation" again in 1997.
13. "Toward a New Conception of the Environment-Competitiveness Relationship," *Journal of Economic Perspectives* (Fall 1995), pp. 97–118.
14. Michael E. Porter and Claas van der Linde, "Green *and* Competitive: Ending the Stalemate," *Harvard Business Review* (September/October 1995), pp. 120–134.
15. Joann Lublin, "An Overseas Stint Can Be a Ticket to the Top," *Wall Street Journal,* 29 January 1996, p. B1.

Chapter 9. People and Profits: A Win-Win Global Strategy for the 21st Century

1. Robert Reich, "Who Is Us," *Harvard Business Review* (January–February 1990), pp. 53–64.
2. Paul Krugman, *Pop Internationalism* (Cambridge, MA: MIT Press, 1996).
3. *The World Bank Research Observer,* Vol. 11, No. 1 (February 1996), pp. 3–22.
4. Jere R. Behrman, "The Impact of Health and Nutrition on Education," *World Bank Research Observer,* Vol. 11, No. 1 (February 1996), pp. 23–37.
5. Dasgupta, "The Population Problem," p. 1898.
6. *The Economist,* "Economic Freedom: Of Liberty and Prosperity," 13 January 1996, p. 21–23.
7. James Gwartney, Robert Lawson, and Walter Block, *Economic Freedom of the World: 1975–1995,* co-published by eleven institutes including the Fraser Institute in Vancouver, the Cato Institute in Washington, D.C., and the Institute of Economic Affairs in London. January 12, 1996.
8. We should note that some of the nations of East Asia with relatively high economic freedom rankings have not yet achieved comparable political or press freedom.
9. Michael Novak, *Business as a Calling: Work and the Examined Life* (New York: The Free Press, 1996), p. 37.

INDEX

Hungary, 54, 65

Immigration flows, 69, 70
Imports. *See* International trade
India, 30, 31, 58
  demographic transition, 101,
    104, 107
  economic growth and
    development, 123, 149,
    153–154, 162
  economic reforms, 83
  fertility rate, 104
  foreign direct investment (FDI),
    84
  population, 71, 75, 83, 85, 107,
    153–154
  purchasing power, 39–40
  telephones, 83–84
Indonesia, 30, 56, 57, 73
  demographic transition, 101
  economic growth and
    development, 119, 123, 149,
    154–155
  fertility rate, 80
  financial aid to, 227
  foreign direct investment (FDI),
    18, 43
  population, 126, 154, 156
Industrialized trading nations
    (ITN), 28–29, 31
  exports, 32, 33
  foreign direct investment (FDI),
    43–45
  GDP measurement, 39
  information technology
    network, 28, 32, 33–37
  Internet access, 37
  population, 32, 33, 68–70
Infant mortality, 94–95
  dehydration and, 97–98
  demographic transition and,
    103–108

Inflation, 2–3, 172, 177, 181
Information technology network,
  8, 28, 32, 33–34, 81
ING Barings, 12
Integrity, of global managers,
  205–206
Intel, 195
Inter-American Development
  Bank, 186
Interest rates, 122–123, 177, 179,
  182
Interface, Inc., 167
International Conference on
  Population and Development
  (1994), 96
International Finance Corporation
  (IFC), 42–43
International investment. *See*
  Foreign investment
International Monetary Fund
  (IMF), 227
International trade, 1–2
  communication and information
    technology and, 8
  exports, 2–5, 11, 26, 115–116,
    140
  global growth in, 5, 6–11
  measurement of, 24–26
  population vs. trade divide,
    41–42
  U.S. growth in, 2–6
Internet, 8–10, 34, 81, 82
  disparity in access to, 37
  growth of, 37
Interpersonal skills, 211
Investing, personal and global,
  192–199
Investment Biker (Rogers), 81
Iran, 31
  fertility rate, 80
  oil exports, 82
  population, 82

ABOUT THE AUTHOR

JEFFREY A. ROSENSWEIG teaches finance and international business at Emory University's Goizueta Business School, where he is a six-time winner of the Distinguished Educator Award. A graduate *summa cum laude* from Yale, Professor Rosensweig received a Ph.D from Massachusetts Institute of Technology, where he was selected to be a Marshall Scholar at Oxford University. Professor Rosensweig has served as senior international economist at the Federal Reserve Bank of Atlanta and is Keynote International Lecturer at the Metro Atlanta Chamber of Commerce.